# Philosophies of Polar Law



Analysing the most important concepts and problems of the philosophy of polar law, this book focuses on the legal regimes relating to both the Arctic and the Antarctic.

The book addresses the most fundamental concepts and problems of polar law, looking beyond the apparent biophysical similarities and differences of the two polar regions, to tackle the distinctive legal problems relating to each polar region. It examines key legal–philosophical areas of the philosophy of law around legal interpretation; the role of nation states, reflected in concepts of territorial sovereignty – whether recognised or merely asserted, the exercise of jurisdiction, and the philosophical justifications for such claims; as well as indigenous rights, land rights, civil commons and issues of justice.

The book will be of interest to students and scholars of polar law, land law, heritage law, international relations in the polar regions and the wider polar social sciences and humanities.

**Dawid Bunikowski** is Senior Lecturer in Law at the State University of Applied Sciences in Wloclawek, Poland, Leader of Sub-group of Philosophy of Law at the University of the Arctic, Finland, and Visiting Researcher in the School of Theology (Philosophical Faculty) at the University of Eastern Finland.

**Alan D. Hemmings** is an Adjunct Associate Professor at Gateway Antarctica at the University of Canterbury, New Zealand.

Routledge Research in Polar Law

**Emerging Legal Orders in the Arctic**
The Role of Non-Arctic Actors
*Edited by Akiho Shibata, Leilei Zou, Nikolas Sellheim & Marzia Scopelliti*

**China's Role in the Arctic**
Observing and Being Observed
*Nong Hong*

**Philosophies of Polar Law**
*Edited by Dawid Bunikowski and Alan D. Hemmings*

For a full list of titles in this series, visit https://www.routledge.com/law/series/RRPL

# Philosophies of Polar Law

Edited by
Dawid Bunikowski and Alan D. Hemmings

Routledge
Taylor & Francis Group
LONDON AND NEW YORK

First published 2021
by Routledge
2 Park Square, Milton Park, Abingdon, Oxon OX14 4RN

and by Routledge
52 Vanderbilt Avenue, New York, NY 10017

*Routledge is an imprint of the Taylor & Francis Group, an informa business*



*British Library Cataloguing-in-Publication Data*
A catalogue record for this book is available from the British Library

*Library of Congress Cataloging-in-Publication Data*
Names: Bunikowski, Dawid, editor. | Hemmings, Alan D., editor.
Title: Philosophies of polar law / edited by Dawid Bunikowski and Alan D. Hemmings.
Description: Abingdon, Oxon ; New York, NY : Routledge, 2020. |
Series: Routledge research in polar law |
Includes bibliographical references and index.
Identifiers: LCCN 2020011175 (print) | LCCN 2020011176 (ebook) |
ISBN 9781138618558 (hardback) | ISBN 9780429461149 (ebook)
Subjects: LCSH: Polar Regions--International status.
Classification: LCC KZ4110.P65 P45 2020 (print) | LCC KZ4110.P65 (ebook) |
DDC 341.40911--dc23
LC record available at https://lccn.loc.gov/2020011175
LC ebook record available at https://lccn.loc.gov/2020011176

ISBN: 978-1-138-61855-8 (hbk)
ISBN: 978-0-367-52819-5 (pbk)
ISBN: 978-0-429-46114-9 (ebk)

Typeset in Times New Roman
by Taylor & Francis Books

# Contents

# Illustrations

## Figures



## Table

# Introduction – Emerging philosophies of polar law

*Dawid Bunikowski and Alan D. Hemmings*

## I Introduction

This is (as far as we are aware) the *first* volume to consider the philosophy, or philosophies, of polar law. There is, perhaps, a curious coincidence in the publication in 1861 of the first volume, to our knowledge, to attempt a coverage of both the Arctic and Antarctic, and the first to employ the term "polar regions" – John Richardson's *The Polar Regions*[1] – and the appearance of the definitive three-volume second edition of John Austin's *Province of Jurisprudence Determined*, his lectures on "Jurisprudence or the Philosophy of Positive Law".[2] Neither, of course, said anything concerning the focus of the other. This is hardly surprising. However, the subsequent absence of any consideration is more so. Even contemporary overviews of the philosophy of international law,[3] and a specialist journal with that title published since 2006,[4] do not mention the Arctic, Antarctic or Polar areas, far less give them any substantive consideration.

Given this, one could argue that the menu of core topics for consideration in this volume should be guided by the current or historic (and perhaps resolving the temporal coverage *is* a critical first step) main issues presenting to polar law in general. There is also another question to resolve – does one consider only international law, or also domestic law? If the latter is included, plainly the scope and complexity of the consideration – already extending over the two separate and gigantic areas of the Arctic and Antarctic –

1 John Richardson, *The Polar Regions* (Edinburgh: Adam and Charles Black, 1861).

2 John Austin, *The Province of Jurisprudence Determined*, 2nd Edn (London: John Murray, 1861).

3 Samantha Besson and John Tasioulas (eds) *The Philosophy of International Law* (Oxford: Oxford University Press, 2010) – its single reference to the Arctic is in the context of the fact of shrinking ice (p. 467); Andrei Marmor (ed) *The Routledge Companion to the Philosophy of Law* (London: Routledge, 2012); Anthony Carty *Philosophy of International* Law, 2nd Edn (Edinburgh: Edinburgh University Press, 2017).

4 *Journal of the Philosophy of International Law.*

*Figure I.1* Austin's *Jurisprudence* and Richardson's *The Polar Regions* of 1861
Source: Alan D. Hemmings

dramatically increase. Alternatively, one could take the generic issues that have arisen in philosophy of law works and seek to interrogate whether and if so how these issues manifest in the polar regions, and introduce anything that seems pertinent in the polar regions but has not apparently arisen in the generic considerations of the philosophy of law. The approach that we, as editors, have adopted is to leave the scoping of appropriate fields of coverage, and the particular "line of attack" to the judgement of the individual chapter authors. They are, we feel, best placed to resolve wherein the core foci for the issues that they are considering actually reside. We merely reminded the contributors that the distinguishing feature of the volume is its consideration of the *philosophy of law* aspects of these issues.

One should also note here that polar law (and particularly, in a bi-polar sense, international polar law) seems a well-developed and "distinctive body" of law.[5] It is obvious that the polar regions, both Antarctica and the Arctic, are regulated by both international and domestic law. But is its philosophy also so well-developed? Seemingly not, judging by the absence of critical philosophical attention to the polar regions, aside from some very recent and still limited works. Accordingly, we think that scholars and decision-makers need to attend to deeper and philosophical, theoretical or ethical/axiological considerations about polar law and problems concerning the polar regions. As a new proposed perspective this might be very fruitful and refreshing for the future development of polar law.

## 2 The structure of the volume

The book consists of four parts. Part I is entitled "Fundamental concepts of the philosophies of polar law"; Part II "Western legal framings"; Part III "Indigenous and non-Western framings"; and Part IV "The environment".

### *Part I Fundamental concepts of the philosophies of polar law*

In Chapter 1 – "The philosophy of law in the Antarctic" – Alan Hemmings notes that the southern polar region has not attracted any significant attention to the philosophy of law. As a place devoid of indigenous human residents, and only relatively recently reached by colonising peoples from the northern hemisphere, and then also from European settler-societies in the southern hemisphere, such philosophy of law as was evident was that implicit in the European colonial project. Territory was claimed here as elsewhere globally – even if most other states did not recognise these claims. As a nominally internationalised space post-World War II, Antarctica was framed in essentially Western terms, devoid of the sensibilities of post-colonialism elsewhere. This internationalisation, whilst limited, led to an international Antarctic legal system, again Western-orientated, and particularly Anglo-centric in its institutional and structural norms. A limited suite of resource issues, conjoined to a commitment to environmental protection, drove this system and its emerging legal and ethical norms. At the present moment, as part and parcel of the transforming global order, the Antarctic sees increasing anxiety and friction between Western states and emerging global south powers – most notably China. In time this unfolding of a new regional order will likely have effect on the philosophies of law guiding interests and practice in the Antarctic.

5 Donald R. Rothwell and Alan D. Hemmings, 'Introduction: The Context of International Polar Law', in Donald R. Rothwell and Alan D. Hemmings (eds) *International Polar Law* (Cheltenham: Edward Elgar, 2018) at xxxiv.

In Chapter 2 – "The philosophy of law in the Arctic" – Dawid Bunikowski tries to find the answers to two questions posed in his earlier (2016)[6] consideration of philosophy of law in the Arctic: (1) What is "Arctic Indigenous peoples' law" from the point of view of Western philosophy of law?; and (2) What is "law" for indigenous peoples in the Arctic? The chapter analyses the main topics of the philosophy of law in the Arctic, namely: (1) fundamental concepts: law in the Arctic, Arctic legal tradition, the Arctic as common good and legal pluralism; (2) Arctic cosmologies, beliefs, art and shamanism; (3) Arctic lands and waters and the environment; (4) indigenous rights and customary law in the Arctic; and (5) the future of philosophy of law in the Arctic: teaching via new tools, and global governance. To Bunikowski, philosophy of law in the Arctic is specific, peculiar and idiosyncratic.

### *Part II Western legal framings*

In Chapter 3 – "Decolonising Antarctica" – Alejandra Mancilla claims that it has become a trope in the field of Antarctic humanities that the history of Antarctica was no exception to world politics (as once thought), but just another instance of the colonial project at the global level. However, the wrongs of colonialism are normally tied to the subjugation of native populations, and in Antarctica there were none. So what is wrong with Antarctic colonialism? In this chapter, she points to three such wrongs: first, the unilateral appropriation by a few states of extravagant expanses of land, in a context where the finitude of land and resources worldwide was already well-known; second, the constitution of a political system (i.e. the Antarctic Treaty) where the majority of those who should have been consulted were not; and, third, the maintenance of a system where not all members are treated under equal and reciprocal terms. She makes some suggestions in relation to decolonising Antarctica.

In Chapter 4 – "The Arctic as civil commons" – Giorgio Baruchello builds upon, and engages with, Ko Hasegawa's contribution to the previously mentioned 2016 e-book.[7] Specifically, Hasegawa's claims about the holistic and invaluable character of any genuine common good are deepened and articulated further by means of the notion of *civil commons*, which life-value onto-axiology considers paramount, as exemplified in the compendium of philosophical works on sustainable development comprised within UNESCO's monumental *Encyclopedia of Life Support Systems* (2002–17). By exploring and explaining how the common good can be identified and best served *qua* civil commons, i.e. all social constructs enabling universal access to life goods,

6 D. Bunikowski (ed), *Philosophy of law in the Arctic* (Rovaniemi/Oulu: UArctic, 2016) (e-book).

7 K. Hasegawa, 'The Arctic as Common Good', in D. Bunikowski (ed), *Philosophy of law in the Arctic* (Rovaniemi/Oulu: UArctic, 2016) (e-book).

the present chapter also refers to, and makes use of, Karol Dobrzeniecki's chapter in the same 2016 e-book.[8]

In Chapter 5 – "Philosophy of science and legal disputes over whaling in the Southern Ocean" – David Coady, Brendan Gogarty and Jeffrey McGee observe that despite widespread public interest on the topic of whaling there has been relatively little work on how philosophy might contribute to an analysis of the status of whaling in international law. When philosophers have looked at whaling they have confined their attention to a narrow set of ethical questions, such as whether international law should permit certain forms of traditional indigenous whaling or even extend legal rights to whales themselves. They suggest that there is another important issue which has so far been largely neglected, even though it is at the forefront of recent international legal disputes over the status of whaling: namely the issue of "scientific whaling" in the International Whaling Commission (IWC). Their chapter considers the international legal dispute between Australia, New Zealand and Japan over the last's lethal harvesting of whales in the Southern Ocean and the recent attempt at resolution of this dispute by the International Court of Justice. On its face, this required that the Court demarcate "scientific" from "unscientific" activity. However, they argue that the Court effectively balked at this task, and characterise this as unfortunate. Demarcating science from commerce is not only achievable in philosophy, they argue, but might also better inform international legal practice. Resolving this issue is important if genuine progress to be made in the international legal dispute over whaling, but also in other contexts in which in the concept of scientific research appears in international law. Coady et al. reflect that with the recent Japanese withdrawal from the IWC, the issue is very unlikely to return for international judicial consideration in the near future.

### *Part III Indigenous and non-Western framings*

In Chapter 6 – "Legal (non) recognition of Sámi customary relationship with the land in Finland: challenges so far and prospects in the modern human rights era" – Leena Heinämäki, Sanna Valkonen and Jarno Valkonen claim that so far, international and domestic policies and legal instruments regarding indigenous peoples have been created by a majority representation of non-indigenous actors, who do not, according to indigenous peoples, necessarily understand the reality in which an indigenous people lives. Legal instruments based on Western value premises may, for instance, emphasise individual rather than collective aspects of the rights, or dichotomy between nature and culture, which is alien to indigenous peoples. This chapter discusses the ontological basis of an indigenous Sámi People's customary relationship with

8 K. Dobrzeniecki, 'Legal Pluralisms', in D. Bunikowski (ed), *Philosophy of law in the Arctic* (Rovaniemi/Oulu: UArctic, 2016) (e-book).

their traditional land in Finland with the aim to review the current legal challenges to recognise and thus protect this relationship, which is an integral part of the culture and identity of the Sámi. Viewing both domestic and international law, the chapter asks whether there are prospects in the modern human rights era, especially after the adoption of United Nations Declaration on the Rights of Indigenous Peoples, to better underpin and take into account indigenous peoples' ontological bases concerning their relationship with their cultural environments.

In Chapter 7 – "Assimilation policy *contra* cultural viability in the North" – Tom G. Svensson points out that historically indigenous people in the Arctic have been subject to enforced assimilation, a process of change that has caused most detrimental effects on their cultural viability. Such Norwegianisation, Japanisation, Sovietisation and Canadianisation turned out to be explicit attacks especially on hunting-gathering and pastoralist ways of life, where sedentarisation by the majority society was considered a predefined ideal. In the same fashion is the school system, which assumed that the language and traditional beliefs should be adapted to mainstream practice. The issue of assimilation being of moral-philosophical order is still discussed and actualised among indigenous people in the political domain, not the least in the North. What is at stake is the right to their own lifestyle. After all, it is a human right to enjoy and preserve cultural distinctiveness, to be culturally unique in the world of peoples. This opens a discussion of law in a broad sense, i.e. in both philosophical and anthropological terms. A topical issue currently refers to the discussion in Norway (pro and con) about an official Commission dealing with the sensitive question of reconciliation and truth (Sanningskommission), the intention of which is to investigate the past and present implications of the assimilation policy. In this chapter the author refers to the Sámi, the Ainu, and the Nisga´a.

In Chapter 8 – "The predicates of Chinese legal philosophy in the Polar Regions" – Nengye Liu and Qi Xu recognise that a key question in contemporary polar affairs, particularly since President Xi Jinping took office in 2013, is to what extent a rising China will shape polar governance. This question, and musings on China's supposed polar ambitions, has been the focus of much speculation in the West. However, China differs from the Western liberal tradition in many ways, including in its values and philosophical foundations. Accordingly, in order to draw a fuller picture of China's likely future role in polar governance, it is critical to consider *Chinese* perceptions and legal philosophy in relation to the current Arctic and Antarctic governance regimes. Most Chinese officials participating in contemporary polar fora were trained by academics in prominent mainland Chinese universities such as Peking, Tsinghua, Renmin and Wuhan. Although they spent their formative years in an open-door China, their view of the world order has been shaped by values and philosophies that are not necessarily the same as their American, European or Australasian colleagues. This chapter therefore applies the idea of "Comparative International Law" to the polar regions by examining Chinese academics' work over the past decade (2009–2019). By examining over 350 papers published by Chinese scholars, the chapter facilitates comparison and inclusion of a broader array of world views. After presenting a brief overview of Chinese legal philosophy in relation to international law, the authors examine the evolution of Chinese research on polar law and policy. They conclude with some predictions about the future of China's role in polar governance.

### *Part IV The environment*

There are just two chapters in this part, and both address the Arctic. The apparent omission of a chapter addressing Antarctic environmental issues is in fact deliberate, given the coverage of these matters in the earlier chapters by Hemmings and by Coady, Gogarty and McGee. The latter chapter could as well have been placed in Part IV.

In Chapter 9 – "Climate change and the role of indigenous peoples in preserving nature and biodiversity with special emphasis on the Arctic" – Agnieszka Szpak considers the dangers brought by climate change on the global scale, and to indigenous peoples in particular. The Arctic merits special attention as it is the area where climate change effects are most acutely visible. In this chapter, the role of indigenous peoples in the preservation of the environment and biodiversity in the context of climate change is examined. Some solutions, including an agro-ecological model, are proposed. The author analyses legal (hard as well as soft law) regulations on the protection of indigenous lands and the environment in the context of climate change and biodiversity preservation. Its aim is to indicate the normative basis of the role of indigenous peoples in preserving nature and biodiversity. The chapter seeks to address the following research questions: (1) What is the role of indigenous peoples in the mitigation and adaptation to climate change, as well as in environmental preservation? (2) Are the international legal, hard and soft law regulations, sufficient to protect the rights of indigenous peoples in the context of climate change? (3) Is the law capable of facing the reality? (4) Does it give the indigenous peoples instruments necessary to realise their rights and potential in the preservation of the environment? And, lastly (5) What are the indigenous alternative ways of development?

In Chapter 10 – "Environmental perceptions and values of the Russian northern indigenous peoples" – Elena Gladun and Olga V. Zakharova write that the Russian indigenous nations living in the Arctic for many centuries preserve their national identity and traditional knowledge that helps them to survive and live sustainably in the severe northern conditions. These nations have also retained traditional attitudes towards nature and deep wisdom regarding the interaction between humanity and the natural environment. Large-scale industrial projects in the Yamal region of the Russian Arctic are altering the culture and traditional way of life of indigenous peoples, and their historic experience and traditional attitudes are not considered in the decision-making process. The chapter sheds light on environmental values and traditional perceptions of the Russian northern indigenous peoples, proving they should be understandable and acceptable in the changing Arctic. It seems very important to preserve and transmit indigenous traditions and values as basic principles and criteria in environmental legal frameworks, which form the basis of the coherent and sustainable management of natural environment, thereby enabling Russia to efficiently transit to sustainable development.

## 3 Concluding remarks

While the diverse foci of the chapters in this volume, and the fact that the volume as a whole extends across both the Arctic and Antarctic, does not lend itself to producing a single convergent assessment around the philosophies of polar law that are evident, we are reassured by our assumption – reflected in the title of the volume – that we are talking about philosophies in the plural. The prevailing philosophy of law has varied with place (most obviously between an Arctic that has an indigenous presence in its diverse peoples of long residence, and an Antarctic which was not occupied by anybody until less than a hundred years ago); across time; and across the actors and interests being pursued. The poles are of course different, and there are different or peculiar problems in each, but some problems concerning the poles are common or similar. These bi-polar problems include territorial "ownership". Issues of territorial sovereignty and jurisdiction arise in both regions, with perhaps more superficial differences than is sometimes assumed. In the Antarctic the disputation (albeit contained by the Antarctic Treaty) is essentially a three-way contest between claimants and non-claimant members of the regional regime, and of the regime with non-regime states. Antarctica presents the novel situation as a result of the territorial uncertainty that includes the last massive part of the planet that is not the subject of any assertion of territorial sovereignty by any state (the so called "unclaimed" sector) and uncertainty about whether the absence of generally agreed coastal states in Antarctica mean that high seas extend to the coastline of the continent. In the Arctic, with the exception of Hans Island, the land areas are all subject to generally accepted national territorial sovereignty, but both in relation to the limited high seas area at the centre of the Arctic Ocean, and in relation to Arctic sea passages around North America and Eurasia, there are tensions between Arctic states themselves (whether the Arctic 5 or the Arctic 8 – and that divide itself speaks to some issues) and between them and non-Arctic states, in relation to navigation and resource access. Integral to the Arctic mix are the rights and interests of Arctic peoples, whose own spatial sense need not correspond to the boundaries of the present Arctic states, and for whom both "internal" and "international" territorial issues are profoundly important.

At the present moment, the commonalities between the Arctic and Antarctic also surely include the opposition between divergent philosophies of law. These are perhaps most intense and immediate around whether the appropriate polar legal framing in each should be predicated upon the facilitation of further resource exploitation under market mechanisms and inter-state competition, or a more constrained collective restraints model that emphasises global environmental protection and international justice in an age of manifest anthropogenic climate crisis. The question of hydrocarbon exploitation in both the Arctic and Antarctic surely raises quite profound international legal philosophical questions. The idea that in the places where we have gained much of our critical understanding of anthropogenic climate change, and which areas we know to be even more impacted by climate change than the planet in general (grim as that general picture is), where we have issues of equity between peoples (both within and between states), governments are in large part supporting research and other activity with hydrocarbon exploitation in mind, may seem quite extraordinary.

So, a legal-philosophical perspective is important for a deeper understanding of both the problems relating to the polar regions, and to any hope of being able to craft common purpose in resolving these, and this is the reason for this volume. The thoughts expressed herein are necessarily preliminary and tentative. We do not offer the collection as a final determination, but as a stimulant to the necessary systemisation, classification and determination of the imperative foci for a study of philosophy of law in the polar regions. This is the challenge for Antarctic and Arctic scholarship – and for those early-career scholars (and those yet to become scholars) who must take up the task.

Dawid Bunikowski, Alan D. Hemmings
February 2020
Finland, New Zealand

Part I

# Fundamental concepts of the philosophies of Polar law

Chapter 1

# The philosophy of law in the Antarctic

*Alan D. Hemmings*[1]

## 1 Introduction

In contrast to the Arctic,[2] the philosophy of law in the Antarctic has barely attracted comment, let alone explicit scholarly consideration, within either the regional Antarctic literature or (perhaps consequentially) in general works on the philosophy of law. There is a now quite massive literature on public international law in the Antarctic – albeit one historically dominated by Anglo-Saxon and Latin American scholars, or otherwise Euro-centric in tradition and orientation. Emilio Sahurie comes closest to considering philosophy of law in Antarctica, in his reflections in *The International Law of Antarctica*,[3] on, inter alia, what he terms "Identifications" which he sees as "largely repetitive of … other processes with global significance",[4] in his observation on the centrality of "Enlightenment" as an Antarctic value,[5] and in his concluding "Appraisal" where he sees a common purpose in the maintenance of "the current premises of the current order of Antarctica".[6] But Sahurie is unusual in the intellectual breadth of his legal engagement with the Antarctic, and his work is now inevitably dated, since it was conceived and published almost 30 years ago, at the hinge point of the end of both the Cold War and the decade-long negotiation of three separate Antarctic legal instruments and the beginnings of the new global order, whose unfolding is still underway today.

1 Gateway Antarctica Centre for Antarctic Studies and Research, University of Canterbury, New Zealand, alandhemmings@xtra.co.nz.
2 See Dawid Bunikowski, Chapter 2 in this volume.
3 Emilio J. Sahurie, *The International Law of Antarctica* (New Haven: New Haven Press and Martinus Nijhof, 1992).
4 Ibid., at 90–94.
5 Ibid., at 98–100.
6 Ibid., at 574–586.

Philosophers have, until very recently,[7] demonstrated very little interest in Antarctica.[8] So, with both lawyers and philosophers looking elsewhere, the lack of attention to philosophy of law in the Antarctic is perhaps not surprising. With the caveat that the present author is neither an international lawyer nor a philosopher, but a specialist on the structure and functioning of the Antarctic politico-legal regime, centred on the Antarctic Treaty System (ATS), this chapter alongside three other chapters in this collection,[9] thus seeks to open the consideration of philosophy of law in the Antarctic. It is inevitably preliminary in scope.

Boundaries are generally more contingent and porous than their proponents perceive, and this certainly holds for both the Arctic and the Antarctic. But some sort of bounding seems essential, and in the case of the Antarctic there is happily an oceanographic/biophysical/geopolitical/legal convergence on a convergence – the Antarctic Convergence – as a useful boundary for "the Antarctic". This convergence is not haphazard. It was arrived at by taking the Antarctic Convergence (also termed the Antarctic Polar Front) as the sensible northern boundary for the key international legal instrument regulating the Antarctic marine environment, the Convention on the Conservation of Antarctic Marine Living Resources (CCAMLR).[10] The Antarctic Convergence extends around the continent of Antarctica, varying in its position, being at its most southerly in the Pacific sector, where it is at about 60°S; around 50°S in the Atlantic sector, and as far north as 45°S in the Indian Ocean sector. CCAMLR defines its boundary by precise points of latitude and longitude.[11] Since CCAMLR is an integral component of the wider ATS, the Antarctic Convergence becomes in effect the northern boundary of this ATS.[12] The maritime area falling within this boundary is colossal, some 32 million square kilometres, constituting just under 10 percent of the

7 Most significantly with the Norwegian-based 'Political Philosophy Looks to Antarctica', https://www.hf.uio.no/ifikk/english/research/projects/political-philosophy-looks-to-antarctica/

8 With the notable exception of Holmes Rolston III, who has addressed environmental ethics there – see his 'Environmental Ethics on Antarctic Ice', *Polar Record* 36 (2000): 289–290; 'Environmental Ethics in Antarctica', *Environmental Ethics* 24 (2002): 115–134; and 'Antarctica' in Baird Callicott and Robert Frodeman (eds) *Encyclopedia of Environmental Ethics and Philosophy* (Detroit: Macmillan, 2009) 53–58.

9 See David Coady, Brendan Gogarty and Jeffrey McGee, Chapter 5, 'Philosophy of science and legal disputes over whaling in the Southern Ocean'; the Antarctic consideration in Nengye Liu and Qi Xu, Chapter 8, 'The predicates of Chinese legal philosophy in the polar regions'; and Alejandra Mancilla, Chapter 3, 'Decolonising Antarctica'.

10 Convention on the Conservation of Antarctic Marine Living Resources, 20 May 1980, 1329 UNTS 47.

11 Ibid., Art. I.4.

12 Although the ATS does not regulate all activities across this entire area.

global marine area.[13] The Antarctic continent adds a further 14 million square kilometres, so that the total area of "the Antarctic" as defined here is 46 million square kilometres – just under 9 percent of the total surface area of the earth.

Thus, this Antarctic is a gigantic area of ocean, continent and islands. It is, variously, subject to the metropolitan legal codes of the states that operate there (whether asserting jurisdiction over only their own citizens and entities, or in the case of claimants notionally more generally), generic international legal instruments, and international law elaborated at the Antarctic regional level by the now more than 50 states (and the European Union) which are party to one or more of the ATS component instruments. North of 60°S coastal state jurisdiction is unimpeded, but this is essentially restricted to nine sub-Antarctic island groups;[14] south of 60°S, unresolved territorial sovereignty and Antarctic Treaty constraints (considered later in the chapter) necessitate consensus decision-making beyond states' immediate jurisdiction over their nationals. Unlike the Arctic (see other contributions to this volume), no issues of indigenous peoples' law within the area arise.[15] Indigenous peoples reached the extremities of South America, just north of the Drake Passage, and, remarkably, Polynesian people briefly settled on Enderby Island (Auckland Islands group, at 50°S) in "the late thirteenth century",[16] but despite apparent Antarctic myths amongst several indigenous peoples,[17] no clear records of penetration, let alone residence in the Antarctic are proven. So, in David Day's emphatic words, there were "no people who could be demeaned and dispossessed".[18]

13 John Croxall and Stephen Nicol, 'Management of Southern Ocean fisheries: global forces and future sustainability', *Antarctic Science* 16 (2004): 569–584.
14 Running clockwise from the South Atlantic: South Georgia and South Sandwich Islands (under effective UK jurisdiction but contested by Argentina); Bouvet Island (Norway); Prince Edward and Marion islands (South Africa); Crozet and Kerguelen islands (France) and Heard and McDonald islands (Australia). All of these groups fall within the CCAMLR area, but are not within the area of application (south of 60°S) of the other ATS instruments. Even under CCAMLR, the sub-Antarctic coastal states' positions are reserved through the *Statement by the Chairman of the Conference on the Conservation of Antarctic Marine Living Resources*, which was promulgated when CCAMLR was adopted.
15 In relation to indigenous peoples, see also Adrian Howkins, *The Polar Regions: An Environmental History* (Cambridge: Polity, 2016); and Ben Maddison, 'Indigenising the heroic era of Antarctic exploration', in Elizabeth Leane and Jeffrey McGee (eds) *Anthropocene Antarctica: Perspectives from the Humanities, Law and Social Sciences* (London: Routledge, 2020) at 135–155.
16 Atholl Anderson, *Te Ao Tawhito The Old World 3000 BC – AD 1830: Tangata Whenua, An Illustrated History, Part One* (Wellington: Bridget Williams, 2018) at 73.
17 See, e.g. Elizabeth Leane, *Antarctica in Fiction: Imaginative Narratives of the Far South* (New York: Cambridge University Press, 2016) at 24–25.
18 David Day, *Antarctica: A Biography* (Sydney: Knopf, 2012) at 521.

In the sections which follow, I first make some general propositions about the nature of any philosophy of law in Antarctica. I then examine the colonisation of Antarctica and the consequential assertion of claims to territorial sovereignty there; the internationalisation of Antarctic legal arrangements through the adoption of the Antarctic Treaty in 1959,[19] and the subsequent expansion of the legal regime through the ATS;[20] then the drivers of Antarctic legal development – both activities and norms; before concluding with an examination of the consequences of the global world order in Antarctica, with all that this may mean for the future legal system there.

## 2 General propositions concerning a 'philosophy of law in the Antarctic'

It may be argued that there is now:

> "a distinctive body of international polar law … not only reflected in the now longstanding regional legal framework that applies to the Antarctic, but also to the developing legal framework in the Arctic [and] … that there are distinctive legal principles that have been developed and applied in the polar regions, especially relating to sovereignty and territoriality, environmental and resource management, and cooperation and regional governance."[21]

But this proposition says nothing about the substructure of the putative body of international polar law. Critically, it risks overlooking the variability therein in relation to motives, interests and underlying norms that diverse states (and now other actors) bring to the process of elaborating (perhaps often without awareness of the emergence of any sort of "body"); and assumptions of a sort of "permanent present",[22] which ignores temporal changes to norms and at least some of the motives and interests.[23]

19 Antarctic Treaty, 1 December 1959, 402 UNTS 71.
20 The ATS is defined in the Protocol on Environmental Protection to the Antarctic Treaty, 4 October 1991, 30 ILM 1461 (hereinafter 'Madrid Protocol'), Art. 1e: "'Antarctic Treaty system' means the Antarctic Treaty, the measures in effect under that Treaty, its associated separate international instruments in force and the measures in effect under those instruments."
21 Donald R. Rothwell and Alan D. Hemmings, 'Introduction: The Context of International Polar Law', in Donald R. Rothwell and Alan D. Hemmings (eds) *International Polar Law* (Cheltenham: Edward Elgar, 2018) at xxxiv.
22 The expression of Eric Hobsbawm, *Age of Extremes: The Short Twentieth Century 1914–1991* (London: Michael Joseph, 1994) at 3.
23 On temporal considerations in the Antarctic, see Alan D. Hemmings, 'From the New Geopolitics of Resources to Nanotechnology: Emerging Challenges of Globalism in Antarctica', *Yearbook of Polar Law* 1 (2009): 55–72; Mônica Heinzelmann Portella de Aguiar, 'Tripartite periodization of the Antarctic Treaty system

Notwithstanding some continuities (including most obviously the institution of the Antarctic Treaty itself), the Antarctic of 1959 with its 12 original signatories (seven of whom were claimants, and two others 'semi-claimants') is different to the Antarctic of 2019 with its 54 signatories, greater diversity of membership (participation of at least part of the post-colonial global south – including a number of actual or incipient great powers such as China, India and Brazil), and profound developments across technology, scientific knowledge, resource interests, and so on. To suppose that a unitary philosophy of law has informed, let alone underpinned, the development of the international legal regime in the Antarctic over a period of 60 years seems inherently improbable. In Antarctica, as elsewhere, a plurality of 'philosophies' of law, varying across actors, issues and time has likely been evident.

States have brought to the Antarctic the legal norms, the political traditions and the geopolitical interests reflected in both their domestic spheres and their wider international engagements. Great powers globally have been great powers regionally in Antarctica, and the prevailing world order – throughout the Cold War, the bipolar world organised around the United States and the Soviet Union; increasingly today a new sense of bipolarity with Western states on one side and China on the other – is reflected too in Antarctic affairs. Being present at the creation has provided (they insisted upon this) privileged standing for the original signatories, and formally sheltered the positions of the territorial claimants, although as Shirley Scott has argued:

> "the Antarctic Treaty fits into a broader pattern of the US consciously choosing to promote or at times to lobby against, the development of multilateral treaties to institutionalize its global freedom of movement and behaviour … [and] in this light the Antarctic Treaty could be viewed as not simply freezing the colonial claims of others, but as an act of imperialism on the part of the US."[24]

Original signatories are decision-making Consultative Parties to the Antarctic Treaty in perpetuity, irrespective of whether they continue to be active in Antarctica, whereas subsequent Consultative Parties formally retain this right only:

> "during such times as that Contracting Party demonstrates its interest in Antarctica by conducting substantial research activity there, such as the establishment of a scientific station or the despatch of a scientific expedition."[25]

from a systematic perspective', *Relaciones Internacionales* 56 (2019): 37–56; and Alessandro Antonello, 'The Antarctic Treaty as a temporal order', *Polar Record* (2019) https://doi.org/10.1017/S0032247419000408.

24 Shirley V. Scott, 'Ingenious and innocuous? Article IV of the Antarctic Treaty as imperialism', *The Polar Journal* 1 (2011): 51–62 at 58.

25 Antarctic Treaty, Art. IX.2.

In some sense one can see an analogue here to the historically-contingent Permanent Five of the United Nations Security Council, where institutional embedding and the modalities of decision-making make it difficult to change the status quo. Whether this is a positive or a negative depends of course on whether 'your' state is a beneficiary or not.

The ATS is a notionally open access system with a very thick glass ceiling in terms of the technical, scientific, administrative and financial prowess necessary to break through and actually operate substantially in the Antarctic and thereby demonstrate the bona fides requisite to acquire decision-making status. Few small developing states and surely no least developed states have any realistic prospects of joining such a system, and this has a bearing on the legal norms and issues considered within the ATS, or likely to be discussed – to say nothing of international equity in relation to an area regarded by some as a global commons. Neither benefit sharing, nor technology-transfer, for example, have appeared on the agenda of any Antarctic Treaty Consultative Meeting (ATCM), nor obviously during the negotiations for any of the resource-focussed legal instruments of the evolving ATS.[26]

## 3 Antarctic 'colonialism' and claims to territorial sovereignty

Notwithstanding the singular fact that the continent of Antarctica had no indigenous human inhabitants, the arrival of European voyages of discovery at its shores from the early 19th century was followed within 100 years by assertions of territorial sovereignty, involving the usual symbolic acts or ceremonies of possession (cairns, flags, speeches, dedications to one's sovereign, etc),[27] associated with European colonisation everywhere else on the planet (see Chapter 3 by Alejandra Mancilla for a fuller discussion of the issues and the question of decolonisation). The legal and geopolitical engagement at First Contact reflected the then prevailing European philosophy of law that sanctioned the occupation, dispossession, disenfranchisement and oppression of the colonial project everywhere. It was just, as David Day observed, that there were no people in the Antarctic to dispossess.

26 In addition to CCAMLR and the Madrid Protocol, already mentioned, these are the Convention for the Conservation of Antarctic Seals, 1 June 1972, 11 ILM 251 (hereinafter CCAS); and the Convention on the Regulation of Antarctic Mineral Resource Activities, 2 June 1988, 27 ILM 868 (hereinafter CRAMRA), which has not entered into force, is not likely to, and thus formally does not form a part of the ATS as defined in Art. 1 of the Madrid Protocol.

27 See Arthur S. Keller, Oliver J. Lissitzyn and Frederick J. Mann, *Creation of Rights of Sovereignty through Symbolic Acts 1400–1800* (New York: Columbia University Press, 1938); Patricia Seed, *Ceremonies of Possession in Europe's Conquest of the New World 1492–1640* (New York: Cambridge University Press, 1995).

But these acts, through the maritime expeditions from the late 18th century,[28] which whilst not landing in Antarctica did land on some sub-Antarctic islands, to the expeditions from the end of the 19th century which landed (and often overwintered) on the continent, and the expeditions post-World War II which established permanent stations (particularly during the International Geophysical Year) that persist today, established a Eurocentric legal framing on Antarctica from the word go. The prime actors in the human arrival in Antarctica were the usual suspects – European states (most notably the United Kingdom and France; but also Norway and Belgium) and the United States and the other settler states that had evolved from the European imperial project in the Southern Hemisphere (Argentina, Chile, Australia and New Zealand). Japan was active in the 'Heroic Era' but made no claims, and was anyway explicitly required to abandon any Antarctic rights under the terms of the 1951 Treaty of Peace with Japan that ended World War II,[29] in a more rigorous version of the general abandonment of territorial rights visited upon Germany by the after World War I which may also apply in the Antarctic.[30] Russia (as the Soviet Union) only became an active Antarctic participant after World War II, although it had contributed one of the great early circumnavigations of Antarctica in 1819–1821 under Bellingshausen.[31]

The variant *mission civilisatrice* in Antarctica was pursuit of knowledge – inter alia Sahurie's "Enlightenment".[32] First in quite coarse geographical terms – charting, mapping, surveying (which anyway had utility in terms of territorial assertions); ascertaining where the magnetic pole was; elucidating sea-ice and oceanographic conditions to aid navigation; and improving meteorological forecasting through better understanding the Antarctic drivers. These and other enquiries could be claimed (as indeed they are) as contributions to a collective public-good, but in the process they provided the grounding for a regional hegemony and (later) a defence against assertions

28 Perhaps most notably James Cook's second expedition of 1772–1775, which circumnavigated the continent and penetrated south of the Antarctic Circle as far as 71°S.

29 Treaty of Peace with Japan, San Francisco, 8 September 1951. Chapter II, Territory, Article 2e 'Japan renounces all claim to any right or title to or interest in connection with any part of the Antarctic area, whether deriving from the activities of Japanese nationals or otherwise'.

30 Treaty of Peace between the Allied and Associated Powers and Germany (Treaty of Versailles), 28 June 1919. Article 118, wherein Germany was required to '[renounce] all rights, titles and privileges whatever in or over territory [outside her European frontiers]'. In relation to both the Japanese and German instances, see Alan D. Hemmings, Donald R. Rothwell and Karen N. Scott, 'Antarctic security in a global context', in Alan D. Hemmings, Donald R. Rothwell and Karen N. Scott (eds) *Antarctic Security in the Twenty-First Century: Legal and Policy Perspectives* (London: Routledge, 2012) at 329–330.

31 Rip Bulkeley, *Bellingshausen and the Russian Antarctic Expedition, 1819–21* (Basingstoke: Palgrave Macmillan, 2014).

32 See above, and note 5.

that Antarctica had been appropriated by the 'rich man's club' (as Malaysian Prime Minister Mahathir bin Mohamad characterised it in the 1980s). If it was all being done in pursuit of scientific knowledge, who could object?

Within the Eurocentric framing, one can drill down deeper and see the Antarctic legal norms as essentially Anglo. This was facilitated first through the clear global dominance of the United Kingdom throughout the 19th century, which enabled it to be the dominant Antarctic player until the mid-20th century, by which time it was surpassed and succeeded by the United States. The United Kingdom was the effective initiator of the territorial claims sequence with its 1908 assertion of claim to the Antarctic Peninsula (Falkland Island Dependencies) and the inter-war British Empire allocation of two further sectors to New Zealand ('Ross Dependency') and Australia ('Australian Antarctic Territory'), in relation to which the boundaries for the Norwegian claim ('Dronning Maud Land') and the French claim ('Terre Adélie') were reconciled. These four secondary claimants – two of which are Anglo – have themselves become significant actors in the Antarctic politico-legal arena. The Argentine and Chilean claims, whatever their roots in the earlier Spanish Imperial arrangements, and the regional significance of the doctrine of *uti possidetis*,[33] which influences their approach to their Antarctic territorial claims,[34] were also given their present codification during World War II in reaction to the UK claim to the Antarctic Peninsula.[35] But, whether as a direct continuation of the long and so frequently dismal European practice of appropriating new lands everywhere, or via a second-order variation such as *uti possidetis*, the engagement with Antarctica as territory reflects a particular and long-standing European philosophy of law. Thus we arrived at the situation by the end of World War II of seven states asserting claims to sectors of the Antarctic Continent (Figure 1.1) and other states framing their own stances in reaction to this reality.

First in support of its 19th century sealing and whaling interests around Antarctica (and consequential US geographical discoveries in the region), then in reaction to the United Kingdom and associated state territorial claims, the United States rose in importance in the Antarctic. Through the motive force of its burgeoning economic and geopolitical heft, its own inter-war Antarctic expeditions under Richard E. Byrd, and subsequently with its emergence as the dominant power after World War II and further expeditions,

33 On the doctrine generally, see Giuseppe Nesi, 'Uti posseditis Doctrine' in Rüdiger Wolfrum (ed), *Max Planck Encyclopedia of Public International Law* (Oxford: Oxford University Press, 2011); and Marcelo G. Kohen, *Possession Contestée et Souveraineté Territoriale* (Paris: Presses Universitaires de France, 1997) at 425–487.

34 Donald R. Rothwell and Alan D. Hemmings, 'Introduction: The Context of International Polar Law', in Donald R. Rothwell and Alan D. Hemmings (eds) *International Polar Law* (Cheltenham: Edward Elgar, 2018) at xviii.

35 All three claims substantially overlap and are mutually contested.

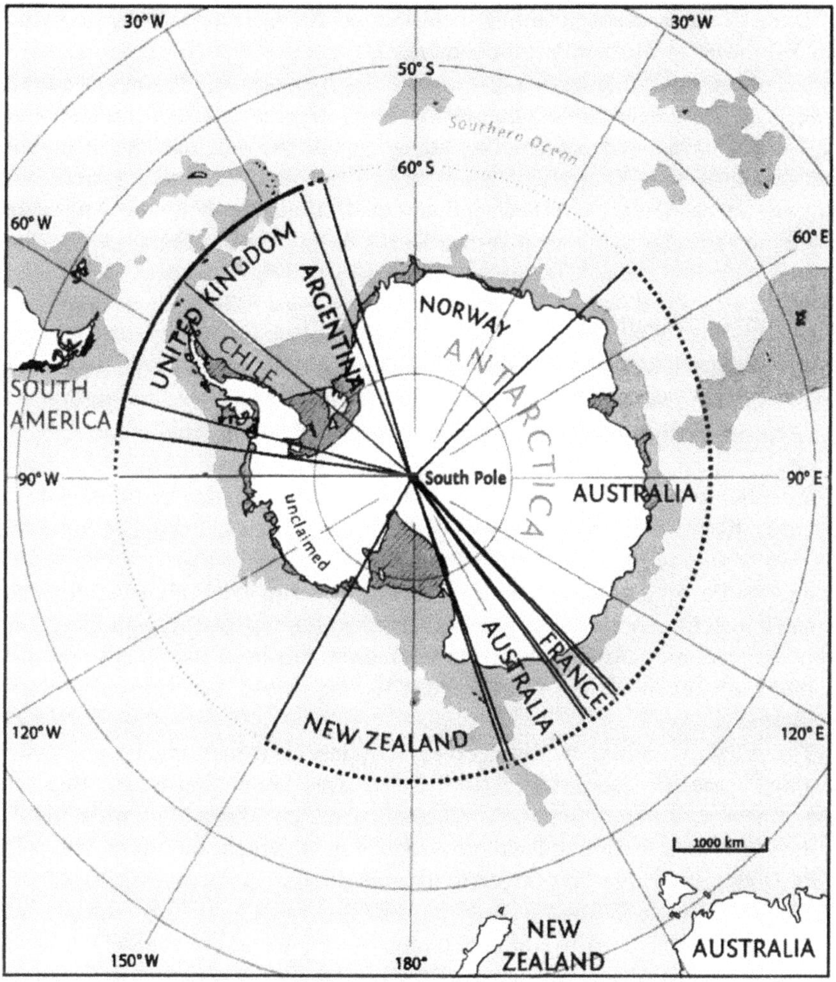


*Figure 1.1* Antarctic territorial claims
Source: Alan D. Hemmings, 'Security beyond claims', in Alan D. Hemmings, Donald R. Rothwell and Karen N. Scott (eds) *Antarctic Security in the Twenty-First Century: Legal and policy perspectives* (London: Routledge, 2012) at 71.

the United States displaced the United Kingdom as the key Antarctic power and shaped the new regional dispensation under the Antarctic Treaty. The United States and the Soviet Union, whatever their differences, adopted a common policy in both refusing to recognise any of the seven territorial claims, and whilst not making claims themselves (despite British Empire hopes inter-war that the United States might claim the 'unclaimed sector', and thus ensure that control of the continent was largely an Anglo affair) each reserving a basis-to-claim if such became desirable at a later date (which has led me to term them 'semi-claimants').[36]

So, in quite tangible ways, the Antarctic legal system has been substantially influenced by Anglophone states, and their interests and legal philosophies. This is not to deny agency to other states outside the Anglosphere in shaping the detail of the Antarctic legal system – Argentina, Chile, France and Norway in particular have been influential. But as elsewhere, the Anglo role in shaping the Antarctic legal system seems to have been dominant.

## 4 An international Antarctic legal system

An essentially unregulated Antarctic was plainly untenable in the new world order following World War II, and under US auspices a new dispensation was ushered in through the 1959 Antarctic Treaty.[37] The resulting regime reflects US cultural and legal norms. It is a permissive legal environment – what is not explicitly prohibited is allowed; there is no general requirement for authorisation of activities as there might be under some European legal traditions. There is little institutional development that would impede discretionary state action. Obligations are cast in terms that allow compliance through meeting procedural process – rather than necessarily judging substantive outcomes. And so on. If another state had been the global hegemon at that moment, no doubt the Antarctic regime would reflect its cultural and legal norms.

The ATS that subsequently evolved,[38] added legal instruments addressing sealing,[39] marine harvesting,[40] minerals exploitation (although this was abandoned without coming into force),[41] and environmental protection.[42] Antarctica's international legal governance is still centred upon the ATS. Whilst one may argue that there are in practice some gaps (perhaps widening) between the historic formal structure and norms of the ATS and the way human activity is actually conducted today (see later in the chapter), it is still useful to identify that normative framing. To the extent that one can see commonalities and/or consistency in a philosophy of law in Antarctica, it is in relation to the foundational norms of the ATS. The three most obvious are

36 Alan D. Hemmings, 'Beyond Claims: Towards a non-territorial Antarctic security prism for Australia and New Zealand', *New Zealand Yearbook of International Law* [2008] 6 (2009): 77–91 at 79–80.
37 The seminal work remains Francis M. Auburn, *Antarctic Law and Politics* (Canberra: Croom Helm, 1982).
38 See Arthur Watts, *International Law and the Antarctic Treaty System* (Cambridge: Grotius, 1992); and Ben Saul and Tim Stephens, *Antarctica in International Law* (Oxford: Hart, 2015).
39 CCAS.
40 CCAMLR, note 9.
41 CRAMRA.
42 Madrid Protocol, note 19.

Antarctic exceptionalism, the containment of territorial sovereignty positions, and the privileged role of science.

The Antarctic regime was historically predicated on Antarctic exceptionalism.[43] That is, parties to its instruments – most critically, the Antarctic Treaty, which set the tone and remains the keystone of the regime – construed the Antarctic as *sui generis*. Activities to be regulated in Antarctica were to the maximum extent possible to be regulated as and when they arose by specially elaborated *Antarctic* rules (under existing instruments if possible, through negotiation of new Antarctic instruments if necessary), determined by the decision-making parties to the relevant instruments of the ATS. Concurrence on this approach by states that varied in other aspects of their Antarctic legal, geopolitical and operational preferences and practices, has been critical in providing a unitary approach – and is surely evidence of some degree of convergence on a philosophy of law. After all, this goes to the heart of what legal regulation was to be sought, and how it was to be effected. Exceptionalism had two further advantages for its proponents (the top-tier of Antarctic decision-making states). First, it underpinned their collective hegemony over the region in relation to *external states*, and it protected the accommodation over the most sensitive issue (differing positions on territorial sovereignty) *within* the parties to the ATS. Second, in practice it resulted in a minimalist regulatory development which minimised constraints on autonomous state action and prevented too great an internationalisation of Antarctica. A fuller internationalisation of Antarctic governance (as with the doctrine of common heritage) was seen as a threat to the positions of the territorial claimants, and as risking the entry into the region of (and at worst, its take-over by) the United Nations. A zero-sum-game for those who presently controlled the Antarctic.

Exceptionalism was made possible by what one might term the *three limitations* obtaining in the Antarctic space: (i) the limited number of states with decision-making standing; (ii) the limited suite of human activities underway in Antarctica; and (iii) the limited extent of extra-ATS or global legal instruments having application in Antarctica. With time all three limitations have come under pressure, but the commitment to exceptionalism has not formally dimmed.[44]

Containment of the unresolved territorial positions was a core imperative of the Antarctic Treaty. As is well known (at least in the small community that attends to Antarctic legal affairs!) this was achieved through the celebrated Article IV of the Treaty, which covered the positions of those who

43 Alan D. Hemmings, 'From the New Geopolitics of Resources to Nanotechnology: Emerging Challenges of Globalism in Antarctica', *The Yearbook of Polar Law* 1 (2009): 55–72 at 63.

44 One consequence of which, essentially outside the scope of the present chapter, is increasing difficulty within the ATS in developing new legal obligations.

claimed territory, those who did not claim and rejected the existing (or theoretically future) territorial claims, and the position of the two states (the two superpowers of the day, the Soviet Union and the United States) which made no claim, rejected existing claims, but reserved their basis-of-claim. This *modus vivendi* was considered so significant that Article IV was reiterated as Article IV of CCAMLR, and the Madrid Protocol was drafted so that it could not undermine this commitment.[45] All subsequent parties to the ATS instruments thus necessarily buy-into the Article IV arrangement at the point of, and in order to, gain entry. The commitment to an essentially open-ended agreement to disagree on a significant legal matter – rights to territory – is a position of legal convergence, novel to the Antarctic regime. This is not to say, however, that the continuing territorial claims, howsoever politically contained through Article IV of the Antarctic Treaty, are necessarily justified on other grounds.[46]

The third foundational norm to consider here relates to the framing of science in Antarctica and the ATS. Science is both the sanctioned main human activity (ashore at least) and the raison d'être for the infrastructure of Antarctica (stations, airstrips, shipping routes, etc), which plainly also serve other purposes associated with national presence. Science as the Antarctic version of the *mission civilisatrice* and the pursuit of knowledge or enlightenment, have already been noted. This reflects Western rationalist norms that have structured its political and legal systems more generally, and the Antarctic role is therefore not unexpected. But science has also been made integral to the ATS as a legal regime – science is part of the purpose of the instruments, is given particular standing within these as an authority advising decision-making, and science is still to a very considerable extent the glue that holds much of the ATS together, notwithstanding the emergence of other human activities in the region. Various reasons can be adduced for this substantive position. In part it is historical: science could be done in Antarctica when much else could not be. Science was (and is) an activity that states can cooperate around. Accordingly, every Antarctic state necessarily has a national Antarctic programme, whereas not every state fishes there or has an Antarctic tourism industry. The principles upon which it is predicated, and the modalities of its conduct, are generally common across political and ideological divides. A commitment to science provided the restricted community of states that were, in fact, taking control of the Antarctic with a

45 Specifically: Art. 4 (Relationship with the other components of the Antarctic Treaty system) and Art. 5 (Consistency with the other components of the Antarctic Treaty system).

46 For critiques, see Alan D. Hemmings, 'Security beyond claims', in Alan D. Hemmings, Donald R. Rothwell and Karen N. Scott (eds) *Antarctic Security in the Twenty-First Century: Legal and policy perspectives* (London: Routledge, 2012) at 70–94; and Alejandra Mancilla, 'The moral limits of territorial claims in Antarctica', *Ethics & International Affairs* 32 (2018): 339–360.

mechanism to underpin their claims to be acting in the interest of the broader world community ("the interest of all mankind" in the Preamble to the Antarctic Treaty). It may also be conceived of as, and argued to be, politically neutral and disinterested, whether or not this is actually the case.[47]

The general political failure of Antarctic states to adopt the responses necessary in relation to anthropogenic climate change, when so much of the scientific evidence has been accumulated in Antarctica, indicates that it is not necessarily the substantive insights of science but its other functions that explain its role there.[48] Whereas Antarctic exceptionalism and the containment of territorial positions are peculiarly Antarctic legal norms, the Antarctic science norm – and a putative philosophy of law that enables it – is more ambiguous. In a general sense science is everywhere what it is in Antarctica; with purposes, logic and standards that transcend national borders; a truly universal human endeavour at the heart of the technocratic structures that everywhere now underpin governance and what is taken as expertise. Is science in the Antarctic materially in a different legal framing from anywhere else? If it is not, then perhaps it is the function of the science structure and administration (i.e. the institutional aspect) rather than the substantive heart of science per se that is being deployed.

## 5 Drivers of Antarctic legal development

The international legal regime of the ATS can be seen to have committed parties to its instruments to three substantial meta-principles around *peace, science* and the *environment*. Preservation by the Antarctic Treaty of the area for "peaceful purposes only",[49] and by implication applying this to the wider area embraced when CCAMLR is considered,[50] was a foundational purpose of the regime. Likewise, for the reasons considered earlier in the chapter, the establishment and promotion of science as the core human activity in the area. While the 1959 Antarctic Treaty itself said nothing explicitly about the environment (although plainly its contingent demilitarisation and denuclearisation provisions implicitly made a substantive contribution), protecting and managing the environment became an early major

47 For an examination of "technocratic governance", see Jessica O'Reilly, *The Technocratic Antarctic: An Ethnography of Scientific Expertise and Environmental Governance* (Ithaca: Cornell University Press, 2017).

48 For one example, concerning the geopolitical aspects of ice-core drilling, see Alan D. Hemmings, 'Subglacial nationalisms' in Elizabeth Leane and Jeffrey McGee (eds) *Anthropocene Antarctica: Perspectives from the Humanities, Law and Social Sciences* (London: Routledge, 2020) at 33–55.

49 Article 1.

50 The 9th recital of the Preamble to CCAMLR reads: "believing that it is in the interest of all mankind to preserve the waters surrounding the Antarctic continent for peaceful purposes only and to prevent their becoming the scene or object of international discord".

focus for the ATCMs.[51] The ATS was created by the addition of new conventions on seals (CCAS) and marine living resources (CCAMLR) – although the purposes of both conventions included managed harvesting – and the Madrid Protocol, all of which address conservation/environmental protection.[52] Whereas the meta-principles relating to peace and science were established at the inception of the regime and have not subsequently been developed further, the meta-principle of environmental protection has been an ongoing project, and indeed remains the main preoccupation of the diplomatic meetings of the ATS and the Antarctic Treaty and CCAMLR secretariats to this day. Indeed, in parallel with global developments, concern about the nature and trajectory of environmental change as a result of the climate emergency is deepening,[53] and increasingly the Antarctic presents environmental ethics questions.[54] For all their differences in detail, in relation to states' interpretation of what the obligations are, how these are to be realised, and irrespective of their preferred Antarctic futures, formal commitment to these meta-values appears to be solid across the membership of the ATS. Since these meta-principles are codified in the instruments and decisions of the ATS, they are substantially legal obligations. Is this a demonstration of the emergence of a particular pan-ATS philosophy of law in relation to Antarctic affairs (or at least some part of those affairs), or are the participant states arriving at an apparently common position through pragmatic application of quite different legal and philosophical approaches to their particular engagement with the area? Or are we seeing an amalgam of pan-ATS and particularist approaches?

If we stand back from the present Antarctic moment, and do not assume a sort of permanent present, we see that with the passage of time the situation in the Antarctic (as both a geographical place, and – through the ATS – as a politico-legal regime) has been challenged by various developments.[55] First, the technical enabling of resource exploitation required regulatory structures to adjudicate competing interests – entailing, as noted, the development of the ATS from the anchor of the Antarctic Treaty, and a slowly increasing cast of participants as the issues arising in the region became of general

51 The Third ATCM adopted the 'Agreed Measures for the Conservation of Antarctic Fauna and Flora' in 1964.

52 For a general consideration of these matters, see Christopher C. Joyner, *Governing the Frozen Commons: The Antarctic Regime and Environmental Protection* (Columbia: University of South Carolina Press, 1998).

53 See e.g. Steven L. Chown, 'Antarctic environmental challenges in a global context', in Klaus Dodds, Alan D. Hemmings and Peder Roberts (eds) *Handbook on the Politics of Antarctica* (Cheltenham: Elgar, 2017) at 523–539.

54 Tina Tin, 'From the Anthropocentric to the Abiotic: Environmental ethics and values in the Antarctic wilderness', *Environmental Ethics* 39 (2017): 57–74.

55 For a general overview by the present author, see Alan D. Hemmings, 'Antarctic politics in a transforming global geopolitics', in Klaus Dodds, Alan D. Hemmings and Peder Roberts (eds) *Handbook on the Politics of Antarctica* (Cheltenham: Elgar, 2017) at 507–522.

international (including economic) interest. Second, the penetration of Antarctic affairs by external actors and events – including the G77 critique of the ATS regional hegemony in the course of the calls for a New International Economic Order in the 1980s; the consequences of the global reach of the UN Law of the Sea Convention;[56] environmental concerns across civil society about the propriety and environmental consequences of Antarctic resource exploitation (first marine harvesting, then more rigorously around mineral resources); the ending of the Cold War and the rise of the global south; globalisation and then the re-emergence of nationalism (events that were variously coupled causally and temporally). In other words, the various transformations in the international system over time. Third, through the paradox of "success" – whereby the very durability of the ATS inevitably meant that temporal factors became manifest, with the accumulation of inconsistencies, increasingly divergent expectations and interpretations of duties and rights, and the spill-over of expectations, practice and norms from global developments outside the ATS. The 'constructive-ambiguity' of legal drafting may aid in the achievement of consensus and the adoption of an instrument, but at some point, perhaps much later, as the instrument is operationalised, ambiguities arise and may prove vexatious or even fatal to the supposed purposes of the instrument. Even foundational provisions of the Antarctic legal dispensation, such as demilitarisation, become more nuanced in an era of fuzzy military-civil boundaries, joint-use technologies and networked global systems, so different from the military picture of the 1950s.[57]

In the early 21st century, the nature of human engagement with the Antarctic is vastly more complex than it was in the late 1950s when the Antarctic Treaty was negotiated. For all their differences, the 12 original signatories were a tight group – in terms of capabilities, the types of activities they were seeking to conduct, and in the generally low intensity of those activities. And states, whatever their form, were more substantively in control of the activities that could occur there than they are today. The legal obligations were limited, and entirely in their hands. Today, the body of regional Antarctic and global law, institutions and norms is denser, and the relationships across these vastly more complex. In a region where there may be fewer impediments to non-state entities conducting the dominant human activities than elsewhere in a still largely Westphalian world order, there are profound and unresolved issues around whose rights and purposes do and should have standing in the Antarctic and where this will be decided. Antarctic actors (whether states or other operators) pursue different goals (and within states, goals vary with the

56 United Nations Convention on the Law of the Sea, 10 December 1982, 21 ILM 1261.

57 Alan D. Hemmings, 'Challenges to substantive demilitarisation in the Antarctic Treaty Area', Presentation at the 12th Polar Law Symposium, 'The Fundamental Principles of Polar Law', Hobart, Australia, 1–4 December 2019.

actor); the foci and purposes of legal obligation are contested; and the historic dominance of Western conceptions of law may be under challenge from the now emergent global powers of the south, even if these states presently accept large parts of the global legal order, and from critiques of historic Western legal norms *within* some Western states.

## 6 The changing world order in the Antarctic

One may conclude that philosophy of law in the Antarctic is *not* demonstrably "specific, peculiar and idiosyncratic" in the way that Dawid Bunikowski (Chapter 2 of this volume) characterises philosophy of law in the Arctic. This polar difference reflects in part the long indigenous human presence in the Arctic, compared to the more recently initiated and overwhelmingly Western Eurocentric presence in the Antarctic. With the exception of Japan, non-European states substantially engaged with the Antarctic, and became part of the politico-legal Antarctic system (the ATS) only from the 1980s. Even then, there was a substantial lag time between their joining the ATS and their becoming (whether actually or potentially, in the eyes of other parties and perhaps themselves) significant actors within it.

That process is still unfolding, and that is at the heart of the present Western anxiety about a relative shift in capabilities, intention and power within the Antarctic regime, particularly in relation to China. There is no doubt that this is happening. The fact that the ATS has been in a sort of institutional hiatus since the entry into force of its last component instrument (the Madrid Protocol) in 1998[58] has also been of significance. No further major instrument has been under negotiation, let alone adopted since the Madrid Protocol in 1991. Second order legally binding obligations – in relation to tourism,[59] through Antarctic Treaty Measures adopted in 2004 and 2009; and the 6th Annex to the Madrid Protocol concerning Liability,[60] also adopted as a Measure in 2005 – have not been brought into force; and no further comparable Measures are even under development. This has meant that there have been no material developments of the ATS legal regime underway, within which one might see any evidence of non-Western states' influence and any reflections of differing legal traditions or norms.

Some common (albeit still largely historic Western) philosophy of law seems evident in relation to the foundational elements of the ATS – most particularly in relation to exceptionalism and containment of territorial positions. Here one may, indeed, see a particular philosophy of Antarctic law in

58 Annex V to the Madrid Protocol entered into force in 2002.

59 India, 'Towards a Comprehensive, Proactive and Effective Antarctic Tourism Policy: Turning Recommendations into Action', *Information Paper* 104 rev. 1 (38th Antarctic Treaty Consultative Meeting: Sofia, 2015).

60 Alan D. Hemmings, 'Liability postponed: the failure to bring Annex VI of the Madrid Protocol into force', *The Polar Journal* 8 (2018): 315–332.

evidence. In relation to the position of science, the picture is less clear, and may be becoming even less clear. A continued failure of global society to take onboard the findings of science in Antarctica (or elsewhere) rather undercuts the validity of the supposed centrality of science in the governance system of the ATS. But, beneath this superstructure, what we see in Antarctica is a constellation of philosophies of law, with clusters around particular suns – European/Western framings; the Anglosphere; the Sinosphere (see Nengye Liu and Qi Xu, Chapter 8 in this volume); non-Western approaches more generally; environmental/scientific and corporate framings. This may be unavoidable, given the growth in the Antarctic-engaged community globally, and the challenge to the historic exceptionalism that is posed by globalism. Whether such a diversity of philosophies of law will aid or complicate our collective governance of the Antarctic is at this point unclear.

## Acknowledgements

I thank colleagues with whom I have worked in Antarctic fora, and/or written about the underpinnings and functioning of the ATS, over the past several decades, most notably: Kees Bastmeijer, the late David Bederman, Sanjay Chaturvedi, Klaus Dodds, Neil Gilbert, the late Chris Joyner, Daniela Liggett, Michelle Rogan-Finnemore, Don Rothwell, Ricardo Roura, Juan Francisco Salazar, Karen Scott, Tim Stephens. However, none of these people should necessarily be implicated in the interpretations, analyses or positions adopted in the chapter, for which sole responsible rests with the author.

Chapter 2

# The philosophy of law in the Arctic

*Dawid Bunikowski*[1]

## 1 Introduction

The philosophy of law in the Arctic is not a new topic. A group of lawyers, philosophers and anthropologists wrote a book on this subject in 2016.[2] This chapter highlights and develops many ideas from that book. The book put on the table two questions for which answer is "the essence of the philosophy of law in the Arctic"[3]: "1) What is 'Arctic indigenous peoples' law' from the point of view of Western philosophy of law?, 2) What is "law' for indigenous peoples in the Arctic?"[4] In the book, the authors considered the answers to those questions. Thus, first of all, the idea was that we should think of how Western philosophy of law thinks of Arctic indigenous peoples' law and what Arctic indigenous peoples' law means for Western legal theory/philosophy. Here we use Western concepts and methodologies. Then, second, we have to think of how Arctic indigenous peoples perceive law (both Western and indigenous) and what law is for them. Indigenous concepts and methodologies are applied in this point. Altogether, research concerning philosophy of law in the Arctic is interdisciplinary: between law, philosophy, anthropology, politics, history, cultural studies, etc.

More generally speaking, for example, when one focuses on Arctic indigenous peoples' law from the point of view of Western philosophy of law, one may speak of indigenous human rights and self-determination in

1 Department of Public Administration, State University of Applied Sciences in Wloclawek, Poland; School of Theology, Philosophical Faculty, University of Eastern Finland, dawidbu@uef.fi.

2 D. Bunikowski (ed), *Philosophy of law in the Arctic*, Rovaniemi/Oulu, UArctic, 2016 (e-book). The motto of this e-book was taken from the Finnish anthropologist Juha Pentikäinen's book: "The term 'Arctic' is not only ecological but also mythical. The term refers to the areas which were thought to be located under the constellation 'Ursa Major' (the Great Bear)". See J. Pentikäinen, *Shamanism and Culture*, Helsinki, Etnika Oy, 2006, 120.

3 D. Bunikowski, note 2 at 10.

4 Ibid.

general,[5] the right of indigenous peoples to their own law[6] or interlegality as a mix of indigenous customary law and Western law.[7] While thinking of "law" for indigenous peoples in the Arctic, one can pay attention to, for example, cosmology and law: the logic of the gift,[8] (Sámi) old customary law[9] and indigenous constitutionalism in Canada's context.[10]

However, the aim of this chapter is to enable the reader to find out the answers to these two questions. This aim is to be realised by analysing a selection of the main topics of the philosophy of law in the Arctic. These topics are as follows:

1 Fundamental concepts: law in the Arctic, Arctic legal tradition, the Arctic as common good and legal pluralism.
2 Arctic cosmologies, beliefs, art and shamanism.
3 Arctic lands and waters and the environment.
4 Indigenous rights (IR) and customary law in the Arctic.
5 The future of philosophy of law in the Arctic: teaching via new tools, and global governance.

Sometimes scholars in Finland ask why philosophy of law in the Arctic is different and why it should be so idiosyncratic. In my view, philosophy of law in the Arctic is different from general philosophy of law (as it is understood in the West) and its crucial problems and main topics, because the concept of law in the Arctic is peculiar, the environment of the Arctic is specific, the ways

5 See e.g. T.G. Svensson, 'Indigenous rights and customary law discourse: comparing the Nisga'a and the Sámi', *Journal of Legal Pluralism and Unofficial Law*, 47, 2002, 1–35; Ch. Allard and S. Funderud Skogvang (eds), *Indigenous Rights in Scandinavia: Autonomous Sami Law*, Farnham, Ashgate Publishing, 2015; W. Twining, *Globalisation and legal theory*, Cambridge, Cambridge University Press, 2000, 240.
6 See D. Bunikowski, 'The Right of Indigenous Peoples to their Own Law', *Nordic Journal of Law and Justice, Retfærd*, 2, 2017, 47–63.
7 See e.g. A. Hoekema, 'European Legal Encounters Between Minority and Majority Cultures: Cases of Interlegality', *Journal of Legal Pluralism*, 51, 2005, 1–28.
8 See e.g. R. Kuokkanen, 'The Logic of the Gift: Reclaiming Indigenous Peoples' Philosophies', in T. Botz-Bornsteinand and J. Hengelbrock (eds), *ReEthnicizing the Minds? Cultural Revival in Contemporary Thought*, Amsterdam/New York, Rodopi, 2006, 251–271.
9 See e.g. M. Åhrén, 'Indigenous Peoples' Culture, Customs, and Traditions and Customary Law – the Saami People's Perspective', *Arizona Journal of International & Comparative Law*, 21 (1), 2004, 63–112. By the way, Åhrén is against the idea of legal pluralism, because legal pluralism means that there are at least two normative orders in one sphere (social, geographical). Åhrén suggests that it should go back to the Sámi old customary laws concerning natural resources management instead. No state law should be applied then. State law is understood as something external and strange here.
10 See J. Borrows, *Freedom and Indigenous Constitutionalism*, Toronto, University of Toronto Press, Scholarly Publishing Division, 2016.

of doing things in the Arctic remain harsh, and the future of the Arctic seems unclear. Some scholars say that maybe this topic should be interpreted in context of postcolonial studies. I guess that the political history of the Arctic seems difficult, but philosophy of law is a wider forum than postcolonial studies in order to discuss issues such as environment, indigeneity, rights, etc. Briefly, it is about five topics: concepts, cosmology, lands, rights and customs/customary law, and future. Usually, philosophy of law in a Western sense or any philosophy of law that claims to be universal and common for all cultures and countries is not so interested in cosmologies, IR, customary laws or lands. Mostly, philosophy of law focuses on sources of law, validity of law, law and morality relations, law and justice, legal interpretation, legal argumentation, law application, law making, etc. These are general topics, while philosophy of law in the Arctic has its own specific and peculiar topics. These will be presented in the following section.

## 2 Fundamental concepts: law in the Arctic, Arctic legal tradition, the Arctic as common good and legal pluralism

### *2.1 Law in the Arctic*

Law in the Arctic might be understood in different ways. There are different kinds of law in this region: international law, state (national) law, local law, customary law, indigenous customary laws. Obviously, all these kinds of law interact with each other. Sometimes clashes between these kinds of law appear, because there are, in fact, clashes between the values that are behind these kinds of law; and there are different interests of different agents who make or develop their kind of law. In this section, we are not to answer the never-ending question of definition what law is – rather we are to answer how law might be described in an Arctic context. Law might be understood not only as international treaties or acts passed by parliaments or governments (or local authorities), but also as unwritten customary laws of indigenous peoples, which exist as different legal "orders".[11] Law in the Arctic is related to indigenous cultures. However, law is also about a mix of understandings of what law is: law is between the state and the indigenous, between the written and the customary. It is necessary to understand and interpret indigenous customary laws in the Arctic as well as it is important to analyse positive law coming from official legal orders (state and international legal frameworks). The concept of law in the Arctic is more sophisticated than it is in Western legal orders. In this sense, philosophy of law in the Arctic has its non-positivist and non-centrist character while perceiving the diverse nature of law.

11 In the case of indigenous customary law, it is difficult to clearly admit that it is *an order* in a Western sense. It is an order, but the indigenous order. It is a *system* of rules of behaviour, beliefs, power, etc. The word "system" is also Western.

## *2.2 Arctic legal tradition*

What is an/the Arctic legal tradition? Jaakko Husa, a comparative legal scholar (originally from Finland), thinks that what we need to do first "in order to discuss the possibility of an Arctic legal tradition" is to "look at how Arctic has been and how it can be conceptualised from the viewpoint of comparative law".[12] Husa is aware of the fact that "From a narrow legal point of view, international law questions concerning mostly territorial claims are at the centre of Arctic issues, like, for instance, contesting national claims of sovereignty over the Arctic area".[13] However, for Husa, "The Arctic is an interesting and challenging area not only geographically and politically but also in a legal sense".[14] This is why one can speak of an Arctic legal tradition. Husa analyses H. Patrick Glenn's theory of legal traditions while thinking of describing "the legal tradition of indigenous peoples' Arctic law": "Glenn distinguished several legal traditions, none of which seems specifically fit to describe the legal tradition of indigenous peoples' Arctic law. In the terminology used by Glenn, this is chthonic law (…)".[15] So what is this chthonic law then? This is "a system of law centred on the sacred character of the cosmos. In other words, it is built upon a certain kind of an idea of nature and man".[16] Husa adds that "In Glenn's analysis the chthonic legal tradition emerged through experience, orality and memory. He regarded this legal tradition as the oldest of all legal traditions. Glenn specifically describes the chthonic legal tradition as a way to live in close harmony with earth".[17] It is necessary to mention that the word χθ⊠ν (khtón) means "earth" or "ground" and "refers to a certain kind of relationship between man and earth".[18] But what about other indigenous peoples and their chthonic legal traditions? Why are Arctic indigenous peoples and their legal tradition so distinctive? "Northness" expressed by the Northern conditions such as ice, snow and special animals (reindeer, caribou) makes a difference.[19] To Husa, there is, indeed, an Arctic legal tradition. "Chthonic Arctic legal tradition" has the following five features. First, an Arctic legal tradition is "not Western positive (State) law, as it has emerged through long experience, orality and memory of indigenous group".[20] Second, it

12 J. Husa, 'Arctic Legal Tradition?', in D. Bunikowski (ed), note 2, 19–25 at 19.
13 Ibid.
14 Ibid.
15 Ibid., at 22.
16 Ibid., at 22–23.
17 Ibid., at 23.
18 Ibid., at 23, footnote 29. Husa rightly mentions in footnote 30 that "Of course, other indigenous peoples may be part of the larger chthonic legal tradition but they lack the 'Northness' which is distinctive for the Arctic indigenous groups. In other words, the Arctic groups' relation to nature is labelled by the Northern conditions (e.g. animals, ice, snow etc.)".
19 Ibid.
20 Ibid., at 23.

"covers the indigenous peoples of the geographical Arctic, who have inhabited this area for thousands of years".[21] To Husa, it is "not the laws or legal systems of Western colonizers, nor is it the laws or customs of non-Arctic indigenous peoples".[22] Third, it "builds especially on the specific connection to the land (earth) that the indigenous peoples have inhabited for very long periods of time".[23] Fourth, it seems "intimately connected to indigenous languages and traditional livelihoods such as reindeer herding, fishing and hunting".[24] Fifth, it is "in danger because of industrialization, social change and environmental issues (e.g. climate change)".[25] Briefly, this tradition is more spiritual and land- and nature-oriented. In this sense, philosophy of law in the Arctic has its spiritual nature.

This last (fifth) factor seems especially important nowadays as Husa concludes that an Arctic legal tradition is "threatened by the tightening grip of Western State laws and their imperialistic embrace". However, it is also clear to Husa that there comes the light at the end of the tunnel: it is "the growing recognition of indigenous rights and the renaissance of self-governing indigenous institutions",[26] and this leads "to a legal recognition of the value and significance of an Arctic indigenous legal tradition".[27] There is no contradiction of this in the Canadian legal scholar Diana Ginn's metaphorical words on the philosophy of law in Canada's North "as a bridge": "The philosophy of law in Canada's North can best be understood through the metaphor of a bridge. This metaphor is explored here in three contexts: recognition of aboriginal customary law; resolution of land and self-governance claims through the doctrine of aboriginal rights; and devolution of jurisdiction to territorial governments".[28]

21 Ibid.
22 Ibid.
23 Ibid., at 24.
24 Ibid.
25 Ibid.
26 Ibid.
27 Ibid. For instance, on the Sámi legal culture and its recognition by Norwegian law, see Ø. Ravna, 'Sámi Legal Culture – and its Place in Norwegian Law', 2009, available online at https://sa.uit.no/Content/219672/cache=20172704050328/Sami%20Legal%20Culture%20%20and%20its%20Place%20in%20Norw.%20Law%2C%20in%20Rendezvous%20of%20European%20Legal%20Cultures.pdf.
28 D. Ginn, 'The Philosophy of Law in Canada's North', in D. Bunikowski, note 2, 26–31 at 26. Ginn claims that "Using the metaphor of a bridge is not intended to portray an unrealistically rosy picture of the Canadian North: there is still a great deal of work to be done in building healthy communities, as is evident from high levels of illness, addictions, poverty and suicide, and in promoting sustainable economic development while respecting traditional ways of life" (at 29). Ginn's aim is not to talk about a Utopia. However, she is aware that "by providing a bridge between different legal systems, between aboriginal use and occupation of the lands and the assertion of Crown sovereignty, and between more and less autonomous models of government, each of these has played some role in

### *2.3 The Arctic as common good*

Also, "common good" as a concept is significant for philosophers of law in the Arctic. Ko Hasegawa, a Japanese legal theorist, treats the Arctic as a common good. What does he mean by that? Hasegawa thinks that "the moral nature of the Arctic" is a "fundamental problem of the philosophy of law in the Arctic", but particularly, "the idea of common good in the Arctic looks much relevant when we see many political, legal, or economic issues concerning the Arctic".[29] Hasegawa puts on the table a question on "the fundamental issue for the preservation and utilization of various conditions and resources in the Arctic": "Should the region of the Arctic be shared by all the relevant societies and peoples, or be appropriated severally by each of those societies and peoples?"[30] This is not only an economic or political problem or question but, in fact, a deep philosophical, moral and cosmological problem, according to Hasegawa.[31] He also distinguishes the concepts of common good, collective goods (such as oil) and public goods (such as water supply). Thus, "the point that common good is invaluable for human life is the difference from collective goods and public goods"[32] and "common good indicates the very necessity of communal hold for the intrinsic and essential basis of human lives".[33] Also, as Hasegawa thinks, the idea of common good is mostly related to "the holistic condition for all human beings in a society, as well as the idea of global common good for all the peoples on this globe".[34] What is common good then? It is "the good that is invaluably basic for any individuals, classes, groups, or communities of divergent people in society, without regard to their political, economic, or cultural variations".[35] What is also interesting in Hasegawa's consideration on common good in the Arctic is his statement that "Common good in a society can be a part of a global common good".[36] The Arctic as a common good might be global while

offering pragmatic, contextual and pluralistic responses to the challenges and conundrums of the Canadian North" (at 29). She speaks of pluralistic legal systems, in fact.

29 K. Hasegawa, 'The Arctic as Common Good', in D. Bunikowski, note 2, 32–38 at 32.

30 Ibid.

31 Ibid, at 37. Hasegawa points out *expressis verbis* in footnote 57 at 37: "To understand why we have to live under common good is to answer the meaning of life for human being, which, I believe, must face another problem about her communal nature. It might become the problem of the communality of communalities in the Arctic".

32 Ibid., footnote 53 at 34.

33 Ibid., at 34.

34 Ibid., at 33. He adds as an example that "(...) it is evident that clean air is an invaluable life condition for all the people in a society, as well as for all the peoples on this globe. This means not simply that clean air is non-exclusionarily sharable but rather that anyone in society cannot live well at all without that condition".

35 Ibid.

36 Ibid., footnote 51 at 33.

thinking of only Hasegawa's two examples: clean air and "climate condition".[37]

However, Hasegawa tries to classify the most important problems concerning the Arctic as a common good. He mentions these four problems: "the problem of *circumstance*", "the problem of *distribution*", and "the problem of *participation*", and "the problem that is the common thread of them, namely the problem of *communality*".[38] The problem of *circumstance* relates to "the possibility of the recognition of common good: how can some good or goods be grasped as invaluably common?"[39] The problem of *distribution* is about "the standards of distribution or redistribution of common good among the relevant peoples, organizations, or states around the Arctic: how can common good be shared equally among relevant societal units?"[40] The problem of *participation* concerns "the conditions of human decision-making for the effective use of common good: how can the relevant units around the region in question decide the administrative issues on the common good in question in a fair way?"[41] The problem of *communality* is connected with "the prerequisites of the three problems explicated so far: how the circumstance, distribution, and participation concerning common good can be relevantly common among the relevant units in the region in question?"[42] These all are "empirical problems".[43]

37 Ibid. Hasegawa rightly writes that "the climate change in a region might influence other changes in other regions on the globe".
38 See ibid., at 34.
39 Ibid.
40 Ibid.
41 Ibid.
42 Ibid.
43 See ibid., at 36, where Hasegawa writes as follows about the most important current concrete issues in the Arctic "from the viewpoint of common good in the Arctic":

(1)"whether and to what extent natural resources and conditions in the Arctic are to be preserved for the stable natural environment in the region and on this globe" – this is the question of preservation of natural resources and climate conditions;

(2)"whether and to what extent the important species should be protected and preserved for the maintenance of the bio-diversity in this region" – this is the question of protection of significant species and bio-diversity;

(3)"whether and to what extent the Arctic is to be geographically arranged to share by the societies or peoples concerned and thereby important resources are to be explored for the common or universal interests of the peoples in this region or on this globe" – this is the question of the use of the region and its resources by different actors for the common good or for interests of the peoples of the region;

(4)"whether and to what extent the interests of minority peoples in the Arctic, whose livings are endangered by capitalistic globalization and other private exploitations from the advanced parts of the world, should be respected in harmony with relevant global considerations" – this is the question of protection of

All these questions are of significant importance for many practical reasons. and it is "hasty" to "advocate" some "particular positions" without deeper considerations, "deep reflections". This is why, Hasegawa claims, "we need the exploration of the philosophy of law in the Arctic".[44] Hasegawa suggests that we should "answer to these issues affirmatively or negatively" but also "properly" as these are "significant problems for the philosophy of law in the Arctic as common good".[45] Lastly, Hasegawa's theory seems cosmology-oriented, as said before: in his words, "the exploration of the Arctic as common good is ultimately a cosmological problem on the very meaning of life for human beings in that vast region in determining the communality of the common good in question".[46] In this sense, philosophy of law in the Arctic has its cosmological nature.

### 2.4 Legal pluralism

Legal pluralism is another important concept of philosophy of law in the Arctic. The theory of legal pluralism is very well described in the worldwide literature and, here, there is no sense in mentioning all the most important scholars who have worked on it so far. What is legal pluralism and why is it so important in the Arctic? It is "a situation in which there are at least two normative systems in the same social sphere, and there is no rule of recognition" (in Hart's sense) about "which rule is more important and which rule to choose and apply".[47] This theory describes and explains tensions between laws such as state and unofficial laws, or international and domestic laws, or domestic and local laws. This helps to resolve the tensions by proposing relevant models. These models recognise customary laws.[48] In this context, we bear in mind Arctic indigenous customary laws. There are successful attempts to combine the theory of legal pluralism with the theory of cultural ecology in order to build a legal-pluralistic model which may help recognise indigenous customary laws in the Arctic.[49] In this sense, philosophy of law in the Arctic has its legal-pluralistic nature.

indigenous rights. These rights are broadly understood as political, economic, social, cultural and linguistic rights.

44 Ibid., at 36.

45 Ibid., at 37.

46 Ibid.

47 See how the theory of legal pluralism is discussed in an Arctic context, how the theory of legal pluralism is combined with the theory of cultural ecology and what a new model of relations between indigenous and state laws/communities is proposed in: D. Bunikowski and P. Dillon, 'Arguments from cultural ecology and legal pluralism for recognising indigenous customary law in the Arctic', in L. Heinämäki and T.M. Herrmann (eds), *Experiencing and Safeguarding the Sacred in the Arctic: Sacred Natural Sites, Cultural Landscapes and Indigenous Peoples' Rights*, Cham, Springer, 2017, 37–64 at 41.

48 Ibid.

49 Ibid. Bunikowski and Dillon's mentioned paper proposes such a model based on the two theories. See D. Bunikowski and P. Dillon, note 47 at 42–45. Also, see

## 3 Arctic cosmologies, beliefs, art and shamanism

Paradoxically and idiosyncratically, cosmology(ies), beliefs, art and shamanism matter greatly for philosophy of law in the Arctic. It is interesting that, usually, philosophy of law in the West or elsewhere is not interested in such issues, but philosophy of law in the Arctic pays attention to them. First, cosmology concerns the beginning and structure of the universe. It includes also eschatology, i.e. the sense and destiny of the universe. Cosmology is somehow related to philosophy or theology, but it seems wider as a point of view or system of views. Arctic indigenous cosmology is deeply spiritual. Second, beliefs are related to religion, which in an Arctic context means that the "religion" of Arctic indigenous peoples seems to have been nature, in which nature was appreciated like a mother of the Earth. Third, art was always the most important form of aesthetical expression of people living in the Arctic. Rock paintings, craft or drums in Finland are a great example of this human activity. Fourth, shamanism is a traditional way of life. It is not a religion in a Western sense. A shaman is a healer, a man who travels through the *worlds*, a spiritual person, a leader of a given community, and a foreteller. Shamanism was always very important in the indigenous Arctic. However, it has been limited due to the pressure made by Christianity and different Christian denominations supported by state tools (restrictive law; state educational system; limited freedom of religion). Interestingly, some scholars may also combine Arctic indigenous cosmology or cosmologies with nomadism as a traditional way of life.

As Dawid Bunikowski and Patrick Dillon claim, cosmology and indigenous customary laws in the Arctic are very interconnected. The authors clearly say that "Indigenous customary rules are inseparable from cosmology, way of life, morality, beliefs, and traditions".[50] For example, Dawid Bunikowski, a Polish legal philosopher from Eastern Finland, analyses the legal-philosophical and anthropological-cultural dimensions of Sámi reindeer husbandry, and comments that Sámi philosophy of life "is based on unwritten, traditional rules of conduct and the system of beliefs. Nature is like a mother for the Sámi people".[51] The English cultural ecologist Patrick Dillon, who worked in

their other paper: P. Dillon and D. Bunikowski, 'A framework for location-sensitive governance as a contribution to developing inclusivity and sustainable lifestyles with particular reference to the Arctic', in K. Hossain and A. Petrétei (eds), *Current Developments in Arctic Law, 5*, Rovaniemi, University of Lapland, 2017, 16–28.

50 D. Bunikowski and P. Dillon, note 47 at 43.

51 D. Bunikowski, 'Sámi reindeer husbandry: legal-philosophical and cultural: anthropological dimensions', *Rajshahi University Law Journal*, 9, 2014 (the journal also mentioned that it was actually published in 2016), 42–56 at 44. Bunikowski also admits that the Sámi people knew the concept of sustainable development (in terms of exploitation of natural resources) and believed in harmony between humans and nature.

Eastern Finland for 25 years, makes connections "between art, environment and nomadic cosmologies" and interconnected "these to matters concerned with customary laws".[52] Dillon states that "Customary laws are primarily reflected in people's *behaviour* within an environment, but they can also be given form and meaning through *art*".[53] The English historian of religion Francis Joy working in Lapland rejects this common statement that shamanism is dead and does not exist in the Arctic.[54] Shamanism as an indigenous way of life is still alive in the Arctic. It has its own rules which are traditional, spiritual and mystical. Both Dillon and Joy seek cosmologies, myths, beliefs in cultural artefacts of the Sámi people. Dillon is known for his research on their art[55] and craft. Joy's expertise in Sámi drums and rock paintings seems significant as well.

It is clear that Arctic indigenous cosmologies are expressed in customary laws. These laws have been developed for centuries in processes of adaptation to the environments indigenous peoples traditionally occupy and inhabit.[56] Beliefs are part of this social order. Art always helped indigenous peoples express their perception of the world, their values, but also their fears and joys. Shamanism helped them to "translate" and understand the world and to travel between the *unseen worlds*.

## 4 Arctic lands and waters and the environment

Fishing waters, hunting grounds, grazing or pasture fields, forests and other lands are at the core of life in the Arctic, especially for indigenous peoples (but

52 See P. Dillon, 'Customary Laws and Nomadic Cosmologies of Art and the Environment', in D. Bunikowski, note 2, 46–52.

53 Ibid., at 47. This is curious how Dillon defines cosmology: it is "a form of universal or divine law which becomes internalised as beliefs and values, and these, in turn, are expressed within a community as customary laws" (at 47).

54 See more: F. Joy, 'Sámi Shamanism Past and Present and the Desecration of the Sacred in Finland', in D. Bunikowski, note 2, 53–60 at 57. Joy made interviews with shamans living in Finland and observed shamans living in Sweden and Norway. He noticed: "In interviews carried out with Sámi shamans in Finland, the mentality surrounding the destruction of shamanism has been expressed in terms of a constant struggle to keep what is left alive with regard to the fragments of history" (at 57), but also added that "The Sámi shamans in Finland, for the most remain invisible and work in secret, which is part of the traditional ways and customs and also as a way to help protect what is left of the culture and religion. The situation in Sweden and Norway is very different" (at 58).

55 Dillon speaks of Sámi art that "The art is an integral part of lived experience, celebrated through handicraft, performance and oral tradition" (at 49–50).

56 See e.g. Dillon, who puts it in this way: "The customary laws of nomadic people have developed over centuries of adaptation through the people having to respond to the immediate opportunities and challenges of the environments through which they travel and in which they live. These laws are part of cosmologies: customary rules that come from traditions based on common, long-standing beliefs and understandings of the world and of the universe" (at 48).

not only for them – they also seem crucial for non-indigenous peoples). Of course, a style of life changes, which means that many indigenous peoples in the Arctic are completely modern and Westernised now: they do not keep up with their ancestors' traditional ways of life and activities. Of, course, this – as it is sometimes presented in the media – "lost meaning of life" implies personal and social consequences (such as depression, alcoholism, drug addiction, trauma, unemployment, poverty, suicides, abortion, etc.). The most well-known examples of this negative process came to light at the end of the 20th century and the beginning of the 21st century, and concerned some indigenous communities in Canada and Greenland.[57] Notwithstanding this social phenomenon, it is enough to claim that narratives on Arctic lands, waters and environment as a whole are an important part of philosophy of law in the Arctic.

As we can read in the section entitled "Philosophy of the Agreement" of the James Bay and Northern Quebec Agreement of 1975 (JBNQA), which was a deal/treaty (in terms of constitutional law) between the government of Quebec and the *native peoples* of this province: "Land is the very basis of the Cree and Inuit cultures. And it is not just a matter of sustaining themselves with the harvest of the land, which of course they do. They have a mystique about the land, and what it contains. They have a special relationship with the land that their ancestors inhabited, a link, something indefinable but real and genuine nevertheless".[58] This axiological framework perceives a great understanding of indigenous belonging to their land.[59] Also, the Finnish international lawyer Leena Heinamäki and the Sámi social scholars Jarno and Sanna Valkonen, while interestingly discussing "ontological basis of the Sámi belongingness to the land and lack of legal

57 Mostly, this meant the Inuit people.

58 The James Bay and Northern Quebec Agreement of 1975 (JBNQA), at 11. The Agreement adds that "The native peoples who will be parties to this Agreement are not the people you see in our cities selling artwork and handicrafts. They are not people who offer themselves as a tourist attraction. They are not people who do odd jobs and live on pizzas and other delicacies of our supposedly advanced southern civilization. They are flesh-and-blood people who live and work in communion with the land they inhabit and who express, in their everyday activities, the continuity of a long, long tradition. They are living, if I may say so, a wholesome life in harmony with the land. They are at peace with nature" (at 11).

59 See also D. Bunikowski, 'Human security as philosophy of law and legal pluralism in Arctic indigenous areas', in K. Hossain and Anna Petrétei (eds), *Unconventional Aspects of Human Security. Cases from the Barents Region*, Rovaniemi, University of Lapland, Juridica Lapponica 45, 2018, 4–62. Generally, for instance, in Sámi culture, land has both a material and immaterial (spiritual) entity. Also, since the Sámi people traditionally occupied (and still live in) northern parts of Sweden and Norway, Finnish Lapland, and northern Russia, then they name this region "Sápmi". It is a material (physical) and spiritual land – homeland. See more: J. Porsanger, 'A Close Relationship to Nature: The Basis of Religion', in J. Pennanen and K. Näkkäläjärvi (eds), *Siidastallan. From Lapp Communities to Modern Sámi Life*, Inari, The Inari Sámi Museum, 2003, 151.

recognition", point out that "The connection to the land in Sámi culture is an ethnic underpinning of all Sámi groups and the foundation from which Sámi culture dwells", so "Any examination of the Sámi connection to the land must take into consideration that the connection involves both the intangible and material cultural components. The Sámi worldview makes no distinction between nature and culture (...)".[60] For example, in Sámi culture it is also renowned that there are some places called *sieidi* – these are sacred sites.[61] Such sites are also known in other indigenous traditions (e.g. for the Nisga'a people in British Columbia in Canada[62]).

In addition to this, as René Kuppe, an Austrian legal theorist, analyses John Locke's theory of sovereignty in the light of the colonisation of the territories occupied by indigenous peoples in North America and the Nordic countries, and interestingly claims, "The consequences of political theories about indigenous people, living in a so-called state of nature, can be detected not only in overseas territories discovered in remote parts of the world, but also in Nordic indigenous territories conquered by settlers from neighbouring civilized nations".[63] Indigenous peoples lived in the Hobbesian-Lockean "state of nature". They did not know Western concepts of private or public

60 L. Heinamäki, J. Valkonen and S. Valkonen, 'Sámi Relationship with the Land: What Does the Law Fail to Recognize?', in D. Bunikowski, note 2, 71–84 at 76. They refer to another Sámi scholar: "E. Helander-Renvall writes how the Sámi language does not even have the word 'culture', and the word for 'nature' relates rather to inner aspects of nature (such as the nonhuman mind) than to the natural environment or landscape. Nature can also be transformed into culture through different activities, such as handicraft, fishing and healing, and culture may be transformed into nature. 'All places and lands have their special character.'" (at 77–78). This is somehow related to "the philosophy of the gift" in Sámi culture. As Rauna Kuokkanen writes: "Further, the Sámi gift philosophy is apparent in the central role of the female divinities in giving the gift of life (to both human beings and domestic animals, mainly reindeer) and their connection to the land". See R. Kuokkanen, note 8 at 263.

61 There are places (hills, rivers, islands, fields with rocks, etc.) where people can worship, pray, give a gift (such as antlers or some decoration) to the master/spirit of the place, and expect good luck, e.g. in hunting, fishing or personal life. See more: D. Bunikowski, note 51 at 45–46. These offerings are important part of the Sámi culture. As D. Bunikowski and P. Dillon write, "Traditional rules or rituals concerning the offerings were recognised as eternal natural law or customary law. Sámi law in this field was coherent with customs, natural religion, beliefs". See D. Bunikowski, P. Dillon, note 47 at 51.

62 Sacred sites are not only a part of indigenous ("aboriginal", as they say in Canada – see art. 35 of their Constitution of 1982) cultures in Canada but are also recognised by Canadian public/constitutional law. The Nisga'a Final Agreement of 1999 defines "heritage sites" as including "archaeological, burial, historical, and sacred sites". In paragraph 36 ('Protection of Heritage Sites') of chapter 17 ('Cultural Artifacts and Heritage') it is stated that Nisga'a Government "will develop processes to manage heritage sites on Nisga'a Lands in order to preserve the heritage values associated with those sites from proposed land and resource activities that may affect those sites".

63 R. Kuppe, 'The Agricultural Argument and Sami Reindeer Breeding Rights: Reflections on Legal Philosophy in the Arctic', in D. Bunikowski, note 2, 62–70 at 63.

ownership, borders, states, etc., but they had their own unwritten legal systems regulating ownership, use of natural resources and of lands, inheritance, marriage, rituals, wars, etc. Western colonisers depreciated these systems, because they were interested in conquering new lands and people as well as in exploiting natural resources and people. Christianity may have played an important role here, since the mission of Christianity is to spread the Word of God. This is absolutely not to blame Christianity but to state this as a historical fact.

Indigenous lands and waters in the Arctic are problematic. Some indigenous groups such as some First Nations in Canada (e.g. the Crees and Inuit – see the earlier mentioned JBNQA) manage their traditional lands, but only to a certain extent. For example, in Quebec the aim is to reconcile two values/principles ("the two guiding principles") which are sometimes in conflict but should be in balance: economic development of the province and appreciation of indigenous cultures of the province.[64] One may suggest that politicians and lawyers should leave Western legal ideologies and ontologies in relation to Arctic peoples' lands. While in Sweden, as Kuppe states, "Swedish law would possibly leave behind its unique and exclusive liberal philosophical foundation of rights over land, based on the ideas of agrarian cultivation and privatization of the commons".[65] According to Heinamäki and the Valkonens, the Nordic states working with Sámi parliaments "could reach out to protect Sámi people's rights, dwelling rather from their own ontologies than solely on Western legal framework".[66] However, there are still some dangers from deliberate policies of lack of protection of indigenous lands and waters in the Arctic, also, for example, in Canada.[67]

## 5 Indigenous rights and customary law in the Arctic

Much ink has been spilled in recent years extolling the merits of IR and customary law in the Arctic.[68] Much has been said about the problems of

64 See more: D. Bunikowski, note 59 at 44.
65 R. Kuppe, note 63 at 68.
66 L. Heinamäki, J. Valkonen and S. Valkonen, note 60 at 80.
67 See more about the federal government's plans in Canada's context: M. Hanrahan, 'Dismantling the Dismantling of Federal Protection for Arctic Waterways: Revisiting Canada's New Navigation Protection Act', in D. Bunikowski, note 2, 85–90. The federal (Harper) government's plans to "dismantle" environmental protection of waters (removing about 98 percent of Canadian waterways from federal protection and substantially touching e.g. Canadian Inuit) caused social protests. As Maura Hanrahan, a Canadian-aboriginal writer and scholar, points out, "The omnibus bill was one of the triggers for Idle No More (INM), a social movement committed to peaceful protest and grounded in Indigenous activism. Its vision was (and is) *to honour Indigenous sovereignty, and to protect the land and water*" (at 87; original emphasis).
68 E.g. in legal philosophy: D. Bunikowski, 'Indigenous peoples, their rights and customary laws in the North: the case of the Sámi people', in M. Lähteenmäki

recognition of indigenous customary laws in the Arctic. Much is known about many movements concerning the improvement of the legal (and social) status of indigenous peoples living in the Arctic. There are even growing ideas related to "women in the Arctic". Thus, in this section, there will be only some signalisations and generalisations.

It seems that while talking about IR we can split the history of Western intervention in Arctic indigenous areas to date to the following three stages of the process:

1 rejection of IR,
2 recognition of IR, and
3 institutional appreciation of IR.

The first stage means that Western colonisers generally rejected indigenous cultures, laws and rights (e.g. to their own law and land). They were interested in exploitation of natural resources, occupation of indigenous territories and bringing Western civilisation to "backward people". Many years after this part of the process – at the second stage of the process – some countries started to recognise the rights of indigenous peoples in the Arctic: from political to social-economic and cultural ones. However, sometimes recognition is only a dead letter. The last, third, stage of the process is about self-determination and self-government of indigenous peoples in the Arctic. It seems that Canada's examples of self-determination of some of the First Nations are a good pattern here.

In different Arctic countries there are different stages of recognition right now, at the end of the second decade of the 21st century. However, it is clear that to recognise IR, one has to recognise indigenous customary laws. There are different tools to make these laws, depending on the legal culture. In the common law tradition, many laws may be made by jurisprudence of the courts (as in Canada in the last 100 years) but also by traditional tools such as legal acts (such as land-claims agreements or self-government agreements in Canada or law on reservations in the United States). In the civil law tradition (let us claim that the Nordic countries and Russia are included here), a traditional legal tool such as law passed by parliaments remains the most important instrument of regulation of indigenous state relations. There are still many interests, tensions and misunderstandings, though. International treaties or even declarations are often the subject of long debates. Ratification or implementation are other issues. Both Western and indigenous legal scholars and philosophers are interested in this particular field.

and A. Colpaert (eds), *East meets North – crossing the borders of the Arctic*, Nordia Geographical Publications, Yearbook, 43(1), 2014, 75–85.

What Western philosophy may propose for an understanding of the current situation is, for instance, a philosophy by Hegel.[69] To Hegel, there are always a thesis and an antithesis. And, then here comes the synthesis. There are always different factors, interests and movements in social processes going on before our eyes. Philosophically speaking, it remains difficult to predict what the synthesis of the current meeting of the thesis and the antithesis will be in a given country. But there will be *something*, and there is always progress – the progress to bring more law and justice to the Arctic, because philosophy of law in the Arctic is about law and justice in the Arctic (in Justinian's terms).[70]

## 6 The future of philosophy of law in the Arctic: teaching via new tools, and global governance

How to teach philosophy of law in the Arctic? Ordinary or classical methods such as lectures can be used. However, there are other ideas on how to do it, two of which are briefly mentioned. First, teaching philosophy of law through documentary films concerning social and legal problems, especially related to the status of vulnerable, indigenous communities, seems a great idea. This idea was proposed by Rebecca Johnson, the Canadian legal scholar.[71] Also, second, teaching philosophy of law in the context of global governance and intercultural justice, as suggested by Brendan Tobin,[72] the Irish-Peruvian legal thinker, seems to be an impressive and breath-taking view.

## 7 Concluding remarks

Philosophy of law in the Arctic is specific, peculiar and idiosyncratic. It is of both a theoretical and a practical nature. It has its own main topics, such as the Arctic as common good, Arctic indigenous cosmology, indigenous lands or indigenous customary laws which I analysed in this chapter. It has also many very detailed topics such as philosophy of reindeer husbandry which are not analysed here. Many new topics may come in the future (such as law and literature in the Arctic), too. Philosophy of law in the Arctic is non-positivist,

69 See e.g. J. Maybee, 'Hegel's Dialectics', *Stanford Encyclopedia of Philosophy*, 2016, available online at https://plato.stanford.edu/entries/hegel-dialectics/.

70 See more: D. Bunikowski, 'Why am I Interested in the Philosophy of Law in the Arctic? On Some Chosen But Essential Ethical Challenges of Conducting Research in the Field', in T. Koivurova and W. Hasanat (eds), *Current Developments in Arctic Law, 4*, Rovaniemi, University of Lapland, 2016, 3–7. "Law and justice" as a traditional topic of jurisprudence comes from the father of Western legal codification (and thought), the 6th century Roman Emperor Justinian.

71 See R. Johnson, 'Notes on Using Film to Engage with Philosophy of Law in the Arctic', in D. Bunikowski, note 2, 123–129.

72 B. Tobin, 'Custom Rising: Indigenous Law and Legal Philosophy as Catalysts for Intercultural Justice and Good Global Governance', in D. Bunikowski, note 2, 130–136.

non-centrist, legal-pluralistic, more cosmological and spiritual, and indigenous customary laws-oriented. It is interdisciplinary, going far beyond law and philosophy. It covers anthropology and history, and environmental and cultural studies, and so on. It shares some topics with Western legal philosophy or theory (the most important concepts such as law, common good). It gets interested in international legal debates on rights of indigenous peoples. However, it does not focus so much on Western debates on legal sources, interpretation or argumentation. Rather, it gives a new meaning to the concept of law. Philosophy of law in the Arctic is both Western and indigenous, uses both Western and indigenous concepts and terminologies and is made by both Western and indigenous scholars. Both Western and indigenous scholars "do" this philosophy of law in the Arctic. Western scholars bring their Western concepts to describe the world in which they did not grow up and are not in their element. Arctic indigenous scholars bring their sensitivity and understanding of many social, "legal" and cultural institutions and problems which are hidden to Western scholars. Their work together is academically crucial and socially desirable. The concept of "Northness" or "the Fourth World", referring to the special geographical, environmental and socio-cultural conditions of the Northern communities, influences, in practice, this philosophy. Indeed, there is a future before philosophy of law in the Arctic. Many – often very concrete, detailed, socially and globally fundamental, not only general, philosophical-legal – topics have to be explored for the common good. As mentioned previously, both law and justice are merged in the Arctic legal philosophy nowadays, but this also means that what is just and universally moral and should be done in international and state law seems politically, economically and socially problematic. In addition to this, instead of narratives on legal interpretation of positive law, there is much to say about a transcendental character of philosophy of law in the Arctic: it goes beyond the letter of the law or beyond some texts and needs a change in order to tackle things – about experience, beliefs and the spirit of the law – on two levels.

Part II

# Western legal framings

Chapter 3

# Decolonising Antarctica

*Alejandra Mancilla*[1]

## 1 Preliminaries

In 1960, the General Assembly of the United Nations adopted the Declaration on the Granting of Independence to Colonial Countries and Peoples (hereinafter, Declaration on Decolonisation).[2] By virtue of the Declaration, the General Assembly recognised, among other things, that "the peoples of the world ardently desire the end of colonialism in all its manifestations", that its continued existence "prevents the development of international economic co-operation, impedes the social, cultural and economic development of dependent peoples and militates against the United Nations ideal of universal peace".[3] Bringing colonialism in all its forms and manifestations to "a speedy and unconditional end" was therefore a necessity.[4] To ensure that this would happen, two years later a Special Committee on Decolonisation was established, and in 1990 the first International Decade for the Eradication of Colonialism was proclaimed.

Today, almost sixty years later, the efforts made to decolonise occupied territories can be celebrated. Even though 17 non-self-governing territories still remain (home to nearly two million people), most of the former European colonies have gained independence.[5] That decolonisation is, as the Declaration asserts, an "irresistible and irreversible" process has become part of the politically correct discourse.

But there is still a whole continent where colonial claims are preserved. In approaching the end of the Third Decade for the Eradication of Colonialism,

1 Department of Philosophy, Classics, History of Art and Ideas, Faculty of Humanities, University of Oslo, alejandra.mancilla@ifikk.uio.no.
2 UN General Assembly, Declaration on the Granting of Independence to Colonial Countries and Peoples, 14 December 1960, A/RES/1514(XV).
3 Ibid.
4 Ibid.
5 Since the creation of the United Nations, more than 80 former colonies comprising some 750 million people have gained independence: 'The United Nations and Decolonization', United Nations, https://www.un.org/dppa/decolonization/en, accessed 13 April 2020.

Antarctica remains an enclave mostly run by the same colonial and wishing-to-be colonial powers that claimed whole wedges of it between 1908 and 1940, or reserved their rights to make a claim in the future under the auspices of the Antarctic Treaty (hereinafter, AT).[6] Ironically, it was by virtue of the latter – signed in Washington DC one year before the Declaration on Decolonisation – that their territorial claims were "frozen". This means that they were not given up, but put in abeyance while the AT remained in force.[7] Today, it is an accepted trope in the field of the Antarctic humanities and social sciences that Antarctica was and still is part and parcel of the colonial project at the global level, and that the once default view regarding Antarctica's "exceptionalism" in world politics does not have much support in historical facts.[8]

6 I say "mostly" because in the course of six decades new actors have appeared. The first unilateral claim was made by the United Kingdom in 1908, when it issued its first Letters Patent, which included a slice of Argentinian and Chilean Patagonia and thus had to be reissued in 1917. It was followed by New Zealand (1923), France (1924), Australia (1933), Norway (1939), Argentina (1940) and Chile (1940). The claims of the United Kingdom, Argentina and Chile partly overlap. By virtue of the AT, moreover, the Soviet Union and the United States reserved their rights to make a claim in the future. By "wishing-to-be colonial powers" I have in mind Argentina and Chile which, while disputing British imperialism in Antarctica, extended – in a colonialist mode – what they conveniently labelled as their own "natural domains" all the way into the South Pole. See Adrian Howkins, 'Appropriating Space: Antarctic Imperialism and the Mentality of Settler Colonialism', in Tracey Banivanua Mar and Penelope Edmonds (eds), *Making Settler Colonial Space* (London: Palgrave Macmillan, 2010), 29–52.

7 Article IV of the AT establishes that:

"1. Nothing contained in the present Treaty shall be interpreted as: a) a renunciation by any Contracting Party of previously asserted rights of or claims to territorial sovereignty in Antarctica; b) a renunciation or diminution by any Contracting Party of any basis of claim to territorial sovereignty in Antarctica which it may have whether as a result of its activities or those of its nationals in Antarctica, or otherwise; c) prejudicing the position of any Contracting Party as regards its recognition or non-recognition of any other State's rights of or claim or basis of claim to territorial sovereignty in Antarctica. 2. No acts or activities taking place while the present Treaty is in force shall constitute a basis for asserting, supporting or denying a claim to territorial sovereignty in Antarctica or create any rights of sovereignty in Antarctica. No new claim, or enlargement of an existing claim, to territorial sovereignty in Antarctica shall be asserted while the present Treaty is in force": Antarctic Treaty, 1 December 1959, 402 UNTS 71.

8 Among others, see Klaus Dodds and Christy Collis, 'Post-Colonial Antarctica', in Klaus Dodds, Alan D. Hemmings and Peder Roberts (eds), *Handbook on the Politics of Antarctica* (New York: Edward Elgar Publishing, 2017), 50–86, at 53; Alan D. Hemmings, Klaus Dodds and Peder Roberts, 'Introduction: The Politics of Antarctica', in ibid., 1–17; Shirley V. Scott, 'Three Waves of Antarctic Imperialism', in ibid, 37–49; Ben Maddison, *Class and Colonialism in Antarctic Exploration, 1750–1920* (London: Pickering & Chatto, 2014); and Adrian Howkins, *The Polar Regions: An Environmental History* (London: Polity, 2016).

In a global scenario where interest in Antarctica and its resources will continue to grow, the question around the present and future governance of the continent becomes pressing. Even though over 60 years the AT's membership has grown from 12 to 54 signatories, only 29 states have the power to "vote" and shape Antarctica's legal framework.[9] Almost three-quarters of the world's states, that is, are total outsiders and not bound by its regulations. The fact that Antarctica remains colonised, in short, impedes rather than allows a stronger development of its governance structures.

In this Chapter, I start from the assumption that humanity as a whole (and not just seven, 12, 29 or 54 states) should be taken to be interested parties on Antarctic matters and should be given, at least *ab initio*, the opportunity to engage in Antarctic deliberations. The lack of native Antarcticans should turn everyone – rather than those who were there first, or did this and that, or discovered so and so – into an 'inchoate' member of the Antarctic club.[10]

With this in the background, in the next section I present some accounts of how colonialism took and takes place in Antarctica, and discuss what I consider to be three specific wrongs connected to it. I then give some suggestions to start the decolonising process in Antarctica, respond to a key objection and conclude.

## 2 What's wrong with Antarctic colonialism?

That Antarctica stands as no exception in world history, but should be seen instead as part and parcel of the colonial project and mindset, has become a commonplace since 1982, when, in a passionate speech to the United Nations General Assembly (UNGA), the Prime Minister of Malaysia, Mohammed bin Mahathir, denounced the AT as "an agreement between a select group of countries [which failed to] reflect the true feelings of the members of the United Nations or their just claims".[11] This discourse slowly gave rise to a "post-colonial engagement" with Antarctica by scholars working in critical

9 The other 24 states are non-Consultative Parties, which means they can attend the annual Antarctic Treaty Meetings (ATMs) and give their opinion on the different matters discussed, but not take part in decision-making (the system operates on the basis of unanimity and does not formally conduct "votes" on any matter). In the last ten years, their presence at the ATMs has been irregular, with only four attending in 2010, and a record number of 16 in 2017: Secretariat of the Antarctic Treaty, 'Final Reports', https://www.ats.aq/devAS/Info/FinalReports?lang=e, accessed 13 April 2020.

10 I have no space here to develop a full argument for this assumption. One way to defend it would be to say that it has to do with a basic requirement of justice in original appropriation. To put it in Lockean terms, "that enough and as good [is] left in common for others [to appropriate]": John Locke, *Two Treatises of Government, Book II*, Peter Laslett (ed) (Cambridge: Cambridge University Press, 1988), §27, at 88.

11 United Nations General Assembly A/37/PV10, 29 September 1982, at 132.

geopolitics and security studies, history, anthropology, international relations and other disciplines.[12] It also challenged the widespread assumption that, because the United States and the Soviet Union (instead of the European powers) were dominant in the AT, the latter was not an appendix of the colonial era. What made this project colonial, as Mahathir suggested, was the fact that only a select group of states took part, imposing their own rules of exclusivity.[13]

It now gets repeatedly mentioned in the literature that the discovery, exploitation of marine resources and subsequent claiming of Antarctica by different states merely echoed what was going on at the time on a global scale: the conquest of land and resources for political, strategic and economic reasons; the projection of capital to the furthest corners of the earth; and a growing pressure over key natural resources by multinational companies that kept pushing the 'resource frontier' further and further.[14] Moreover, as Klaus Dodds puts it, the AT did not eliminate, but rather rewarded these attempts at colonial occupation and annexation. Accordingly, its new members were "forced to replicate the colonizing behavior of earlier parties" via the establishment of scientific bases to prove they were conducting substantial research activity in the continent, and thus accede to Consultative status.[15]

Shirley Scott has retold Antarctic history as three successive imperialist waves performed through colonial practices. The first wave took place in the 16th century, when Spain and Portugal divided the "New World" between them – and therefore, the yet to be discovered *terra australis incognita*. The second wave took place throughout the period where states staked their territorial claims over the continent as if it were *terra nullius* available for acquisition. The third wave is ongoing since the AT was signed, with the United States "using the rhetoric of universal science as justification".[16]

12 Klaus Dodds, 'Post-Colonial Antarctica: An Emerging Engagement', *Polar Record* 42, no. 1 (2006): 59–70.
13 I thank Peder Roberts for pointing this out.
14 For an analysis of Antarctica as a "resource frontier", see Howkins, note 6. In the literature, "imperialism" and "colonialism" are sometimes treated as interchangeable terms, sometimes as two processes that went together hand in hand, and sometimes as if colonialism had been a subset of practices within the wider umbrella of imperialism. For the purposes of the discussion, I will refer to colonialism only, and understand it roughly as a practice of domination through political and economic control over a territory, which standardly included the creation of settlements that kept their political allegiance to the colonising power. Here I draw from the definition offered by Margaret Kohn and Kavita Reddy, 'Colonialism', *The Stanford Encyclopedia of Philosophy* (Fall 2017 edn), Edward N. Zalta (ed), https://plato.stanford.edu/archives/fall2017/entries/colonialism/, accessed 4 February 2019.
15 Dodds, note 12 at 63.
16 Scott, note 8 at 39–44.

Adrian Howkins discusses the mentality of settler colonialism (i.e. 'a desire to conquer nature and to appropriate space') as falling under the umbrella of imperialism, and remarks that it is "no coincidence that all the countries involved in the twentieth-century 'Scramble for Antarctica' were also practicing settler colonial imperialism in other parts of the world".[17]

To give one last example, in the course of criticising the obsession with sovereignty of the seven historic claimants, Alan Hemmings points out that "the present Antarctic dispensation, including the treatment of territory, was arrived at prior to the existence of more than half of the world's present states, as a result of an imperial and colonial model now generally repudiated".[18]

There is thus wide agreement that Antarctica was and remains a colonial enclave. What is harder to find is a categorisation of the moral wrongs specific to this kind of colonialism, and a request for explicit recognition of the colonial origins of Antarctic claims, as well as for a revision of the colonial terms under which the "Antarctic contract" was originally signed, and under which it is currently sustained.[19] In the remainder of this section, I point to three such wrongs.[20]

There are two kinds of theories that have been developed in political philosophy to explain the moral wrong of colonialism that seem relevant for our purposes. A first kind of theory sees the moral wrong of colonialism as lying in the unjust taking of land from indigenous populations for the massive settlement of groups who came from the colonial power, and maintained their allegiance to it. As Margaret Moore explains, this process not only disrupted the affective attachment of the natives to the land, but robbed them of their collective right to be self-determining over *that* territory, to decide what life-plans and projects they wished to pursue *there*.[21] A second kind of theory, defended by Lea Ypi, sees the moral wrong of colonialism as consisting in the political domination of one group over another, where this domination involves "the creation and upholding of a political association that denies its members equal and reciprocal terms of cooperation".[22] According to this

17 Howkins, note 6 at 48.
18 Alan D. Hemmings, 'Security beyond Claims', in Alan D. Hemmings, Donald R. Rothwell and Karen N. Scott (eds), *Antarctic Security in the Twenty-First Century: Legal and Policy Perspectives* (Abingdon: Routledge, 2012), 70–94, at 77.
19 Alan Hemmings comes closest when he analyses four aspects in which territorial claims in Antarctica are wrong: moral, practical, legal and geopolitical. He then advocates for an Antarctic where security is prioritised beyond territorial claims, and where the seven claimants give up their claims to sovereignty in order to be better prepared for future challenges. Hemmings, note 18 at 70–94.
20 The list does not intend to be exhaustive.
21 Margaret Moore, 'Justice and Colonialism', *Philosophy Compass* 11, no. 8 (July 28, 2016): 447–61.
22 Lea Ypi, 'What's Wrong with Colonialism', *Philosophy & Public Affairs* 41, no. 2 (2013): 158–91, 158.

account, the morally problematic feature of colonialism lies not in the occupation of someone else's land per se, but in the terms under which distinct territorial agents (i.e. the colonisers and the colonised) were made to interact.

Because of the lack of native Antarcticans, it might seem odd to try to apply these theories to our case.[23] My contention, however, is that a reinterpretation of each can help to make sense of three distinctive wrongs of Antarctic colonialism.

The first wrong, I submit, consisted in the unilateral appropriation by a few states of extravagant expanses of uninhabited (and mostly uninhabitable) space. In a context where it was already clear that the earth's land and resources were not infinite, and that humans were exhausting them quite rapidly, those who staked claims over Antarctica during the first half of the 20th century did so with a hoarding and overwhelming attitude, almost completely foreclosing the possibility of future takings.[24] Moreover, in so doing they left out the majority of the world's states and the majority of humankind.[25] Following Moore's theory, it was a wrongful taking of land. But departing from Moore, what made it wrong was not the eviction or subjugation of native populations. Rather, what should have been considered as a common bounty of humanity (the last continent to be discovered, the only land left on earth yet to be explored) was divided into pie-shaped wedges among only seven countries, and claimed on grounds that could have at best justified much more modest appropriations.[26]

The second and third wrongs of Antarctic colonialism have to do with political domination and are thus connected to Ypi's account. They consist, first, in the creation of a political association (the AT) whose members appointed themselves as representatives of all mankind when it came to

23 As Ben Maddison points out, because of its lack of inhabitants, Antarctica was "unsettling to [the Europeans'] prevailing understandings and procedures of colonial possession": Maddison note 8 at 52. This fact did not prevent them, of course, from "dispossessing" the native population of penguins. In the words of a midshipman in a British expedition that discovered a new island in the South Shetlands, in 1819, the birds "with most disturbing obstinacy disputed our right to proceed… and it was not until great slaughter had been committed and an opening forced through them [that] we were enabled to further our research": ibid, at 53.

24 I say "almost" because Marie Byrd's Land, the most inaccessible part of Antarctica, remains unclaimed.

25 In 1959, the population of the seven claimant countries taken together represented a mere 4.74 percent of the total world population. At the time, there were 82 members of the United Nations. See, respectively, United Nations, 'World Population Prospects', https://population.un.org/wpp/Download/Standard/Population/, accessed 19 February 2019; and Donald R. Rothwell, 'The Antarctic Treaty as a Security Construct', in Hemmings, Rothwell and Scott, note 18 at 46.

26 The merits of the different grounds for these claims are examined in Alejandra Mancilla, 'The Moral Limits of Territorial Claims in Antarctica', *Ethics & International Affairs* 32, no. 3 (2018), 339–60.

governing the fifth largest continent on earth; and, second, in the maintenance of a system where not all members are treated on equal and reciprocal terms.[27]

The birth of the AT, in 1959, took place with only 12 states taking part: the historic claimants, those who did not make claims but reserved their right to make such claims in the future, and those others which had conducted science in Antarctica during the International Geophysical Year 1957–1958.[28] It has been repeatedly argued in defence of this arrangement that the time was ripe to lay down rules and prevent Cold War tensions from escalating on the "white" continent; that the beauty of the Treaty was precisely that it left sovereign claims suspended in order to focus on peaceful scientific cooperation instead; that keeping it as a demilitarised and nuclear-free zone was a true diplomatic feat.[29] However, it is well-known that some of the claimants blocked from the beginning the idea of establishing a genuinely international association, which would have required them to give up their claims entirely.[30] Because it was better to have a frozen claim than none, the AT was constituted for this purpose by the claimants themselves, and with the approval of a handful of other states.

As already shown, Ypi's theory sees ones of the wrongs of colonialism as consisting in the creation (by the colonisers) of a political system to rule over a group of people (the colonised) who are not treated as equal members in the rule-creating process. The second wrong of Antarctic colonialism, relatedly, lies in the creation of a political system that leaves out from the outset a

27 In the Preamble, the 12 original signatories recognise "that it is *in the interest of all mankind* that Antarctica shall continue for ever to be used exclusively for peaceful purposes and shall not become the scene or object of international discord"; they are "convinced that the establishment of a firm foundation for the continuation and development of such cooperation on the basis of freedom of scientific investigation in Antarctica as applied during the International Geophysical Year accords with the *interests of science and the progress of all mankind*"; and are convinced that using Antarctica for peaceful purposes only "will further the purposes and principles embodied in the Charter of the United Nations": AT, Preamble, my emphases.

28 Argentina, Australia, Chile, France, New Zealand, Norway and the United Kingdom, plus the Soviet Union and the United States, plus Belgium, Japan and South Africa.

29 See, e.g., Francisco Orrego Vicuña, 'Antarctic Conflict and International Cooperation', in National Research Council, *Antarctic Treaty System: An Assessment: Proceedings of a Workshop Held at Beardmore South Field Camp, Antarctica, January 7–13, 1985* (Washington, D.C: National Academy Press, 1986); and Gillian Triggs, 'The Antarctic Treaty System: A Model of Legal Creativity and Cooperation', in Paul Arthur Berkman, Michael A. Lang, David W. H. Walton and Oran R. Young (eds), *Science Diplomacy: Antarctica, Science, and the Governance of International Spaces* (Washington D.C.: Smithsonian Institution Scholarly Press, 2011), 39–50.

30 Peter J. Beck, *The International Politics of Antarctica* (London and Sydney: Croom Helm, 1986), at 39.

group of people who should have been treated as members, but were not – i.e. the international community as a whole. The injustice consists not in the constitution of a political association that was not negotiated under equal and reciprocal terms by its members, but in treating a large part of those who should have been members and deliberators in the initial establishment of the association as wards in need of representation. In constituting the AT, the 12 original signatories appointed themselves not only as guardians of Antarctica, but also as guardians (in the sense of legal representatives) of the rest of humanity.

The third wrong of Antarctic colonialism, lastly, consists in the maintenance of a political association with an unequal power structure, where membership is open in theory to all world states, but 'real' membership (i.e. consultative status with decision-making power) is given exclusively to those capable of conducting "substantial research activity there, such as the establishment of a scientific station or the despatch of a scientific expedition" – a condition that was imposed by the original self-appointed signatories.[31] By turning a politically exogenous feature – i.e. scientific capacity – into the decisive criterion for determining who "votes" and who doesn't, the AT leaves a large group of states (and thus a substantial percentage of humanity) substantively voteless, while giving decision-making powers over a whole, resource-rich continent to roughly one-sixth of them.[32] This restriction of voting rights is a colonial hangover rather than a clean break with Antarctica's colonial past: as many have pointed out, the science criterion may be interpreted as the perfect cover-up for ensuring that only states that are developed enough will ever be able to take an active role in Antarctic politics.[33] Here some could object that, insofar as it is a voluntary association, the two-tiered membership of the AT does not violate any requirements of reciprocity or equal treatment to those who wish to become part. They are, after all, free to choose whether or not to join in the first place. But this objection takes for granted precisely what is being put into question; namely, whether

31 AT, Article IX(2). It is true that this requirement has been broadened in interpretation, so that now collaboration with ongoing scientific programmes and use of already established infrastructure is encouraged. The question remains, however, why science should be required at all.

32 Defenders of the AT might object that the most populated countries on earth are Consultative parties, so that the majority of humanity is in fact represented: as of 2018, around 65 percent of it: Kevin A. Hughes, Andrew Constable, Yves Frenot, Jerónimo López-Martínez, Ewan McIvor, Birgit Njåstad, Aleks Terauds, et al., 'Antarctic Environmental Protection: Strengthening the Links between Science and Governance', *Environmental Science & Policy* 83 (2018): 86–95, at 88.

33 On the uneasy relationship between Antarctic science and politics, see John R. Dudeney and David W.H. Walton, 'Leadership in Politics and Science within the Antarctic Treaty', *Polar Research* 31 (2012), 1–9; and Aant Elzinga, 'The Continent for Science', in Dodds, Hemmings and Roberts, note 8, 103–124.

having the governance of a whole continent come under the aegis of a handful of states was just to begin with.

In the excessive historic claims, in the constitution, and maintenance of the AT as an elitist political association for privileged states only: therein lie three specific wrongs of Antarctic colonialism. In the next section I make some suggestions as to how to move forward.

## 3 Decolonising Antarctica

What should be done, then, to decolonise Antarctica? Rather than a full proposal, what I offer in this section is a brief sketch with some points to consider.

Taking the Declaration on Decolonisation as the model to drive and guide the decolonisation process in Antarctica, the first step should be an explicit recognition by the historic claimants of the colonial spirit in which their unilateral claims were made. Vestiges of a bygone era, and either unrecognised or openly disputed by the majority of world states (including Treaty members), these claims should once and for all be allowed to "melt".[34] Giving up their territorial claims, however, would not mean giving up their presence in the continent. Just like the Declaration on Decolonisation recognises that newly independent states will need to go through a transition, where the old authorities ensure that new institutions are in place before leaving, here a similar arrangement should be reached. Moreover, because the "newly independent state" in this case lacks a permanent human population, the historic claimants would probably continue to have a strong presence and influence on Antarctic matters.[35]

A second step should be the explicit recognition of the way in which the AT was originally constituted, by self-appointed members that unilaterally ruled out the possibility of internationalising Antarctica. That all states are free to opt in is the default response among those who think there is no problem regarding participation in the AT. The truth, nonetheless, is that the majority of developing states remain outsiders.[36] One idea towards revising

34 According to Alan Hemmings, "186 states appear *not* to recognize the Antarctic claims [and] a smaller number have clearly declared this": Hemmings, note 18 at 77. To be sure, this would require Argentinians and Chileans to recognise – against their purportedly anti-colonial attitude – the colonial nature of their claims.

35 Those who find this proposal utterly unrealistic should not forget that international politics is full of unexpected turns, and that some of the claimants in the past have been open to this possibility. See, e.g., New Zealand's position on this issue in Hemmings note 18, at 87–88.

36 Among the consultative parties, 18 out of 29 countries are OECD members, while in the case of non-consultative parties it is 11 out of 24. OECD, 'List of OECD member countries – Ratification of the Convention on the OECD', http://www.oecd.org/about/membersandpartners/list-oecd-member-countries.htm, accessed 25 February 2019.

the terms of accession would be to turn things on their head and consider every world state a member of the AT unless they opted out. Given that this would only give states the right to speak and give their opinion at the ATMs, it couldn't be objected that this nudging strategy would create a huge political upheaval within the system.

Third and finally, there should be an explicit recognition that the maintenance of a two-tiered membership based on science is problematic and should be rethought. It is one thing to say that science is a good thing to have in Antarctica, because it enhances the capacity for decision-making, but quite another to say that the production of scientific knowledge *alone* should be the basis for privileged decision-making rights. A "continent for science" might be a good thing, but from this it does not follow that the political arrangement should be the exclusive property of those who do science. Imposing science as the criterion to determine who should be Antarctic players, in sum, perpetuates the unequal power relations characteristic of colonial structures; removing it would be to remove a real obstacle in the way to a more fair participation in Antarctic decision-making.[37]

## 4 An objection, and a response

In a much quoted article by theorists interested in colonisation and decolonisation, Jeremy Waldron argues for what he calls "the supersession of injustice".[38] In places such as North America, New Zealand and Australia, he contends, heinous injustices were committed against the native populations by the colonial powers, which not only subjugated them, but also settled there for good. So what should we do about those wrongs? What should a theory of reparation demand? Waldron's answer is that, insofar as circumstances have radically changed (through a sharp increase of the world's population and a sharp decline of available resources) what counted as an injustice at $t_1$ may not be so at $t_2$. The message for the indigenous groups is that the initial injustice has been *superseded*: proper reparation should not be about giving the land back to the native people (for, where would the descendants of the settlers go?!), but about creating just conditions for them, now and in the future.

Similarly, some may agree with the analysis offered in section 2 and still object to the idea that the wrongs of Antarctic colonialism should be addressed head-on. Despite the colonial origins of the AT and its associated wrongs, they might say, its accomplishments in 60 years, its growing membership and legitimacy, the efficiency of its legal corpus and its overall stability should be hailed, not jeered. Among the accomplishments, they could mention what Alan Hemmings calls "the new trinity of high values" of the AT since the

37 Thanks to Peder Roberts for pushing me on this point.
38 Jeremy Waldron, 'Superseding Historic Injustice', *Ethics* 103, no. 1 (1992), 4–28.

Environmental Protocol (EP) was signed in 1991: peace, science, and the protection of the environment.[39] In short, rather than becoming obsessed with the unjust beginnings of the Antarctic political setup, we should look forward and secure what the AT has already achieved.[40] What might have been an unjust arrangement at its inception, in other words, may have ceased to be so considering six decades of positive track-record.

I don't think this objection works. For one thing, it is impossible to disprove such a claim, given that we have no access to the possible worlds where the AT did not happen. How can we know if things would not have been even better if Antarctica had not been colonised in the way it was? For another thing, this objection is biased in favour of the status quo, and seems to assume that the list of achievements already set out would be lost if someone dared to reform the AT's structure. But this worry is unwarranted. On the contrary, there are good reasons to think that all the positive aspects already mentioned could be strengthened in a decolonised AT.

In terms of preserving peace and scientific cooperation in the continent, it makes sense to think that bringing in a larger number of members into the Antarctic political association would help, rather than hinder, these goals.[41] The ideals of open science and knowledge-sharing might truly be realised, while a critical discussion could finally be had regarding issues such as bioprospecting – which goes unchecked given the unwillingness of many of the consultative parties to modify the legal status of what today is conveniently treated as *res nullius*.[42]

As for the protection of the environment, Antarctica is usually mentioned as the most protected place on earth, thanks to the provisions of the EP.[43] In practice, however, Antarctica has mostly protected itself thanks to its uninviting climate, geographical remoteness, and costly access. It is these factors – more than any active engagement of the AT – which has kept the continent relatively pristine.[44] To be sure, it has to be acknowledged that it was thanks

39 Alan D. Hemmings, 'Considerable Values in Antarctica', *The Polar Journal* 1 (2012): 139–56, at 145.
40 In this spirit, see Marcus Haward, Julia Jabour and A. J. Press, 'Antarctic Treaty System Ready for a Challenge', *Science* 338, no. 6107 (2 November 2012), 603.
41 At this point, some might worry that if the decision-making procedure through consensus is already problematic, it will become unworkable as membership keeps growing. For a defence of a more democratic procedure, see 'Reform the Antarctic Treaty', *Nature* 558 (14 June 2018), 161.
42 Cristopher C. Joyner, 'Bioprospecting as a Challenge for the Antarctic Treaty', in Hemmings, Rothwell and Scott, note 18, at 197–214.
43 'Protocol on Environmental Protection to the Antarctic Treaty', Umwelt Bundesamt, 27 January 2016, https://www.umweltbundesamt.de/en/protocol-on-environmental-protection-to-the, accessed 12 November 2018.
44 For a critical appraisal of environmental protection in Antarctica, see Justine D. Shaw et al., 'Antarctic Protected Areas are Inadequate, Unrepresentative and at Risk', *PLOS Biology* 12 (2014), 1–5.

to the vision of the EP signatories that there still is a protected Antarctic environment. If the Convention on the Regulation of Antarctic Mineral Resource Activities (CRAMRA) rather than the EP had been signed, the "white" continent would have probably ceased to be so by now.[45] Still, it is not clear why this would change for the worse in a decolonised Antarctic Treaty System, especially considering that those states that more openly wish for the end of the mineral ban are already signatories.[46]

Moving on to its growing membership and legitimacy, it is true that the AT is now more representative – and purportedly, more legitimate – than it was at the beginning. Yet it should be recalled that its growth in terms of members occurred precisely when external criticism increased.[47] Rather than waiting for a new Mahathir to reopen the 'Question of Antarctica' at the UNGA, and rather than waiting for non-parties to publicly reject the AT as the rightful political association to regulate Antarctic matters, starting a decolonising process within the AT might give the system increased legitimacy and standing vis-à-vis potentially rebellious states.

Regarding the efficiency of its legal corpus, this would not have to be affected by a decolonisation process. On the contrary, it is more likely that those areas which have, so far, been left out – such as bioprospecting – could finally become regulated.

Lastly, that the AT has provided stability to the continent during six decades is no guarantee that it will continue to provide it in the future. But, more importantly, stability in itself is not a value: a wrongful arrangement might be very stable, and one might still want to change it. I am not saying that this is the case of the AT; I am only saying that the fact that there is a stable system on its own is no argument against a push toward decolonisation.

45 This is not obvious, though, given that most of the tough environmental regulations found in the EP were actually taken from CRAMRA. I thank Julia Jabour from bringing this point to my attention.

46 See, for example, the recent claim by the leader of the National Antarctic Center of Ukraine, Evgeny Dikiy, that "there is only a little more than 30 years to 2048 and, after this, it is probable that the ban will be lifted. In this process will be those countries that keep scientific stations there and carry out scientific activities. Because of this, it is no coincidence that half of our [2018–19] expedition consists of geologists": Alexander Zagorodny, 'For the First Time in Many Years, Ukrainian Female Scientists Have Been Sent to Antarctica', *TSN Ukraine*, 17 January 2019, https://ru.tsn.ua/ukrayina/vpervye-za-mnogo-let-v-antarktidu-otpravlyayutsya-ukrainskie-zhenschiny-uchenye-1282185.html, accessed 25 February 2019, translation by Hannah Monsrud Sandvik. See also China's purported acknowledgment (at least for the Chinese public) that its main interest in Antarctica is to eventually exploit its resources: Anne-Marie Brady, *China as a Great Polar Power* (Cambridge: Cambridge University Press, 2017), at 38.

47 Twenty-nine new states joined the AT after 1982: Secretariat of the Antarctic Treaty, 'Parties', https://ats.aq/devAS/Parties?lang=e, accessed 13 April 2020.

## 5 Concluding remarks

In this article I have suggested that, being part and parcel of the colonial enterprise, Antarctica should also be part of the world's decolonisation process. After pointing to three wrongs of Antarctic colonialism (the extravagant appropriation of land, the unjust constitution, and the unjust maintenance of a political association where not all parties are treated in equal and reciprocal terms), I proposed some ways forward. An open recognition of its colonial past and an honest willingness to move forward together with those who have so far been left aside are, in my view, the two main routes that the decolonisation process should take in Antarctica. Instead of weakening the achievements of the AT over six decades, this might be a needed step to strengthen and deepen its capacity to confront the challenges ahead.

## Acknowledgements

This article is part of the project "Political Philosophy Looks to Antarctica", financed by the Polar Programme of the Research Council of Norway. I am especially indebted to Julia Jabour and Peder Roberts for their comments on a first draft, and to the editors of this volume, Alan Hemmings and Dawid Bunikowski. I am also grateful for their feedback to the participants at the second workshop of the project, at the Practical Philosophy Seminar, University of Oslo, and at the Ira W. DeCamp Bioethics Seminar, Princeton University, and to Hannah Monsrud Sandvik and Oda Storbråten Davanger for research assistance.

Chapter 4

# The Arctic as civil commons

*Giorgio Baruchello*[1]

## 1 Introduction

In his contribution to a pioneering book on the philosophy of law in the Arctic, Ko Hasegawa asks five inter-related questions:

1 1 “[W]hat sort of particular good(s) should be regarded as invaluably basic for the fundamental conditions of human life without which human beings cannot subsist and act well at all?”[2]
2 “[H]ow can some good or goods be grasped as invaluably common?” (i.e. “the problem of *circumstance*” aka “the possibility of the recognition of common good”)[3]
3 “[H]ow can common good be shared equally among relevant societal units?” (i.e. “the problem of *distribution*”)[4]
4 “[H]ow can the relevant units around the region in question decide the administrative issues on the common good in question in a fair way?” (i.e. “the problem of *participation*”)[5]
5 “[H]ow the circumstance, distribution, and participation concerning common good can be relevantly common among the relevant units in the region in question?” (i.e. “the problem of *communality*”)[6]

According to Hasegawa, these are five fundamental questions upon which we must ponder, and possibly find an answer to, in order to be able to grasp in both theory and practice how the Arctic is much more than a merely geographic or even geopolitical expression, but rather a unique natural and

1 Faculty of Humanities and Social Sciences, University of Akureyri, Iceland, giorgio@unak.is.
2 K. Hasegawa, ‘The Arctic as Common Good’, *Philosophy of Law in the Arctic*, D. Bunikowski (ed), Rovaniemi, The University of the Arctic, 32–38 at 33.
3 Ibid. at 34.
4 Id.
5 Id.
6 Id.

human heritage to be handled with great care, for its enlightened "utilization" is of great importance for the wellbeing of all, not just of the communities living inside it.[7]

Insofar as "[t]he idea of common good indicates … the holistic condition for all human beings in a society, as well as the idea of global common good for all the peoples on this globe",[8] then the Arctic becomes a specific space on earth serving the life-aims of all of its inhabitants in a way that any rational being would recognise as positive and prior to other considerations (e.g. the profitable "utilization of various conditions and resources").[9] As Hasegawa writes: "it is evident that clean air is an invaluable life condition for all the people in a society, as well as for all the peoples on this globe. This means not simply that clean air is non-exclusionarily sharable but rather that anyone in society cannot live well at all without that condition."[10]

Aware of the critical point in history in which we live and sympathetic to Hasegawa's concerns and aims, the present text argues that life-value onto-axiology can offer sensible answers to all five fundamental questions put in his essay or, at least, it can show where exactly the answers will have to be found by clarifying the ground of the common good's goodness. Furthermore, the application of this specific theory of value to the Arctic case can help us conceive of the Arctic as a token of civil commons, namely a conception of shared goods – indeed, of shared good goods, as will become clear – that can integrate, disambiguate and empower Hasegawa's notion of the common good.

## 2 Life-value onto-axiology

Life-value onto-axiology is based upon the reasoned belief that it is possible to identify a universal and objective ground of value. There may exist a so-called "marketplace of ideas" about what is good and what is not (e.g. capital punishment, abortion, pornography), but some preferences are actually better than others, and they are often acknowledged as such, sometimes in universal and uncontroversial ways (e.g. good health over sickness, happiness over unhappiness, knowledge over ignorance, fulfilment of human rights over their abuse). According to its founder, Canadian philosopher and public intellectual John McMurtry, we can "recover step by step the missing *life-ground* of values and the ultimate meaning of how we are to live."[11]

7 Ibid. at 32.
8 Ibid. at 33.
9 Ibid. at 32.
10 Ibid. at 33.
11 J. McMurtry, 'What is Good? What is Bad? The Value of All Values across Time, Place and Theories', *Encyclopedia of Life Support Systems*, Paris and Oxford, UNESCO (EOLSS), 2009–10, para. 1.16 (emphasis added).

The definition of the life-ground is not overly complicated: "Concretely, all that is required to take the next breath; axiologically, all the life support systems required for human life to reproduce or develop."[12] Without enough bread, clean water, breathable air, open spaces in which to move, regular sleep, acceptable education and meaningful socialisation, no value whatsoever that we cherish will ever be expressed in reality. No value whatsoever, whether ethical, political, legal, economic, epistemic, spiritual or aesthetic, can be given independently of this vital platform. Life is the fundamental precondition for any and every other value that there can be – *ergo* the prefix "onto-", i.e. "concerning being" – and, *a fortiori*, it is itself valuable and inescapable whenever reflecting upon evaluations – *ergo* the noun "axiology", i.e. "value theory".

To all intents and purposes, there can be no life as such, not to mention any good life, outside the life-ground. As McMurtry states: "Life support systems – any natural or human-made system without which human beings cannot live or live well – may or may not have value in themselves, but have ultimate value so far as they are that without which human or other life cannot exist or flourish."[13] Logically, it remains possible to distinguish between life's intrinsic value and the life-ground's instrumental value. Ontologically, however, it is not: "All that is of worth consists in and enables life value to the extent of its experienced fields of thought, felt being and action (intrinsic value), and what underlies and enables these fields of life themselves, life support systems."[14]

Life is understood as manifesting itself in three basic modes of being: "action" (also "biological movement" or "motility"), "felt being" (also "experience" or "feeling") and "thought".[15] All that is intuitively saluted as genius, justice, happiness or health is – if truly good – a constructive and comprehensive expression of life-value, in one or more of these mutually non-exclusive modes of being: action (e.g. health and fitness), felt being (e.g. religious and aesthetic wonder at nature's intricate complexity) and thought (e.g. proportionality in judicial sentencing). Consistently with this understanding of being and value, the two fundamental axioms of value adopted in life-value onto-axiology read as follows:

- *"X is value if and only if, and to the extent that, x consists in or enables a more coherently inclusive range of thought/feeling/action than without it"*
- *"X is disvalue if and only if, and to the extent that, x reduces/disables any range of thought/experience/action."*[16]

12 J. McMurtry, 'Glossary', EOLSS.
13 McMurtry, 'What is Good? What is Bad?', para. 6.2.1.
14 Ibid. at para. 6.1.4.
15 Ibid. at para. 6.1.
16 Id. (emphasis in the original).

These axioms apply to all types of human agency. For instance, as contemporary environmental issues are concerned, McMurtry distinguishes between "zero growth" and "zero bad growth", claiming the former to be negative and the latter to be positive, since "growth of production that serves universal human life-needs is necessary and good the more there is deprivation."[17] No good can be given outside the life-ground, the composition and scope of which life-value onto-axiology clarifies by means of two key-concepts: "need" and "civil commons".

As the former key-concept is concerned, McMurtry observes that not anything that we may claim to "need" is, after closer scrutiny, a need: "'n' is a need if and only if, and to the extent that, deprivation of n always leads to a reduction of organic capacity."[18] Only that "without which life-capacities are always reduced" counts as need.[19] We can live, and even prosper, without travel cheques or credit default swaps, but we cannot live, not to mention prosper, without "sufficient nutriment, clean water, sewage facilities, learning of society's symbol systems, home and love, and expert care when ill".[20]

To strengthen the point, life-value onto-axiologist Jeff Noonan neatly separates needs from economic preferences ("wants"):

- "deprivation of needs always leads to harm whereas deprivation of wants is only harmful in light of revisable self-interpretation" (e.g. depriving oneself of food is harmful, even if the person who does it believes it is not; whilst depriving oneself of videogames is not harmful, even if the person undergoing it thinks it is);
- "needs are satiable whereas wants are not" (e.g. the need to eat vanishes when full, and other needs take over, e.g. the need to digest, rest and defecate).[21]

No much-desired expensive consumer goodies will ever be vital in the way water and bread are, whatever the subjective perception of them may be. In this connection, McMurtry identifies humanity's fundamental "means of life" or "vital need[s]… for none can be deprived without reduction of vital life capability."[22] In its formulation for the *Encyclopedia of Life Support Systems* (EOLSS), McMurtry lists seven vital goods that refer to as many vital needs:

17 J. McMurtry, *The Cancer Stage of Capitalism: From Crisis to Cure*, 2nd edition, London, Pluto, 2013, 42.
18 J. McMurtry, *Unequal Freedoms: The Global Market as an Ethical System*, Toronto, Garamond, 1998, 164.
19 McMurtry, *The Cancer Stage of Capitalism*, 19.
20 Id. at 1.
21 J. Noonan, *Democratic Society and Human Needs*, Montreal & Kingston, McGill-Queen's University Press, 2006, xiv and 57.
22 J. McMurtry, *Value Wars: The Global Market versus the Life Economy*, London, Pluto, 2002, 156 (emphasis removed).

1 the atmospheric goods of breathable air, open space and light;
2 the bodily goods of clean water, nourishing goods and waste disposal;
3 the home and habitat goods of shelter from the elements;
4 the environmental good of natural and constructed elements all contributing to the whole;
5 the good of care through time by love, safety and health infrastructures;
6 the good of human culture in music, language, art, play and sport; and
7 the good of human vocation and social justice – that which enables and obliges all people to contribute to the provision of these life goods consistent with each's enjoyment of them.[23]

The seven criteria constitute, in short, a "wellbeing index", which can be applied to any human community in order to determine whether life-ranges are being comprehensively enabled or not, therefore requiring to seek solutions that are truly advantageous to all parties involved, though not necessarily to the same level, inasmuch as needs may differ.[24]

As the latter key-concept is concerned, McMurtry defines "civil commons" *qua* "unifying concept to designate social constructs which enable universal access to life goods."[25] Born in the 1990s, this concept is today a commonplace notion in the social sciences, having found application in several fields of inquiry.[26] McMurtry lists an astounding array of concepts, arrangements and artefacts aimed at fulfilling life-enabling ends under diverse socio-historical contexts:

> "The nature of language, the air we breathe, the common fire, food recipes, universal health plans, the world wide web, common sewers, international campaigns against US war crimes, sidewalks and forest paths, sports and sports fields, the open science movement, the Chinese concept of jen, the Jubilee of Leviticus, public streetscapes, effective pollution controls, birdwatching, city squares and sidewalks, Buddha's principle of interdependent origination, old-age pensions, the rule of life-protective law, universal education, universal hygiene practices, footpaths and bicycle trails, fair elections, unemployment insurance, the global atmosphere, maximum work hours and minimum wages, public parks, clean water, the Tao, community fish-habitats, public broadcasting, the

23 McMurtry, 'What is Good? What is Bad?', EOLSS, para. 10.10.4.
24 McMurtry, *Value Wars*, 156.
25 McMurtry, 'Glossary'.
26 Totally unaware of McMurtry's philosophy, Burns H. Weston and David Bollier reinvented both conceptually and nominally McMurtry's "civil commons", showing *ipso facto* the urgent poignancy of this notion (see their book *Green Governance: Ecological Survival, Human Rights, and the Law of the Commons*, Cambridge, Cambridge University Press, 2013).

ancient village commons before enclosures, the unnamed goal of the Occupy Movement."[27]

Possibly built upon the cooperative inclinations that have helped the survival of many animal species, including ours, these many concepts, arrangements and artefacts have established "commons" that are characterised by the predicate "civil". This predicate reveals the socially constructed and socially aimed dimensions of the institutions nurturing "real capital", i.e. "life-capital – the natural and human-made wealth that produces more through time without loss".[28] Life-value onto-axiology is not referring to, say, pastures available to all without supervision and sanctions for misuse (e.g. Hardin's unregulated natural "commons"), but pastures that the community consciously or pre-consciously (i.e. akin to linguistic syntax) recognises in its symbolic systems and manages in order to yield life-supporting fruits through time for all its members, thus reducing a prime cause of internecine competition (e.g. by fostering life-enabling cooperation and sustainability *via* religious rites and principles of conduct).[29]

## 3 Five answers

Although the account of life-value onto-axiology provided in the previous section is brief and selective, it is nonetheless possible to apply it to Hasegawa's case and therefore offer some answers to the five questions from which we started.

### ***I "[W]hat sort of particular good(s) should be regarded as invaluably basic for the fundamental conditions of human life without which human beings cannot subsist and act well at all?"[30]***

Over the past 150 years, ordinalist, emotivist, relativist and postmodernist schools of thought in economics and philosophy have, *inter alia*, made us accustomed to claims of irreducible pluralism and unresolvable difference in ethical and political matters. At the same time, human rights jurisprudence, jusnaturalism and ethical minimalism have kept alive – each in its own way, degree and domain of intellectual influence – the notion that pluralism and difference have been overly exaggerated, insofar as we belong to one and the same animal species and that our cultures have all developed on the one and only planet, that we know of, which is capable of sustaining human life.

27 McMurtry, *The Cancer Stage of Capitalism*, 240.
28 Ibid. at 199 (emphasis removed).
29 See G. Hardin, 'The Tragedy of the Commons', *Science*, 162, 1968, 1243–1248.
30 Hasegawa, 'The Arctic as Common Good', 33.

Awareness of common human exigencies and aspirations is as old as religious and philosophical thought itself, and it is within this groove that life-value onto-axiology matured, as also signalled by its prominent role within UNESCO's EOLSS *qua* scholarly and scientific emanation of the United Nations' (UN) system and traditions, which find a recurrent and consistent point of convergence and coherence in human rights jurisprudence. Under this perspective, the continuity between the wellbeing index highlighted above and the International Covenant on Economic, Social and Cultural Rights (ICESCR) is noteworthy. The former is a distillate of life-value onto-axiology. The latter lies at the very heart of the UN system and the human rights legal regime that has been growing since the initial experimentations with the League of Nations.[31]

## 2 "[H]ow can some good or goods be grasped as invaluably common?" (i.e. "the problem of circumstance" aka "the possibility of the recognition of common good")[32]

Anyone denying the paramount value of life and of the life-support systems that inevitably and necessarily accompany, sustain and describe it, would instantiate a case of performative contradiction, for she who denies it has been meeting her vital needs for the very long time entailed in developing the faculties required to deny its import. The only coherent denier would be a suicidal one, though not even under all circumstances. Suicides, extreme pessimists and extremist gnostics can still affirm it in fact, albeit *via negativa*, if they take their departure from a better life that is no more, that is dreamt or conceived of, or that is to be gained *post mortem*.[33]

As to those that take it for granted, a short period of deprivation (e.g. life-threatening accidents, illness, impoverishment, imprisonment) is usually more than enough to make them take the life-ground no longer for granted. Vicariously, the same awareness can be gained as well, which is why education, whether formal (e.g. university degrees, scholarly conferences) or informal (e.g. prize-winning documentaries such as Al Gore's 2006 *An Inconvenient Truth*) can play an important role in creating the proper circumstances that are required in order to grasp the common good for what it is.

31 See G. Baruchello and R.L. Johnstone, 'Rights and Value: Construing the International Covenant on Economic, Social and Cultural Rights as Civil Commons', *Studies in Social Justice*, 5(1), 2011, 91–125 and their follow-up contribution, 'Comment on 'Rights and Value': The Committee on Economic, Social and Cultural Rights Assesses the Environment', *Studies in Social Justice*, 7(1), 2013, 175–179.

32 Hasegawa, 'The Arctic as Common Good', 34 (emphasis in the original).

33 See J. Noonan, 'The Debate on Immortality: Posthumanist Science vs. Critical Philosophy', *The European Legacy*, 21(1), 2016, 38–51.

### *3 "[H]ow can common good be shared equally among relevant societal units?" (i.e. "the problem of distribution")*[34]

Need, not want or preference, being the standard, distributive issues are resolved by addressing first the claims of those whose life-ranges are the least met. Growth is certainly good where it is needed, not necessarily where it is wanted, and only inasmuch as it is genuine growth, i.e. growth in real capital (or life capital). Equality matters then as regards having access to means of life, not where it implies equal participation in life-disabling activities (e.g. gender equality in CEO membership of speculative hedge funds or in death squads). Need being the deciding factor, once universal equal access to means of life has been granted and guaranteed, inequalities can still emerge as the natural result of different individual endowments, interests and circumstances, but not as lack of opportunity.

### *4 "[H]ow can the relevant units around the region in question decide the administrative issues on the common good in question in a fair way?" (i.e. "the problem of participation")*[35]

"Civil commons" exist already *qua* institutions dealing with communities' life-needs at many levels, e.g. tribal, village-based, local, national, supra-national. Such institutions must therefore be preserved where functioning, improved where inadequate or diverted from their life-enabling aims, and introduced where absent. The decision-making process is a formal issue rather than a substantive one. How the good is delivered is secondary, as long as the good gets delivered. This wisdom is reflected in standard human rights legislation. For instance, the UN's Committee on Economic, Social and Cultural Rights (CESCR) is ecumenical about the economic system whereby human rights are expected to be respected, protected and fulfilled, and it has taken care to point out that the ICESCR does not exclude, for example, a libertarian model, as long as everyone's rights are in fact fulfilled, noting in 1990 that:

> "[T]he undertaking 'to take steps… by all appropriate means including particularly the adoption of legislative measures' neither requires nor precludes any particular form of government or economic system being used as the vehicle for the steps in question, provided only that it is democratic and that all human rights are thereby respected. Thus, in terms of political and economic systems, the Covenant is neutral and its principles cannot accurately be described as being predicated exclusively upon the need for, or the desirability of a socialist or a capitalist system,

34 Hasegawa, 'The Arctic as Common Good', 34 (emphasis in the original).
35 Id. (emphasis in the original).

or a mixed, centrally planned, or laissez-faire economy, or upon any particular approach."[36]

It is thus quite reasonable for the State to assume that individuals will be able to a large extent to satisfy their own rights, with a minimum of State intervention. For example, individuals should be likely to be able to satisfy their rights to work and to an adequate standard of living, with the State stepping in for those who are unable to do so independently.

There is in fact only one notable exception in the ICESCR: the right to education, which, at least at primary level, must be compulsory and free.[37]

At the same time, the CESCR has not eschewed criticism of the libertarian model when this has proven life-disabling rather than life-enabling. In its standard review of the 2001 report about Hong Kong, the CESCR stated that the region's "philosophy of 'positive non-interventionism'" was hampering the implementation of the ICESCR, to which they are party: this business-centred philosophy "had a negative impact on the realization and enjoyment of the economic, social and cultural rights of Hong Kong's inhabitants, which has been exacerbated by globalization."[38]

From a life-grounded perspective, the ends are the obligation; the means can vary. Any "economy succeeds or fails to the extent to which it provides or does not provide its members with th[e] means of life severally and as a whole."[39] Instrumental and institutional pluralism is therefore a reasonable conclusion. Dogmatic adherence to means is, instead, illogical.

## *5 "[H]ow the circumstance, distribution, and participation concerning common good can be relevantly common among the relevant units in the region in question?" (i.e. "the problem of* **communality***")*[40]

"Civil commons" refers to the life ground upon which all stand in order to live and, if possible, thrive; hence to the common and good ground *par excellence*, i.e. that which is needed to take the next breath, so to speak, and then seek higher satisfaction in life. Some of its manifestations are obvious, others are subtler. Disagreement about the latter group may ensue and, given human imperfection, they are likely to persist even in the most prosperous societies. Life-value onto-axiology tells us what good and bad decisions are

36 CESCR, General Comment No. 3, in *Compilation of General Comments and General Recommendations Adopted by Human Rights Treaty Bodies*, 1989–2009, para. 8.
37 See the UN's ICESCR, Articles 13(2)(a) and 14.
38 CESCR, *Report on the Twenty-fifth, Twenty-sixth and Twenty-seventh Sessions* (U.N. ESCOR, Comm. on Econ., Soc. and Cultural Rts., 58th Sess., Supp. No. 2, U.N. Doc. E/2002/22), para. 176.
39 McMurtry, *Value Wars*, 156.
40 Hasegawa, 'The Arctic as Common Good', 34 (emphasis in the original).

like and thereby achieves a traditional goal of philosophical inquiry, since it allows for the determination in principle of good and evil, cutting across received dualisms, e.g. geoengineering vs sustainable retreat, free choice vs paternalism, free trade vs protectionism, individualism vs collectivism, etc.

In theory, the definitive axiological criterion is sharp: *comprehensive life-enablement is good; life-disablement is bad.* In practice, there are going to be simpler and more complex evaluations to be made. Thorny cases and dilemmas are part of the fabric of the human world. Not even the most perceptive philosophy can save us from having to face them. Nevertheless, if life-value onto-axiology is correct, then the better option is bound to be always the result of comparisons of coherent, comprehensive and compossible life-value.

## 4 A tale of two justices

In addition to answering the five questions put by Hasegawa, or at least pointing in the direction where such answers can be found, the conceptual armoury of life-value onto-axiology can also solve a sticky point that, in my judgment, affects Hasegawa's approach. Specifically, as most clearly exemplified by his first two interrogatives, Hasegawa is uncertain about talking of the common "good" in the singular or "goods" in the plural. Reflection on life-value onto-axiology and the common good can untie this knot.

The notion of the common good has ancient roots and, though Hasegawa does not explore such roots himself, in the same book in which Hasegawa's essay was published, there is another essay that, instead, refers explicitly to them: Dobrzeniecki's chapter, entitled "Legal Pluralisms", mentions "ius-naturalism", which Thomism (or neo-Thomism) has been championing in modern times.[41] Without addressing the whole tradition, I believe that, within it, an important distinction is contained, which standard economics fails to identify and address.

Since Hasegawa relies on standard economic categories of thought in his essay, it is the absence of this distinction that causes him to face the ambiguity between "good" in the singular and "goods" in the plural. On top of that, as seen in my answers to Hasegawa's five questions, life-value onto-axiology clarifies to what extent and in which ways their being common is good. As the forgotten yet important distinction at issue is cast in the work of a major 20th-century Thomist scholar, Arthur Fridolin Utz OP (i.e. Thomas Aquinas' monastic order), it is a matter of recognising, on the one hand, "particular justice" and, on the other hand, "general justice" (also called "legal" or "social justice").

The former kind of justice is itself distinguished into "commutative" and "distributive" justice, which are understood, respectively, as fairness in the

41 K. Dobrzeniecki, 'Legal Pluralisms', *Philosophy of Law in the Arctic*, 39–44 at 42.

commercial and contractual exchanges between particular individuals or groups (e.g. trade unions, professional associations), and fairness in the distribution of whatever socially acknowledged benefits and responsibilities there may be for the same particular individuals or groups (e.g. progressive taxation of different income brackets).

These are the two species of particular justice insofar as they address that which is due to specific individual members of the community (e.g. certain customers, employers, spouses, etc.) or associations thereof, i.e. particular people, not all people at large.

However, there can also be general justice, meaning fairness towards the whole community, inside which particular individuals and associations thereof operate and upon which they rely throughout. Whilst particular justice, whether commutative or distributive, is owed to particular members of society, i.e. to this or that person, legal justice is owed to all persons – past, present and future – in general (hence its name) and is best expressed in abstract universal terms, such as ethical norms, moral maxims, constitutional provisions, basic laws (hence its synonym "legal justice") that apply not to specific persons, but to society in its entirety (hence its synonym "social justice").[42]

Utz refers explicitly to Aquinas' "general" or "legal" justice, calling it though "social justice", and claims it to have "priority over" both forms of "particular justice", also in the economic sphere (i.e. "market law" or "commutative justice").[43] Without the prior recognition of the common humanity of its members, there can be no viable society in which commutative and distributive justice truly apply. Quite the opposite, as Utz argues, the relations that should embody them turn far too promptly and far too easily into instruments of injustice.

For example, when social justice is absent or hampered, "prices" and "contracts" can be formed devoid of "good faith", e.g. unbalanced transactions occurring because of another person's state of urgent need, such as "hunger".[44] In this case, speaking of "free contracts", "free trade" and "individual responsibility" is either naïve or hypocritical. It is like accepting

42 "Social justice" *qua* Aristotelian "general justice" or Thomist "legal justice" appears for the first time in the work of Luigi Taparelli, mentor to the future pope Leo XIII, the initiator of the Social Doctrine of the Church (see his *Saggio di diritto teoretico appoggiato sul fatto*, Rome: Civiltà Cattolica, 1855, vol. I, para. 354).

43 A.F. Utz, *Wirtschaftsethik*, Bonn, Scientia Humana Institut, 1994, para. 5.2.6 (all translations are mine).

44 Ibid. at para. 10.1. For a recent example of this kind of behaviour, consider price gauging in 2017 hurricane-devastated Texas, see M. Hiltzik, 'Memo to economists defending price gauging in a disaster: It's still wrong, morally and economically', *Los Angeles Times*, 28 August 2017, available online at http://www.latimes.com/business/hiltzik/la-fi-hiltzik-price-gouging-harvey-20170828-story.html.

as valid "sport performances" by athletes taking forbidden drugs, or the "legal order" established by "dictators" who violate "human rights".[45]

For the system of "commutative justice" known as the market economy to be justified, the conditions for "social justice" must be in place.[46] In the terms of life-value onto-axiology, the priority of social justice over particular justice means that effective civil commons are the precondition for just commutations and distributions.

That social justice is prior to particular justice is no revolutionary or particularly original realisation, though it is likely to sound somewhat radical in our time and age, when libertarian stances receive much credit in political rhetoric, the current Pope is accused by popular media pundits of being a dangerous Marxist for merely recalling the Scriptures' admonitions against the wealthy's greedy neglect of the poor,[47] and individualistic self-maximising rationality is taken seriously *qua* foundational anthropological assumption in socio-scientific methodology.

*Pace* Utz's unswerving adherence to the long-lived Aristotelian and Thomist conceptions of the human being as inherently social and of the family *qua* fundamental social unit, many social scientists, especially in economics, operate today under the presumption that, somehow, Hobbes' thought experiment of a state of nature in which individual humans are merciless beasts that prey on one another – *homo homini lupus* – is candid enough a depiction of human nature, aspirations and relationships.[48]

Self-interested individuals are therefore the starting point of standard economic theories and models, even if such a Hobbesian state of nature has never existed prior to communal life. Scientifically, the opposite is true. We are social primates and require prolonged parental care before even being able to conceive ourselves as individuals. Personally, it takes years for an individual to become an individual. Socially, it took centuries, because all pre-modern communities were family-or clan-based in their laws and mores, rather than individualistic.[49] We can only subsist occasionally and for a very short time as mere individuals in constant comprehensive mutual competition – *bellum omnium contra omnes* – which

45 Ibid. at para. 10.1.

46 Ibid. at para. 10.2. Although complete perfection is not possible in this life, the Catholic doctrine assumes the possibility of progressive improvement, or at least of worthy attempts in this sense.

47 E.g. T. Bradford, 'Limbaugh: I Told You Pope Francis Was a Marxist', *Truth Revolt*, 17 June 2015, available online at https://www.rushlimbaugh.com/daily/2015/06/16/the_pope_s_leaked_marxist_climate_rant/.

48 See G. Slomp, *Thomas Hobbes and the Political Philosophy of Glory*, London, Palgrave Macmillan, 2000.

49 See M.S. Weiner, *The Rule of the Clan*, New York, Farrar, Straus & Giroux, 2013.

occurs whenever pre-existing societies collapse (e.g. the British civil war witnessed by Hobbes in the 17th century).

Operating within today's individualistic and competitive conceptions of the human being, which are as commonplace in social science as they are mistaken, only "distributive justice" is mentioned in Hasegawa's text, while "commutative" and, above all, "general" justice (or "legal" or "social") are nominally absent.[50] Yet, in his text, the requirements arising from "commutative" and "general" justice persist conceptually. The former appears *qua* assumption of fair interpersonal exchanges in the commercial or economic sphere under "capitalistic globalization and other private exploitations" for the sake of genuine "development" in the Arctic region.[51] The latter appears *qua* concern with regard to how we can think of "the Arctic, or some important aspect of the Arctic, can be a common good, and, if so, in what sense and for whom."[52]

That latter concern is exactly where the distinction between particular and general justice would be required and most fruitful. It is by its application that we can make sense of the notion that, on the one hand, there can be goods, in the plural, that are owed to some people and not to others, i.e. under conditions of particular justice, whether distributive or commutative. On the other hand, there is also a good, in the singular, that is owed to all equally or, which is equivalent, to the entire social body, i.e. under conditions of general justice. It is in the name, and for the sake, of such a common good that certain resources or "goods" can and ought to be seized, kept aside, managed, and/or otherwise utilised by civil commons institutions, i.e. institutions providing universal access to life-goods over generational time.

The notion of general justice being absent from his adopted conceptual framework, Hasegawa is forced into choosing a second-best, poorer candidate, which is the technical term "non-exclusionar[y]" (or non-excludable) – and a revealing related footnote (i.e. number 52), in which Hasegawa shows an implicit pining for a better conceptual armoury, indeed one that may be akin to jusnaturalism: "Although I am not a Thomist, I maintain that this invaluableness, and thus basicness, is the key to the genuine idea of common good for human beings."[53]

## 5 A tale of two economies

Hasegawa's unresolved ambiguity between "good" and "goods" is the unfortunate result of an over-reliance on the conceptual framework of orthodox economics, which is far from capable of addressing fundamental issues of life

50 Hasegawa, 'The Arctic as Common Good', 35.
51 Ibid. at 35–36.
52 Ibid. at 35.
53 Ibid. at 33.

and death. The characterisation as "non-eclusionar[y]" of the goods that he has in mind is insufficient to grasp the "invaluableness" and "basicness" that he aims for.

In mainstream economics, anything that provides satisfaction to its user is called a "good", even if it can be as carcinogenic as cigarettes, as morally debasing as pornography, as socially degrading as separate entrances for high- and low-income tenants in Upper West Side New York, as environmentally devastating as ordinary cars, or as addictively pathological as junk food sold to juveniles. Being excludable (or exclusive or exclusionary) does not cut it. Instead, by identifying genuine needs, human and non-human (e.g. animals', plants', ecosystems'), and separating them from artificially instilled wants, and by determining in principle, if not in each and every possible application, under which conditions anything can be life-enabling or life-disabling, life-value onto-axiology can distinguish between real capital and fake capital, good capital and bad capital, good goods and bad goods.

Methodological individualism is another limitation of orthodox economics, which presupposes the existence of individuals *qua* appetitive machines and the collective good, if and when considered, becomes an aggregate of individual goods. This is a poor account of the common good, and of human life itself, in many ways. Psychologically, it denies altruistic, sociable and empathic tendencies constitutive of our soul. Morally, it denies mutual duties and responsibilities, thus reducing what is right and what is wrong to calculations of individual utility. Historically and politically, it denies the simple fact that, before any individual can ever be an individual, a family or tribe of sorts must be in place, and that human beings have been engaging in the construction of complex social bodies since the dawn of our civilisation. Hasegawa, by assuming the standard individualism of mainstream economics, gets entangled in its inherent limitations.

## 6 Concluding remarks

Life-value onto-axiology, as briefly sketched in this chapter, sets out the criteria for good and bad, which are precisely what is required to determine the nature, scope and direction of human action (and inaction) with regard to the issues that Hasegawa uses to exemplify his chief concerns: "the preservation of climate conditions, the acquisition and use of natural resources in the Arctic, the cooperative use of sky, sea and land for transportation, or socially, the rights of indigenous peoples in the Arctic with each other and against other people and organizations from different areas, the relationship between the necessity of economic development and the maintenance of traditional ways of life, and the communicative exchanges of divergent cultures in the region".[54]

54 Ibid. at 35.

The notions of "life" or "real" capital can help clarify and defend "common capital in society", so as to avoid misunderstandings, whereby "growth" and "development" are shown to be the actual opposite, namely the cumulative destruction of the life-capital required for human survival and wellbeing.[55] Thus, the concept of civil commons and the theory of value behind it are precisely an instantiation of Hasegawa's claim that "we need the exploration of the philosophy of law in the Arctic", insofar as philosophy, by pursuing "deep reflections" into the axiological roots of legal institutions, can reveal what fundamental purposes laws ought to serve, which laws ought to be changed, and which realms of value and/or being laws fail to cover, whether partially or *in toto*.[56]

55 Id.
56 Ibid. at 36.

Chapter 5

# Philosophy of science and legal disputes over whaling in the Southern Ocean[1]

*David Coady[2], Brendan Gogarty[3] and Jeffrey McGee[4]*

## I Introduction

The history of international regulation of commercial whaling, and its movement from diplomacy to litigation, has been discussed in international affairs literatures.[5] As Hurd notes, the International Whaling Commission (IWC) had 'successfully managed the historical transition from open whale hunting to highly restricted hunting [but] ... it has left the hardest part of the problem for last'.[6] Namely, the IWC has for some time reached a deadlock over the remaining states who wished to 'continue whaling under the guise of legal exceptions to the international whaling regime'.[7] He notes that the debate over killing whales has 'been recast as a set of disputes over legal technicalities regarding how and when states are allowed to make reservations to treaties and what amounts to "scientific" research on whales' under international law.[8] As such, Hurd and others saw the (then) pending decision of the

1 This chapter is based on the authors' article 'Scientific whaling and how philosophy of science can help break the international deadlock', which appeared in the *Australian Journal of International Affairs* (2018) 72(1): 49–67.
2 School of Humanities, University of Tasmania, Australia.
3 Faculty of Law, University of Tasmania, Australia.
4 Faculty of Law and Institute for Marine and Antarctic Studies, University of Tasmania, Australia.
5 See: Shirley Scott, 'Australia's decision to initiate Whaling in the Antarctic: winning the case versus resolving the dispute', *Australian Journal of International Affairs* (2012) 68 (1); Ian McArthur, 'Media portrayal of the cultural relationship between Australia and Japan', *Australian Journal of International Affairs* (2016) 60 (4): 574; Mike Iliff and Julia Jabour, 'Theatre sports in the Southern Ocean: engagement options for Australia in whale research protest action', *Australian Journal of International Affairs* (2012) 63 (2): 268; Keith Suter, 'The international politics of saving the whale', *Australian Outlook* (1981) 35 (3): 283; and Ian Hurd, 'Almost Saving Whales: The Ambiguity of Success at the International Whaling Commission', *Ethics & International Affairs* (2012) 26 (1): 103.
6 Hurd 2012 at 111.
7 Hurd 2012 at 104.
8 Hurd 2012 at 104.

International Court of Justice (ICJ) on the legality of Japan's whaling program as an important, if not decisive, mechanism to resolve the dispute through external means.[9]

Other authors were more circumspect about the prospects for the ICJ case. Scott warned that 'the ruling is most likely to be inconclusive, and this on its own would be unlikely to bring about an end to Japanese whaling'.[10] This turned out to be the correct view. In fact, after the ICJ judgment was delivered ('Whaling Case'),[11] Japan's whaling program in the Southern Ocean was renewed and, in some respects, increased in scale from previous years.[12] Many anti-whaling opponents found this surprising, and put it down to Japan's apparent intransigence because it was widely reported that Australia/New Zealand had 'won' the case. While this is technically true, so is it technically true that Japan's new whaling program in the Southern Ocean was not in legal breach of the ICJ ruling.

As will be discussed later, the 1946 International Convention for the Regulation of Whaling ('Whaling Convention') regulates – and in most cases, prohibits – harvesting whales, unless it is for the purposes of 'scientific research'. This has become the legal focus of the 're-cast' dispute between whaling and anti-whaling nations. Australia, in particular, complained that the Japanese lethal whaling program was misusing this exception to undertake commercial whaling activities. However, the Court sidestepped this larger question. Rather it chose to approach the issue by considering whether the (then) Japanese whaling program, as previously implemented, was justified by its own scientific aims. Importantly, the Court found the methods and approach of the Japanese whaling were inconsistent with an earlier program that had largely similar aims and objectives. In other words, the program was internally and externally unjustified.

In approaching the Australia/New Zealand complaint in such narrow terms the ICJ did not articulate a legal test to determine, in advance, when a proposed lethal whaling program is scientific or not. At best, the ICJ Whaling Case suggested that a whaling program is not justified when its conduct over several years is not consistent with its own stated scientific objectives. The ICJ case also did not address *who* might authoritatively decide on whether a whaling program is justified, other than perhaps the state claiming to be conducting the scientific research, or another international court. We

9 Hurd 2012 at 108–111.

10 Scott 2012 at 13.

11 *Whaling in the Antarctic (Australia v. Japan: New Zealand Intervening)* 2014 (International Court of Justice, 31 March), https://www.icj-cij.org/en/case/148/judgments; *ICJ Summary of the Judgment of Whaling in the Antarctic (Australia v. Japan: New Zealand Intervening)* 2014 (International Court of Justice, 31 March), https://www.icj-cij.org/en/case/148.

12 Brendan Gogarty and Peter Lawrence, 'The ICJ Whaling Case: Missed Opportunity to Advance the Rule of Law in Resolving Science-Related Disputes in Global Commons?', *Heidelberg Journal of International Law* (2017) 77: 161–198, at 165.

therefore argue the ICJ has not, however, addressed the 'hardest part of the problem' as was hoped by international relations experts and commentators.

We argue that the failure of the ICJ to break the whaling deadlock was as much related to its own unwillingness to grapple with the nature and character of 'scientific knowledge' as it is Japan's wider resistance to halting its whaling program. Questions about the nature and character of scientific knowledge, like other bodies of knowledge, originate in philosophy, but they should not only be relegated to that field. Indeed, the ICJ Whaling Case shows just how important philosophical questions about the nature and character of science are to international law, relations and governance, particularly in areas such as Antarctica and the Southern Ocean.

International law's primary compliance mechanism is horizontal pressure between states. Judicial arbitration is rare, especially in regard to the global commons. This means that clarity of meaning of international treaty terms is particularly important to its success. Without clarity, treaty terms can become mired in uncertainty and disagreement. More to the point, without a clear and precise way of showing a state is breaching its international legal obligations, other states cannot effectively place diplomatic pressure on them, undermining the legal efficacy of that treaty.

Contemporary philosophy of science provides a substantive and workable understanding of the scope and limits of 'scientific research' which can be clearly, transparently and predictably separated from other activities such as commercial exploitation. Had the ICJ applied such a philosophical lens, we may not have returned to the legal-diplomatic dispute over Japan's new program, because states would have a legal mechanism to evaluate the veracity of claims that a particular whaling program is directed to the pursuit of scientific knowledge. Indeed, such a lens might also have provided much better guidance about the appropriate use of science in other international legal regimes. This, in itself, provides a motivation for greater interdisciplinary engagement between philosophers, lawyers and international affairs experts in working on the governance of the global commons.

## 2 Background to the legal dispute between Australia and Japan

At the root of the dispute before the ICJ were two separate articles of the Whaling Convention: Articles V and VIII. Article V of the Convention allows the parties to set catch limits for whales, so long as they are 'based on scientific findings'. At the 1982 meeting of the IWC, the states present invoked Article V to amend the Schedule of the Whaling Convention so that catch limits for commercial whaling of all whales were reduced to zero, thereby effectively prohibiting all commercial whaling.[13]

13 This was achieved by inserting paragraph 10(e) of the Schedule to the Whaling Convention; see *International Whaling Commission Report*, IWC 34th Annual Meeting, 19–24 July 1982, 72–86.

Japan initially protested against this 1982 commercial whaling moratorium, arguing that it had 'no basis in science' and was instead driven by the domestic socio-political concerns of other states.[14] However, Japan eventually withdrew its objection to the moratorium and instead indicated that it would undertake a 'scientific whaling program', involving lethal sampling of whales, to prove the moratorium itself was not based on 'sound science'.[15] This program was ostensibly undertaken under Article VIII of the Whaling Convention, which reads as follows:

1 Notwithstanding anything contained in this Convention any Contracting Government may grant to any of its nationals a special permit authorizing that national to kill, take and treat whales for purposes of scientific research …and the killing, taking, and treating of whales in accordance with the provisions of this Article shall be exempt from the operation of this Convention. …
2 Any whales taken under these special permits shall so far as practicable be processed and the proceeds shall be dealt with in accordance with directions issued by the Government by which the permit was granted.

Japan pursued two back-to-back whaling programs under this provision. The 1987–2005 Japanese Whale Research Programme under Special Permit in the Antarctic (JARPA) and JARPA II program from 2006 to 2014. These programs had functionally similar objectives but varied in the extent of the lethal take of different whale species. In both programs, whale carcasses were ultimately sold for consumption, as is permitted by Article VIII.

Despite Japan's claim to be harvesting whales to determine the scientific legitimacy for the commercial moratorium, the majority of states in the IWC criticised its use of lethal sampling to achieve this aim.[16] This included IWC non-binding resolutions (by simple majority) that the JARPA/JARPA II programs should be: revised to be more scientifically justified (IWC 1987), limited

14 Government of Japan, *National Diet Debates*, House of Representatives – Agriculture, Forestry and Fisheries Committee – No. 2, 11 October 1983 [excerpt], cited in Memorial of Australia, *Whaling in the Antarctic (Australia v. Japan: New Zealand Intervening)*, ICJ Written Proceedings, https://www.icj-cij.org/en/case/148/written-proceedings (9/5/2011) [hereafter 'Australian Memorial' or pleading party and pleading type if other pleadings], Annex 90, p 77.

15 Joji Morishita, 'IWC and the ICJ Judgment', in Malgosia Fitzmaurice and Dai Tamada (eds), *Whaling in the Antarctic: Significance and Implications of the ICJ Judgment*. Leiden: Brill, 2016 at 240.

16 In the IWC, see IWC Resolutions 2003–3 and 2005–1, 2005–1, 2007–1; Annual Reports of the IWC, (2009), 26–28, (2010), 23, (2012), 41–43. IWC Resolutions and reports available at https://iwc.int/home. See also Reuben Ackerman, 'Japanese Whaling in the Pacific Ocean: Defiance of International Whaling Norms in the Name of "Scientific Research", Culture and Tradition', *Boston College International & Comparative Law Review* (2012) 25 (2) at 323.

to exceptional circumstances (1995, 1998, 1999), use non-lethal techniques (1995–1999), establish whale sanctuaries (1995–1998), or be stopped altogether JARPA II (IWC 2003, 2005, 2007). However, the Whaling Convention lacks a mechanism for the IWC, or any of its related bodies (such as the Science Committee) to develop these resolutions into binding restrictions on Japan, or override the 'scientific whaling' permits it has granted to its citizens (in this case state funded organisations) under Article VIII. Indeed, Article VIII allows for permits to be issued 'notwithstanding anything contained in this Convention', effectively restricting the capacity of the IWC to amend the schedules to prohibit or regulate such permits as part of the Convention system. Amending the entire Whaling Convention would require that it be negotiated by all state parties, something Japan and other whaling states would likely block.

Australia was one of the most vocal critics of Japanese whaling in the Southern Ocean, arguing that Japan's harvesting of whales was for commercial purposes, and as such, that 'Japan's so called "scientific" whaling is contrary to [Japan's] international obligations and should stop'.[17] In 2008 a Small Working Group of states (33 states in total participated at different stages, including Japan, Australia and New Zealand) was established outside the main chamber of the IWC to help build consensus on a range of controversial issues, but especially lethal whaling. It operated on the premise that 'nothing is agreed until everything is agreed'.[18] Unfortunately, when it came to lethal whaling, nothing was ever agreed.

In 2010, Australia, frustrated by the impasse in the Small Working Group, tabled a proposal to the working group demanding: 'an immediate end to unilateral so-called "scientific" whaling purportedly conducted under Article VIII' and the establishment of a reform process for the Article. However, Japan blocked the proposal and it failed to reach consensus. In May 2010 Australia instituted proceedings in the ICJ complaining that:

> 'While Japan indicated a willingness to negotiate on the numbers and species targeted by its programs in the context of a negotiated package, it continued to reiterate the "scientific" justification for JARPA II and its purported legality under international law. It has become clear that current and proposed IWC processes cannot resolve the key legal issue that is the subject of the dispute between Australia and Japan, namely the legality of large-scale "special permit" whaling under JARPA II.'[19]

17 International Whaling Commission 64th Annual Meeting (2–6 July 2012) Opening Statements from Contracting Governments, IGOs and NGOs Press statement by (the then) Australian Federal Environment Minister, Hon Tony Burke, cited in: Minister for Australian Antarctic Division, 'Australia continues push for reform at International Whaling Commission', *Press Release*, 2 July 2012, http://www.antarctica.gov.au/news/2012/iwc-minister.

18 IWC 2009.

19 Government of Australia 2010.

These complaints were repeated in Australia's memorial (i.e. formal court document) filed with the ICJ. In the memorial Australia claimed that Japan was breaching the Whaling Convention by not acting in good faith to its 'obligation not to kill whales for commercial purposes' and that the issue of special permits by Japan allegedly under Article VIII of the Whaling Convention purportedly authorising whaling 'for purposes of scientific research' is not consistent with the Whaling Convention.[20]

New Zealand later joined as an intervenor (co-complainant) against Japan. It argued similar grounds to Australia, although they were more directed to the 'proper construction of Article VIII of the Convention', which it said could not be used in bad faith to justify 'whaling for other purposes … even if it involves the collection of some scientific data'.[21]

Japan in its counter-memorial, argued that its lethal whaling was conducted pursuant to a 'legitimate scientific programme, permitted under Article VIII of the ICRW [Whaling Convention] … fully consistent with the text as well as with the object and purpose of the ICRW'. It argued that in fact the opposition to its program was anti-scientific, because the complainants were 'opposed to any form of whaling … regardless of science or law' and their views on whale conservation and management were not 'based on science'.

The Whaling Case was therefore predominantly a contest about the meaning or interpretation of the words 'scientific research' in Article VIII of the Whaling Convention.[22] On the one hand, Japan claimed the states behind the 1982 commercial moratorium were motivated by the ethical and social politics of their domestic populations – rather than scientific evidence of overfishing of whales or threats to whale population. On the other hand, Australia and other anti-whaling states argued that Japan's so-called 'scientific research' was merely commercial harvesting of whales dressed up in the lab-coat of science.

### *2.1 A contest about 'legitimate' science*

During legal proceedings before the ICJ the parties variously agreed – admittedly to different degrees – that the question of what is scientific research for the purposes of Article VIII was not an arbitrary decision to be decided entirely by the state issuing the permit. With the assistance of the bench, the parties had moved even closer together by the close of proceedings, such that Japan conceded that any decision to issue a permit must be 'objectively reasonable, or supported by coherent reasoning and respectable

20 Government of Australia 2011 at 3.
21 Government of New Zealand 2012 at 16.
22 Brendan Gogarty, 'Conceptions and (Mis)conceptions of Science in International Treaties; the ICJ Whaling Case in Context', *The Yearbook of Polar Law* (2015) 7 (1): 607.

scientific evidence and … , in this sense, objectively justifiable'.[23] The Court summarised the position to be that, while Article VIII granted discretion to issue a permit to the authorising state, and no other body within the IWC, that state still needed to 'explain the objective basis for its determination'.[24]

While 'scientific' and 'research' are compound conceptions, all parties were primarily concerned with the meaning of 'scientific' as the operative term which would demarcate permissible from non-permissible types of whaling activity. Specifically, the parties disagreed about how to distinguish between scientific and non-scientific activities involving the killing of whales. As noted, this has been an ongoing source of dispute within the IWC regime.

The history of the IWC is, to a great extent, a history of debate on the issue of how to distinguish ostensibly 'scientific' whaling from commercial whaling. One of the earliest disputes concerned whether testing new harpoons on whales could be treated as scientific whaling and hence be exempted from the operation of the Whaling convention under Article VIII.[25] In response to disputes of this sort, in 1957 the United States delegation to the IWC sought to narrow the interpretation of 'scientific research' for the purposes of Article VIII, arguing that 'at the time of preparation of the Articles of the Convention it was in the minds of the framers that scientific research is *essentially biological research*'.[26] Whatever may be the merits of this claim, or the merits of focussing on the original intent of states as a theory of interpretation in international law, the IWC has not been able to resolve or clarify this issue internally. Its own Scientific Committee has explicitly refrained from offering a 'practical definition of science' in the context of Article VIII, saying that 'it would be very difficult to make any such definition or to draw a line between one branch of science and another'.[27] It has therefore never revisited this technical-legal question.

These are certainly difficult tasks, but given the importance of the issues, it is worth trying. In fact, it seems that members of the Scientific Committee were not merely baulking at a difficult task. Rather, they had a principled objection to it. Neil Mackintosh explained the Committee's position by saying 'we felt that it would be anti-scientific to make any limit on scientific research of any kind'.[28] This attitude, we submit, is itself thoroughly anti-scientific. If it is wrong to place limits on scientific research by defining it, then what is to prevent activities such as astrology or tarot card reading from

23 ICJ 2014 at 29.
24 Ibid.
25 Graham Burnett, *The Sounding of the Whale: Science and Cetaceans in the Twentieth Century*. Chicago: University of Chicago Press, 2012 at 411.
26 Ibid; original emphasis.
27 IWC. 1957. *Scientific Committee Report for 1957*. International Whaling Commission, paragraph 12.
28 IWC. n.d. *Scientific and Technical Committee Recommendation*. International Whaling Commission, at 47.

claiming the status of scientific research? The Scientific Committee and Mackintosh seem to confuse the (generally laudable) view that science requires a degree of freedom from the restraints of orthodoxy, especially when those restraints come from regulatory bodies such as the IWC, and the wrongheaded view that science can be anything at all and that there is no way of distinguishing one branch of science from another.

The Science Committee's position equally seems contrary to the intention of the law which constitutes it and sets out its roles and duties. The Whaling Convention specifically provides for scientific research as an exception to conduct that is otherwise prohibited. By incorporating that rule into law, the parties to the agreement have agreed that the phrase 'scientific whaling' has meaning that is capable of producing a desired and predictable outcome. Hence, by refusing to commit to binding, limiting terms, the Committee was arguably not acting in accordance with the original intention of those who drafted the agreement. Ultimately, the lack of engagement with the problem by the Science Committee has contributed to an impasse between the IWC parties and the referral of the dispute to the ICJ.

## 3 Philosophy's contribution to the debate on whaling (and scientific governance more generally)

Despite widespread public interest in the topic of whaling there is relatively little philosophical work on the status of whaling in international law and international affairs. When philosophers have roused themselves to consider the topic, they have largely confined their attention to a narrow set of ethical questions. For example, philosophers have considered the question of whether international law should permit certain forms of whaling because it is part of a community's traditional 'form of life',[29] and whether international law should extend legal rights to whales themselves.[30]

However, philosophy can offer much more for developing an understanding of the foundations of the dispute in the Whaling Case. As much as this dispute between Australia and Japan has arisen in the context of an international legal dispute, it appears to be at its core a philosophical problem about the boundaries of concepts. At its simplest, the dispute came down to what could be classified as 'scientific research' under Article VIII, and what could not. This is an inherently philosophical question, albeit arising within the context of a legal dispute.

The problem of distinguishing science from non-science (or pseudo-science) is one that has been traditionally addressed by philosophers. Philosophy can

29 Ronnie Hawkins, 'Cultural Whaling, Commodification, and Culture Change', *Environmental Ethics* (2001) 23 (3): 287–306.

30 Robert Garner, 'Animal Welfare, Ethics, and the Work of the International Whaling Commission', *Journal of Global Ethics* (2011) 7 (3): 279–290.

play a key role resolving disputes such as this, or at least help the parties to see clearly what is at stake in their dispute. The most famous approach to the problem of scientific demarcation was offered by Sir Karl Popper. According to Popper, the method of genuine science (as opposed to pseudo-science) involves attempts to falsify (rather than verify) hypotheses which purport to explain observed phenomena. If we succeed in falsifying a given hypothesis, we should reject it. If we fail to falsify it, however, we should not conclude that it is true or even that it is probably true. As Popper himself put it:

> 'I think that we shall have to get accustomed to the idea that we must not look upon science as a "body of knowledge", but rather as a system of hypotheses; that is to say, as a system of guesses or anticipations which in principle cannot be justified, but with which we work as long as they stand up to tests, and of which we are never justified in saying that we know that they are "true" or "more or less certain" or even "probable".'[31]

Despite its influence, few contemporary philosophers of science accept the completeness of Popper's account of science.[32] Scientists do, and should, try both to falsify and to verify hypotheses, and the more often they are verified, the more likely it is that they are true.

So, the common-sense view of science as consisting (at least in part) of a 'body of knowledge', could reasonably be said to reflect a contemporary, mainstream, understanding of the term. The nature of knowledge is, of course, another longstanding philosophical issue, but we won't let it detain us for long. We adopt a minimal (or veritistic) account of knowledge, according to which knowledge is simply true belief. On this account, to say that someone knows *p*, is simply to say that he or she believes *p* and that *p* is true.[33] In this sense, science involves the pursuit of truth as one of its core missions. Scientists *qua* scientists seek to acquire true beliefs for themselves, and to spread those true beliefs to others through academic publication and other forms of dissemination.

It seems clear therefore that scientific research necessarily involves the pursuit of truth. But although this is a necessary condition for an activity to constitute scientific research, it doesn't seem to be a sufficient condition. We don't want to say that every time someone pursues truth that person is engaged in scientific research. Looking up a timetable to see when the next bus is arriving, for instance, clearly does not constitute scientific research.

31 Karl Popper, *The Logic of Scientific Discovery*. London: Hutchinson, 1959 at 317.
32 David Coady and Richard Corry, *The Climate Change Debate: An Epistemic and Ethical Inquiry*. New York: Palgrave, 2013.
33 In adopting this strictly veritistic account of knowledge, we are following Goldman: Alvin I. Goldman, *Knowledge in a Social World*. Oxford: Clarendon Press, 1999.

A natural thing to say is that scientific research involves the pursuit of new truths: ones that have never been known before, or at least which are currently unknown in the community in which they are pursued. This is better, but there still seem to be plenty of activities that involve the pursuit of new truths which (at least arguably) are not scientific research. History, philosophy, legal research and theology all often involve the pursuit of new truth, but to categorize any of these activities as scientific research would be controversial, to say the least.

Fortunately, it is not necessary for us to have a complete definition of scientific research, in the form of necessary and sufficient conditions, to make progress on the whaling dispute between Australia and Japan. The Whaling Convention envisions two primary types of activity relating to whales, commercial whaling and scientific whaling; and to a lesser extent indigenous hunting (which was not a subject of the dispute). Thus, a resolution of the dispute merely requires that we find ways to demarcate scientific research from commercial activity.

## 4 The Whaling Case through a philosophical lens

The Whaling Case before the IWC focused on certain 'broad criteria' which the main expert witness called by Australia, Marc Mangel a professor of mathematical biology, described as 'necessary for a program for purposes of scientific research'. These criteria are as follows:

a Does the program have an over-arching conceptual framework that leads to a set of focused questions (hypotheses)?
b Does the program employ the correct set of empirical tools to answer the questions including setting samples sizes with sound statistical reasoning and linking mathematical models and data appropriately?
c Does the program have proper assessment through the community of scientists?
d Is the program designed to avoid unintended negative ecological consequences?[34]

Lars Walløe, the only expert witness called by Japan, disputed this account of scientific research, describing it as 'restrictive and therefore misleading'.[35] In particular, Walløe argued that Mangel's criteria a and b were unnecessary.

34 Marc Mangel, 'An Assessment of Japanese Whale Research Programs Under Special Permit in the Antarctic (JARPA, JARPA II) as Programs for the Purposes of Scientific Research in the Context of Conservation and Management of Whales', *ICJ* (2013) at 350, https://www.icj-cij.org/en/case/148/written-proceedings.

35 Lars Walløe, 'Scientific Review of Issues Raised by the Memorial of Australia Including its Two Prefaces', *ICJ* (n.d.) at 3, https://www.icj-cij.org/en/case/148/written-proceedings.

He described them as 'perhaps an adequate ... description of research in a fairly advanced biological field', however, Walløe claimed, they are not appropriate to situations where 'existing knowledge ... is very limited', such as work on the Southern Ocean ecosystem, of which he says the following:

> 'it is difficult to tell which observations are likely to be important for an understanding of the dynamics of the system. As a result, all physical, chemical and biological oceanographic data that can be collected may be considered potentially valuable, not only data relevant to specific hypotheses.'[36]

Much will depend on how we interpret Walløe's use of the word 'specific' in this passage. It would be natural, given his claim about the potential value of all oceanographic data, to interpret him as saying that the collection of such data doesn't have to be guided by any hypotheses at all. If all oceanographic data is potentially relevant, the implication seems to be, then the collection of any or (if that were possible) all of it could be scientifically justified. On this interpretation science is, or at any rate can be, nothing more than a collection of truths, or as Mangel dismissively puts it in his response to Walløe, science would be reduced to a mere 'bucket of data'.[37]

This understanding of the Japanese position appears to be confirmed by the Japanese response to Mangel's submission to the ICJ, which characterizes the Japanese whaling programme as 'exploratory data analysis', which it defines as 'summarizing the main characteristics of data sets without using statistical models or formulating hypotheses'.[38] In defence of the scientific status of exploratory data analysis, the Japanese representative points out that if one looks up 'exploratory data analysis' on Google Scholar, one will find over a million articles.

The fact that one can find a lot of references on Google Scholar to a certain practice is no guarantee that it is a scientific practice. Nonetheless, we accept that exploratory data analysis is a genuine aspect of scientific research practice. However, the Japanese representative's characterization of it as proceeding without formulating hypotheses at all is significantly mistaken. It is true that it does not involve the formulation of formal statistical hypotheses, but that does not mean that it does not involve the formulation of any hypotheses at all. Furthermore, exploratory data analysis is not, and was never intended to be, a stand-alone practice. It was devised as a supplement to confirmatory data analysis (i.e. statistical hypothesis testing).

36 Ibid. at 5.
37 Mangel 2013 at 3.
38 Koji Tsuruoka, 2013. 'Observations of Japan on the Statements Submitted by the Experts Called by Australia'. *ICJ* (2013), at 7, https://www.icj-cij.org/en/case/148/written-proceedings.

Exploratory data analysis has been compared to the process of gathering evidence by a detective, while confirmatory data analysis is compared to a court trial.[39] This analogy is, however, potentially misleading since it is not the case that one form of analysis is supposed to precede the other. Rather, as John Tukey himself, the source of Walløe and the Japanese representative's claims about exploratory data analysis, says: 'exploratory and confirmatory analysis can – and should – proceed side by side'.[40]

A more charitable interpretation of the Japanese position, and that of their expert, Walløe, is, however, available. Walløe concedes that there are 'always general hypotheses behind any collection of primary data'.[41] However, he claims, these hypotheses are 'often vague and not easy to formulate in scientific language'. This suggests that he is taking issue with Mangel's use of the word 'focused' in 'focused questions (Mangel's criterion "a")'.

The question then is whether the hypotheses that are being tested in genuine science have to be focussed (i.e. precise), as Mangel would have us believe, or whether they can be vague (i.e. imprecise), as Walløe claims. Vagueness and precision are matters of degree, and the degree of precision that is required of hypotheses will inevitably depend a great deal on the area of science considered. Physics, for example, aspires to a degree of precision that is impossible in the social sciences. Marine biology seems to be somewhere in between physics and social science in this respect; for a hypothesis to be serviceable in biology, it need not be as precise as those found in physics, but it would probably be more precise than many hypotheses of the social sciences. This is because biology relies on fundamental concepts, such as *species* and *genus*, that are somewhat vague (i.e. they admit of borderline cases),[42] but not as vague as many of the key concepts of social science, such as *race*[43] and *social class*, which are notoriously imprecise. Furthermore, given the disagreement between the experts called by Australia and Japan on the issue of how much precision the hypotheses of marine biology should aspire to, it seems that this topic is very much unsettled within the discipline itself.

We don't need to defer to disciplinary experts about one aspect of the Japanese case. Contrary to Walløe's testimony, it doesn't seem to be the case that scarcity of knowledge about a given subject is any reason for operating

39 John Tukey, *Exploratory Data Analysis*. Reading, MA: Addison-Wesley, 1977 at 3.

40 Ibid.

41 Walløe n.d. at 5.

42 'Science' isn't the only undefined and contested word to appear in the Whaling Convention. There is also considerable controversy over what exactly is meant by the imprecise word "whale", see Sean Stephenson, Arne Mooers and Amir Attaran, 'Does Size Matter? The ICRW and the Inclusion of Small Cetaceans', *Transnational Environmental Law* 3 (2) (2014): 241–263.

43 Of course, some people think of race as a biological rather than a social category. Our view is that they are wrong.

with less precise hypotheses. If anything, the opposite would seem to be the case. The less we know about a subject, the more important it is to research it with precise (and hence definitively testable) hypotheses. Otherwise we run the risk of aimlessly collecting data for no particular purpose.

## 5 Does science need empirical tools?

The disagreement between Mangel and Walløe over Mangel's second criterion (criterion b) follows a similar dialectical pattern. Mangel insists that genuine science must employ the correct set of empirical tools to test its hypotheses, claiming that 'the essence of science is to extract knowledge from data and, if one does not know in advance how the data will be analyzed to extract such knowledge, one is not ready to collect the data'.[44] Walløe responds that this is too much to require in the initial stages of an inquiry into a subject matter about which there is little existing knowledge, and that the correct empirical tools may only become apparent at some later stage of the enquiry.

On this issue, we are inclined to side with Walløe. It would clearly be too much to demand that scientists state precisely how data will be analysed prior to collection. That would seem to rule out in advance the possibility of data that is so surprising it cannot be analysed in the way anticipated by the scientists in question, or of those scientists simply changing their minds (on rational grounds) about how the data should be analysed. So Mangel's criterion b seems somewhat too rigid and should be weakened to require, not necessarily the correct set of empirical tools, but those which it is rational to suppose are correct given the evidence available at the time the investigator begins to collect the data.

The empirical tool which is discussed by both experts in greatest detail is the setting of sample sizes. This is a particularly important issue in the ICJ Whaling Case, since a sample size effectively means the number of whales that will be killed. On this topic, Walløe says 'it must be admitted that the Japanese scientists have not always given completely transparent and clear explanation of how sample sizes were calculated or determined'.[45] However, he does mention one factor that he thinks plays a role in determining sample sizes. Japan covered part of the cost of JARPA and JARPA II with the proceeds of whale products, and Walløe states that he 'often had the impression that sample sizes were influenced by funding considerations'.[46]

44 Mangel repeats this point in his response to Walløe, saying that if "scientists do not know how the data will be analysed, they are not ready to collect it" – see Mangel 2013 at 10.
45 Walløe n.d. at 10.
46 Ibid.

On its face, this looks like an admission by Japan's own expert witness that undermines Japan's claim to scientific legitimacy. If something as fundamental as sample sizes is motivated (even in part) by funding considerations then, to that extent, it appears the whaling has a demonstrably commercial rather than a scientific purpose. Walløe defends the practice of partially funding 'scientific' whaling from whale products in the following passage:

> 'As long as an activity is genuinely motivated by an intent to conduct scientific research, other additional motivations, e.g. obtaining some of the funding by selling products, may even be regarded as an advantage and not as a counterargument.'[47]

Walløe points out, in defence of this claim, that it is not uncommon for scientific research to be partially self-funded and he cites a number of examples of this phenomenon, including fisheries research, medical research, and archaeological research, in support of this claim. This is all true, but those are all activities in which commerce is permitted and even encouraged. In the Whaling Case the opposite is true, the Whaling Convention – in its current form, at least – specifically prohibits commercial exploitation, while permitting scientific research. What the Court (and the experts that appeared in front of it) was being asked to do was establish whether the activity was actually about commerce rather than science. Furthermore, assuming, for the sake of argument, that some commercial motivation may legitimately co-exist with a genuinely scientific motivation, in this case (as admitted, it seems, by their own expert) the commercial motivation is not merely a means to doing the research, but is actually determining the nature of the research itself.

The problem is that almost any endeavour can be described as simultaneously motivated by a desire for knowledge and financial benefit. Even the most basic scientific research is often part of a continuum of activity leading to commercial application. Even the most commercial enterprise will provide data which may be analysed in a way that develops our knowledge. However, just because they mix scientific and commercial aspects does not mean these are not two separate things. Walløe tacitly accepts this when he describes the commercial motivations as 'additional' to the scientific ones. Accepting that this is the case, the question in situations such as the Whaling Case – where commercial activity is prohibited and research permitted – is how to distil and measure the potential motivations against each other. When something is clearly much more about commerce than it is about scientific research, it is hard to see how the mere fact it might somehow contribute to our knowledge of the world would allow it to escape a ban on commercial exploitation.

47 Ibid.

## 6 Analysing the ICJ's position on 'scientific research'

As noted, Walløe addressed his criticisms at criteria a and b of Mangel's proposal, without contesting criteria c and d. The Court went one step further and dismissed Mangel's criteria altogether, stating:

> 'the Court is not persuaded that activities [under Article VIII of the Whaling Convention] must satisfy the four criteria advanced by Australia in order to constitute "scientific research" in the context of Article VIII. As formulated by Australia, these criteria appear largely to reflect what one of the experts that it called regards as well-conceived scientific research, rather than serving as an interpretation of the term as used in the Convention. Nor does the Court consider it necessary to devise alternative criteria or to offer a general definition of "scientific research".'[48]

Instead, the ICJ chose to focus its legal analysis on the term 'for the purposes of' within the Article. Specifically, it considered whether JARPA II's stated program's design and implementation are reasonable in relation to its stated scientific objectives – without questioning whether those objectives were, in fact, scientific or not. This involved measuring the internal consistency of the program against its own stated aims, as well as measuring it against what it had previously done in pursuit of the same ostensible aims of the principal JARPA program. In other words, the Court asked whether Japan had succeeded in doing what it claimed it was going to do in relation to both programs. However, the Court did not consider whether what Japan had set out to do was actually scientific in the first place, or was primarily motivated by scientific reasons.

The ICJ's approach is puzzling, since presumably the court must have some idea of the meaning of 'scientific research' if it is able to determine whether an activity is 'for the purposes' of it, and if it does have an idea of what it means, it presumably can convey what it means through some kind of definition. There are of course many different kinds of definition. We have already suggested that providing a set of necessary and sufficient conditions that would capture all uses of the words 'science' or 'scientific research' in all contexts may be overly ambitious. Nonetheless, some indication of how these terms are to be understood in the Whaling Convention and perhaps in other treaties governing global commons areas, would be highly desirable. Indeed, it is clear the Court must have been operating with implicit definitions of these terms. Unfortunately, it fails to make these definitions explicit.

48 *ICJ Summary of the Judgment of Whaling in the Antarctic (Australia v. Japan: New Zealand Intervening)* 2014, 4.

## 7 The aftermath of the decision

The ambiguous nature of the ICJ resulted in different members states of the IWC interpreting the decision differently.[49] For the most part these interpretations accorded with each party's pre-judgment position. Australia and New Zealand thus argued in the IWC that the decision should be read as limiting, if not all-out prohibiting, future lethal whaling.[50] While Japan was generally shocked by the decision of the ICJ it was also reassured by the Court's explicit refusal to prohibit future whaling permits under Article VII. Japan saw this as a green light to issue further permits under a new 'scientific research' whaling program, noting the Court had placed no specific limits on the program's design or methodology.[51] Initial hopes by all parties that the decision would lead to greater clarity, or at the very least, greater dialogue and consensus building within the ICJ subsequently faded.

In November 2014, only a few months after the decision, Japan announced a new 'scientific research' permit program called NEWREP A. Despite Japan's claims the new program was in line with the ICJ judgment, it has received criticism from the scientific community for being largely identical in its approach and use of lethal methods to the previous two programs.[52] The majority of IWC members reacted strongly to the proposal. New Zealand drafted a resolution to clarify and tighten the provisions of Article VIII. Its draft resolution proposed the direct involvement of the Scientific Committee in issuing scientific research permits based on a reasonableness test. New Zealand argued the resolution was necessary to give effect to the ICJ judgment (IWC/65 OS New Zealand). Japan contested the resolution as 'going beyond the ICJ judgment',[53] and blocked its adoption.

While New Zealand's Article VIII resolution was adopted by simple majority (35 votes in support, 20 against and 5 abstentions), it did not achieve the consensus required to be legally binding (IWC/65/14 Rev 1). Japan subsequently ignored it, as it ignored a flurry of activity in the IWC, the popular press and scholarly journals condemning the program,[54] and pressed ahead with its whale hunt in 2015, subsequently killing over 300 whales per year.

Following the ICJ decision Japan has practically blocked any further dispute over whaling being raised against it in the ICJ, by refusing to accept its jurisdiction over future fisheries disputes, as it is permitted to do in international law.[55] Consequently, assertions that Japan's new program NEWREP A

49 Morishita 2016 at 256.
50 Malgosia Fitzmaurice, *Whaling and International Law*. Cambridge: Cambridge University Press, 2015 at 113.
51 Morishita 2016 at 253.
52 William de la Mare, Nick Gales, Marc Mangel. 'Applying scientific principles in international law on whaling' *Science* (2014) 345: 1125–1126.
53 Morishita 2016 at 257.
54 Fitzmaurice 2015 at 116–117.
55 Gogarty and Lawrence 2017 at 165.

is no different than JARPA II – indeed, it is largely identical – are not able to be subjected to legal analysis by an international court. Without that avenue states are only able to rely on the judgment in the Whaling Case, or their own interpretation of Article VIII. As has been discussed, neither is particularly clear about when killing whales is for scientific research rather than commercial ends. Indeed, given that the Court's reasoning only tested the internal justification of a program after it had been carried out (over almost a decade in the case of JARPA II), it would really only become useful in relation to NEWREP A once it had been conducted for a long period of time.

The Court's refusal to offer any criteria to distinguish science from commerce has, in our view, perpetuated the deadlock and ineffectiveness of the Whaling Convention treaty regime rather than solved it. As Clapham rightly noted:

> 'The ICJ decision, while satisfying to Japan's critics as an independent vindication of their views, was little more than a temporary setback for that nation's whaling.'[56]

As already discussed, in late 2018, Japan gave notice of intention to withdraw for the Whaling Convention, which took effect on 30 June 2019. This means that Japan is now able to legally conduct commercial whaling, although it has discontinued its whaling activities in the Southern Ocean. The character of Japanese whaling practices will therefore not be litigated again any time soon.

### *7.1 Towards a more shared understanding of science*

While it would be nice if the Court had provided a set of necessary and sufficient conditions for distinguishing science from other activities, that would perhaps, as already suggested, be too much to ask. A more limited and, we submit, achievable goal would be to provide criteria that would distinguish science from commerce.

Fortunately, the testimony of the expert witnesses in this case gives us some reason for optimism that there might be some, albeit limited, shared understanding of how 'science' and 'scientific research' is to be understood in this context. Both sides of the dispute appear to have accepted implicitly the position that the United States took in 1957 that 'scientific research' referred to in Article VIII should be confined to biological research, since that is the field of research of their expert witnesses, and their arguments all seem to presuppose that if JARPA II was for the purposes of scientific research it was for the purposes of research into the biological sciences. The disagreements between them are about the nature of science, not about the kind of science involved.

56 Philip Claphman, 'Japan's Whaling Following the International Court of Justice Ruling: Brave New World or Business as Usual?', *Marine Policy* (2015) 15 (1): 238–241.

We have said that science is, amongst other things, a knowledge acquiring and propagating enterprise, where knowledge is understood simply as true belief. Commerce, on the other hand, is concerned with acquiring money, usually through contractual based exchange of commodities. So, a natural way to distinguish science from commerce is to consider the primary and dominant purpose of the activity in question. If it is primarily oriented towards knowledge, then it is science. If, on the other hand, it is primarily oriented towards the acquisition of money, it is commerce.

Although there is something clearly right about this common-sense proposal, there are two problems with leaving it there. First, scientific research is often, perhaps usually, directed, at least in part and in the long run, at the goal of making money. There are few scientific projects which receive funding without the prospect of making money for someone. Second, commerce is often, perhaps usually, concerned, at least in part, with acquiring and disseminating knowledge (i.e. true belief). As one of our earlier examples makes clear, whalers need true beliefs about harpoons if they are to successfully engage in commercial whaling.

One possible response to this difficulty would be to insist that money must play no role at all in the motivations of those engaged in scientific research. This would seem to be an overly puritanical approach, disconnected from the realities of modern academic and professional research. For one thing, it would rule out scientists who are motivated, even slightly, by their salaries. We can sidestep this difficulty by distinguishing between the motivation of a project and the motivations of the individuals engaged in the project. We often ascribe properties, including motivations, to collective enterprises that are largely independent of the properties of the people engaged in them. So, we could say that, whatever the motivations of the individuals involved, scientific, as opposed to commercial whaling, is whaling that can be justified entirely by reference to the value of acquiring and disseminating truths about cetology (i.e. whale science) and, perhaps, marine biology and ocean science more broadly. This would mean that testing harpoons on whales could not count as scientific whaling, even if it met all of Mangel's criteria for scientific research (set of focused hypotheses, correct empirical tools, etc.), which it quite easily could. It would also mean that it would be permissible for a whaling country which is in the Whaling Convention to sell whale products, so long as that was merely a by-product of scientific whaling. After all, it seems to be a waste not to use these products if the whales are being killed anyway. This is surely the rational basis for allowing whale meat to be sold after scientific research is conducted under the Whaling Convention.

As we have seen, however, the JARPA II whaling program involved not only the selling of whale products, but also the use of the proceeds from that to fund 'scientific whaling'. In this case, the commerce is not merely a by-product of the 'science', it is playing an essential role in it. Perhaps whaling countries party to the Whaling Convention could argue at this point, with some plausibility, that the commercial aspects of the enterprise are entirely subordinate to the scientific, in the sense that the *goal* of the activity is entirely scientific, even if the *means* to that goal are, in part, commercial. This response loses all of its plausibility, however, if as Japan's own expert witness suspects, the number of whales being killed is, in part, determined by commercial, rather than scientific considerations. This highlights the importance of the hypotheses being tested by any whaling that purports to be scientific being clearly stated by those who seek to engage in it.

Clarity is not the same thing as precision, and a hypothesis can be clear (i. e. unambiguous) and still be vague. As we have seen, there seems to be some room for disagreement about how vague the legitimate hypotheses to be tested by cetology or marine biology more generally need to be. Allowing them to be vague to one degree or another is perfectly consistent with requiring that those hypotheses be articulated with complete clarity.

### 7.2 Choosing which scientific expert to believe

A final suggestion can be drawn from the above discussion. We have seen that the expert witnesses called by the parties in the ICJ Whaling Case disagreed in fundamental ways about the nature of science. This puts the court in a difficult position, since it must resolve these disputes without trying to do science itself, which is not its role and is beyond its competence. The question of what non-experts are to believe when experts disagree is one that has received quite a lot of attention by philosophers lately. Scott Brewer puts the problem like this:

> 'When experts disagree about the truth of some evidentiary proposition, the nonexpert must decide whom to believe on the scientific issue. But, ex hypothesi, the nonexpert does not have sufficient competence in the expert discipline to be able to make the choice on substantive grounds, so how can the nonexpert make that choice? If we assume honesty on the part of each expert, this can seem especially puzzling in that it may look like we are expecting greater ability to discern the scientific truth from the nonexpert than we are from the expert.'[57]

More recently, the philosopher Alvin Goldman has adopted a more optimistic view, citing five forms of evidence which, at least in some circumstances, allow a non-expert, such as a court, to rationally adjudicate between conflicting expert testimonies:

57 Scott Brewer, 'Scientific Expert Testimony and Intellectual Due Process', *Yale Law Journal* (1998) 107: 1535 at 1595.

1 Arguments presented by the contending experts to support their own views and critique their rivals' views.
2 Agreement from additional putative experts on one side or other of the subject in question.
3 Appraisals by 'meta-experts' of the experts' expertise (including appraisals reflected in formal credentials earned by the experts).
4 Evidence of the experts' interests and biases vis-a-vis the question at issue.
5 Evidence of the experts' past 'track-records'.[58]

We don't have space to go through how each of these considerations might apply to the case at hand. However, it is worth noting that each of these five forms of evidence presupposes that the non-expert has already identified the relevant experts (or at least the relevant putative experts). Unfortunately, when the issue is whether a certain practice constitutes scientific research, such an identification is never straightforward.

It is natural to suppose that the relevant experts should be scientists. Science is, however, a very broad and heterogeneous category, and it seems extremely implausible that anyone is an expert in 'science' as such.[59] As we have seen, the actual practice of both disputants in this case suggests that the relevant experts are biologists and we believe those who specialize in cetology would have an even stronger claim. It is worth noting, however, that the people who have expertise on the issue of whether the pre-2019 Japanese whaling program was scientific, and who may be called on by the court as experts, may not themselves be scientists, or at least they may not all be scientists. One prominent philosopher of science, Steve Fuller, has argued with some plausibility that 'knowledge of the history, philosophy and sociology of science provides a better basis for evaluating the scientific standing of a field of inquiry than someone formally trained in science'.[60] Fuller is speaking here about providing criteria that would distinguish science from religion and theology in a legal case about whether so-called 'creation science' is really science. In the Whaling Case, as we have seen, the challenge was somewhat different. Here we are trying, not to demarcate science from religion, but to demarcate science from commerce. If philosophers (and other non-scientists) can be called as experts on the former demarcation issue (as they have been), there seems no reason they cannot be called as expert witnesses on the latter demarcation issue.

58 Alvin Goldman, *Knowledge in a Social World*. Clarendon: Oxford Press, 1999 at 93.
59 David Coady, *What to Believe Now: Applying Epistemology to Contemporary Issues*. Chichester: Wiley-Blackwell, 2012 at 54–55.
60 In fact, Fuller didn't merely argue this. He declared it under oath. See Steve Fuller, 'A Step Toward the Legalization of Science Studies', *Social Studies of Science* (2006) 36 (6): 827.

## 8 Conclusion

Defining science is a notoriously difficult task and it is understandable that the ICJ was reluctant to weigh into this issue. However, it was an essential feature of the dispute before it, and ultimately the source of the paralysis in the Whaling Convention treaty regime designed to regulate commercial whaling. As Hurd argued, it is the last, hardest, problem in that governance system which internal dialogue and debate had failed to solve.[61] The ICJ was called in to break the deadlock *specifically because* the question was hard. That said, we do not consider the question itself to be unanswerable, or the dispute irreconcilable, especially when considering the type of demarcation in question.

As we have shown, the task of demarcating science from commerce is achievable and can inform international legal practice. It is also essential if any progress over the meaning of 'scientific whaling' in the Whaling Convention, and more broadly in international law, is to be made. The ICJ's refusal to engage with this task represents a significant missed opportunity. Whilst the Court did not need to adopt verbatim all of Australia's experts' criteria for science – certainly we agree that some are more compelling than others – it was inadvisable for it to accept Japan's expert view that there is no hope of articulating any criteria at all. As Mangel rightly pointed out, that would lead to science involving the collection of a mere 'bucket of data', something that is not reflected in genuine mainstream scientific practice. More to the point, such ontological nihilism means that international laws that rely on science have no meaningful basis, no clarity and no potential to bind the states which are parties to them, because scientific research can mean whatever those states want it to.

In this chapter we have offered some criteria for guidance over how the Court could have made a distinction between science and commerce. These criteria suggest that both JARPA and JARPA II were commercial, rather than scientific, whaling programmes and as such were impermissible under international law. Ultimately, the analysis shows that the Court – and perhaps international law more generally – must have a much greater engagement with both the philosophy of science and the philosophy of expertise. These are interrelated things; not only does philosophy assist us in settling on appropriate definitions for science, but also it can help us find and evaluate the veracity and authority of the experts to contribute to that task. Or, it might allow the Court to call on its own experts, rather than relying entirely on witnesses called by the disputants in the case.[62] There is no doubt that the Court has the power to do this under Article

61 Hurd 2012 at 11.

62 Brendan Gogarty and Peter Lawrence, 'The ICJ Whaling Case: science, transparency and the rule of law', *Journal of Law, Information & Science* (2015) 23 (2): 134.

50 of its Statute.[63] The Court, to date, has been reluctant to itself call on experts and has only once done so.[64] As we have seen, the task of selecting suitable expert witnesses in this case is far from trivial. However, we have provided some general criteria that we believe could help the Court, and the development of international law more broadly, in this important task.

63 This provides that "The Court may, at any time, entrust any individual, body, bureau, commission or other organisation that it may select, with the task of carrying out an enquiry or giving an expert opinion", Statute of the International Court of Justice, Article 50.

64 *Corfu Channel Case (United Kingdom v. Albania); Assessment of Compensation*, 15 XII 49 (International Court of Justice, 15 December 1949).

Part III

# Indigenous and non-Western framings

Chapter 6

# Legal (non) recognition of Sámi customary relationship with the land in Finland

## Challenges so far and prospects in the modern human rights era

*Leena Heinämäki*[1], *Sanna Valkonen*[2] *and Jarno Valkonen*[3]

## 1 Introduction

As articulated by a Sámi scholar Elina Helander-Renvall, the discursive conditions in Indigenous politics are often determined by the majority people. It is in these terms that Indigenous related issues are considered, interpreted and dealt with. The major problem from Indigenous peoples' perspective is that the majority discourse may not correlate with the reality in which a particular Indigenous people lives.[4] It is the dominant society that sets the conditions in political discussions and decision making also regarding what knowledge is. In doing so, it imposes a semantic field of sorts on Indigenous politics, with this field then forming the context in which an Indigenous people's demands are asserted.[5]

International and, in many places, domestic legal protection of Indigenous peoples is based on the human rights' ideology of equality of all human beings. General human and fundamental rights are grounded on the ideology of guaranteeing the equality of each person independently of his/her gender, race, ethnic background, religion or other such markers. Indigenous peoples' legal protection is justified as "positive discrimination", affirmative action in order to overcome their often unequal position in society due to their

1 Arctic Centre, University of Lapland, Finland, leena.heinamaki@ulapland.fi.
2 Faculty of Social Sciences, University of Lapland, Finland.
3 Faculty of Social Sciences, University of Lapland, Finland.
4 E. Helander-Renvall, *Sámi Society Matters*, Rovaniemi, Lapland University Press, 2016 at 150–151.
5 S. Valkonen, J. Valkonen and V.P. Lehtola, 'An Ontological Politics of and for the Sámi Cultural Heritage – Reflections on Belonging to the Sámi Community and the Land', in A. Xanthaki, S. Valkonen, L. Heinämäki and P.K. Nuorgam (eds), *Indigenous Peoples' Cultural Heritage, Rights, Debates, Challenges*, Leiden and Boston, Brill Nijhoff, 2017, 149–174 at 174.

minority position and special cultural characteristics. Despite the recognition of "equality of differences" being built within the idea of equality, the related positive action, in the form of policies and laws, is by far in most of the cases based on Western value premises. The Western ontology puts emphasis on the protection of individuals rather than groups, or the division between culture and nature, which is alien to Indigenous peoples.

Both international as well as national legal instruments have so far been created mostly by non-indigenous actors, and are hence most commonly based on Western structures. As argued in this chapter, these instruments often fail to recognize Indigenous values and ontological premises. A notable international exception to a relatively high degree is the UN Declaration on the Rights of Indigenous Peoples (UNDRIP), which was negotiated with a wide participation of Indigenous peoples over two decades, and became accepted by the UN General Assembly in 2007.[6]

The relationship to the land is a fundamental question of existence for Indigenous peoples, because, as Tim Ingold puts it, cultures grow from the land and in places. Ingold writes that the relationship to the land bears on the place where an Indigenous people dwells and exists, where its members practice their traditional way of life, and what the people's broader cultural conception is of itself, its identity and its past.[7]

The aim of this chapter is to discuss the ontological basis of Sámi customary relationship with the land and the challenges of legal instruments to recognize this relationship, including ways of living, cultural practices, customs and customary laws, values, worldviews and knowledge.[8] Although international law, significantly stronger than Finnish national legislation, succeeds in recognizing some key features of Sámi and other Indigenous peoples' unique relationship with the land, it most commonly fails to embrace and thus protect its totality, while being based on profoundly different premises than the Indigenous worldview. In other words, the reality of Indigenous peoples, as widely experienced and expressed, is based on a different ontology than that underlying the Western way of seeing the world.[9]

This chapter argues that it is possible, however, to incorporate into legislation and policies Indigenous peoples' values and to recognize their customary

6 United Nations Declaration on the Rights of Indigenous Peoples, 13 September 2007, UN Doc. A/RES/61/295.

7 See T. Ingold, *The Perception of the Environment. Essays on Livelihood, Dwelling and Skill*, London, Routledge, 2000 at 148–150.

8 See more about the concept of ontology: A. Mol, 'Ontological Politics. A word and some questions', *The Sociological Review* 47(S1), 1999, 74–89; S. Woolgar and D. Neyland, *Mundane Governance. Ontology and Accountability*, Oxford, Oxford University Press, 2013.

9 See M. Blaser, 'Ontology and Indigeneity: On the Political Ontology of Heterogeneous Assemblages', *Cultural Geographies* 21(1), 2012, 49–58; T. Ingold, note 7 at 132–152; see also S. Valkonen, J. Valkonen and V-P. Lehtola, note 5.

relationship with the land by engaging with Indigenous peoples in a meaningful way and acknowledging their customary ways of knowing and acting. UNDRIP serves an example of a modern human rights instrument, which has been created with Indigenous peoples, not for them. By implementing its rights and principles into domestic settings, we could have substantial improvements in safeguarding Sámi people's customary relationship and practices in their traditional lands.

## 2 Ontological basis of the Sámi belongingness to the land: values, knowledge and action

An integral part of Indigenous peoples' cultural heritage is their special relationship to the land and the closely connected knowledge related to the environment.[10] The concept of cultural environment describes this relationship. Cultural environments are at the interface between nature and culture, tangible and intangible heritage, biological and cultural diversity. They represent a closely woven net of relationships, the essence of culture and people's identity.[11] The cultural values of natural ecosystems embody far more than tangible services; they are often of a non-material or intangible nature derived from human interaction with ecosystems, and they are part of Indigenous peoples' traditional knowledge, belief systems, spiritual values and worldviews. They play an important role in how people perceive and conserve natural places. Thus, intangible values can help to reduce or prevent human disturbance to ecosystems. For example, spiritual values attributed to sacred places in nature often entail restricted access and use, which shape the safeguarding of these ecosystems.[12] Sacred natural sites of Sámi, *sieidis*, have traditionally been governed by Sámi customs and customary laws, related to access, ownership and secrecy.[13]

10 P. Magga, 'Mikä tekee kulttuuriympäristöstä saamelaisen' ['What makes an Environment a Sámi Environment'], in P. Magga and E. Ojanlatva (eds), *Ealli Biras, Saamelainen kulttuuriympäristöohjelma*, Inari, Sámi Museum – Saamelaismuseosäätiö, 2013, 10–13, at 10–13. See also S. Valkonen, J. Valkonen and V-P. Lehtola, note 5 at 164; J. Valkonen, S. Valkonen and T. Ingold, 'Introduction' in T.H. Eriksen, S. Valkonen and J. Valkonen (eds), *Knowing from the Indigenous North. Sámi Approaches to History, Politics and Belonging*, New York, Routledge, 2019.

11 M. Rössler, 'World Heritage Cultural Landscapes: A UNESCO Flagship Programme 1992–2006', *Landscape Research* 31(4), 2006, 333–353 at 334. See also T. Herrmann, L. Heinämäki and C. Morin, 'Protecting sacred sites, maintaining cultural heritage, and sharing power, Co-management of the SGang Gwaay UNESCO World Heritage Site in Canada', in L. Elenius, C. Allard and C. Sandström (eds), *Indigenous Rights in Modern Landscapes, Nordic Conservation Regimes in Global Context*, Abingdon, Routledge, 2017, 62–81 at 65.

12 B. Verschuuren, R. Wild, J.A. McNeely and G. Oviedo, *Sacred Natural Sites Conserving Nature & Culture*, London, Earthscan, 2010.

13 See, L. Heinämäki and A. Xanthaki, 'Indigenous Peoples' Customary Laws, Sámi People and Sacred Sites', in L. Heinämäki and T.M. Herrmann (eds),

Essential to the Sámi customary relationship with the land is to consider nature and culture as one space – an entirety without categorical functional or philosophical differences between culture and nature. Sámi customary relationship with the land has existed (and still exists) through daily cultural practices such as reindeer herding, fishing, hunting, gathering or handicrafts. The knowledge related to nature, values and goals is adopted and immediately implemented through these practices. This is why, according to Helander-Renvall, there are no major differences between values, knowledge and action.[14] Cultural and nature activities have been intertwined without fundamental differentiation between nature and culture. This kind of knowledge system has made Sámi culture a very nature sensitive and place oriented "nature-culture".[15]

Accordingly, the connection to the land includes not only a material bond but also elements of the intangible heritage, such as place names and the oral tradition. Therefore, in the Sámi worldview, the relationship with nature entails a deeper awareness of, belonging to and obligation towards a natural environment than manipulating and exploiting it.[16] Deborah Rose uses the concept "ecological connectivity", a term that seems to describe the Sámi customary relationship with the nature. It refers to a "mode of existence" in which the land is not only a place or object but also a subject (or "agent") in its own right.[17]

Rodney Harrison argues that because the protection of Indigenous cultural heritage is based on a Western, anthropocentric mentality that emphasizes a distinction between culture and nature and a pre-eminence of human beings over nature, it easily fails to safeguard their intangible cultural heritage which

*Experiencing and Protecting Sacred Natural Sites of Sámi and other Indigenous Peoples, The Sacred Arctic*, Cham, Springer, 2017, 65–82.

14 E. Helander, 'Saamelainen maailmankuva ja luontosuhde', in I. Seurujärvi-Kari (ed), *Beaivvi Mánát. Saamelaisten juuret ja nykyaika*, Helsinki, Suomalaisen Kirjallisuuden Seura, 2000, 171–175 at 175. See also J. Valkonen and S. Valkonen, *Viidon Sieiddit – Saamelaisen luontosuhteen uudet mittasuhteet* [*The New Scales of Sámi Nature Relations*], Kustannus-Puntsi, 2018.

15 See E. Helander-Renvall, note 4; J. Valkonen and S. Valkonen, 'Contesting Nature Relations of Sámi Culture', *Acta Borealia: A Nordic Journal of Circumpolar Societes* 31 (1), 2014, 25–40; J. Valkonen and S. Valkonen, note 14 at 7.

16 E. Helander-Renvall, 'Saamelainen tapaoikeus' ['The Sámi Customary Law'], in P. Magga and E. Ojanlatva (eds), *Ealli Biras, Saamelainen kulttuuriympäristöohjelma*, Inari, Sámi Museum – Saamelaismuseosäätiö, 2013, 132–134. See S. Valkonen, J. Valkonen and V.P. Lehtola, note 5 at 165.

17 D. Rose, 'Sharing Kinship with Nature: How Reconciliation is Transforming the NSW National Parks and Wildlife Service', *NSW National Parks and Wildlife Service*, 2003; D. Rose, D. James and C. Watson, 'Indigenous Kinship with the Natural World', *NSW National Parks and Wildlife Service*, 2003 at 3. See also R. Harrison, 'Beyond "Natural" and "Cultural" Heritage: Toward an Ontological Politics of Heritage in the Age of Anthropocene', *Heritage & Society* 8 (1), 2015, 24–42.

builds on a different ontological basis.[18] As already noted in this chapter, and also discussed by Harrison, there is no boundary between nature and culture in indigenous ontologies and the two are intertwined, meaning that culture can be considered to be everywhere. Thus, Indigenous peoples' connection to the land and notions of protecting their cultural heritage proceed from a wholly different ontological basis than Western ways of perceiving heritage, making its protection challenging.[19] Similarly, the human rights approach to environmental protection and the protection of Indigenous peoples' relationship with the land has been accused of being anthropocentric, failing to recognize Indigenous peoples' holistic worldview, viewing humans as part of nature, not above it, and claiming their role as nature custodians.[20]

For instance, as illustrated in the Sámi context, a natural environment can be a cultural environment regardless of whether it bears traces of human activity. For this reason, the Sámi cultural environment does not not fit into the public categories used in defining and managing cultural environments.[21] A Sámi scholar, Päivi Magga, has developed the concept of Sámi cultural environment and shown that the Sámi perception of nature does not emphasize the human as its cultivator and manipulator. A landscape that seems natural may have been a living environment of local Sámi for centuries without any appreciable traces left of lived life and resource use in the environment and, therefore, can contain deep cultural values and meanings. These values and meanings often remain inaccessible to cultural outsiders, leading them to perceive such an environment as a wilderness.[22] The related legal problematics will be addressed in the following sections.

## 3 (Non)recognition of Sámi's "nature culture" in Finnish legislation

The Sámi culture in Finland enjoys a constitutional legal protection. According to Article 17 (3) of the Finnish Constitution, Sámi have a right to

18 R. Harrison, note 17 at 30.
19 Ibid.
20 See P. Taylor, *An Ecological Approach to International Law; Responding to Challenges of Climate Change*, London and New York, Routledge, 1998 at 233.
21 See e.g. P. Magga and E. Ojanlatva, *Ealli Biras, Saamelainen kulttuuriympäristöohjelma* [*Living Environment – Sámi Cultural Environment Program*], Inari, Sámi Museum – Saamelaismuseosäätiö, 2013; A. Schanche, 'Horizontal and vertical perceptions of Saami landscapes', *Dieđut* 3, 2004, 1–10; P. Magga and T. Elo, 'Johdanto' ['Introduction'], in T. Elo and P. Magga (eds), *Eletty, koettu maisema: näkökulmia saamelaiseen kulttuurimaisemaan*, Rovaniemi, Lapin ympäristökeskus, 2007, 3–4; E. Helander-Renvall, 'On customary law among the Saami people', in N. Bankes and T. Koivurova (eds), *The proposed Nordic Saami Convention: national and international dimensions of indigenous property rights*, Portland, Hart, 2013, 281–291.
22 P. Magga, note 10 at 10–13.

their culture as an Indigenous people. Furthermore, Article 121 (4) of the Constitution grants Sámi a linguistic and cultural autonomy in the home region. In the context of the Constitution, Sámi traditional livelihoods, namely reindeer herding, fishing and hunting, are recognized as a part of their culture.[23] Yet, in the land-use legislation such as reindeer herding, fishing or hunting acts, there is no specific recognition of Sámi culture, let alone recognition of their values or worldviews.

Although land is the basis for the Sámi culture, the Sámi cultural autonomy operates without any land-governance or real influence on the outcomes of the decision-making regarding Sámi traditional territories. Although the task of the Sámi Parliament is to "look after the Sámi language and culture, as well as to take care of matters relating to their status as an Indigenous people",[24] in reality, its decision-making powers are very limited. Authorities are obliged to negotiate with the Sámi Parliament in "all far-reaching and important measures which may directly and in a specific way affect the status of the Sámi as an Indigenous people and which concern matters in the Sámi homeland."[25] In practice, however, this means rather "an opportunity to be heard and discuss on matters", without necessarily any real influence on the outcome of the decision-making.[26]

Sámi have continually, over the last few decades sought legal recognition of their connection to the land as part of the safeguarding of their cultural heritage. Despite several attempts, Finland has not to date been able to ratify the Indigenous and Tribal Peoples Convention, 1989 (No. 169) (ILO Convention No. 169), which grants land rights to Indigenous peoples. Recent years' struggles relate to debates such as who has the right to be Sámi and thus who is the subject of the land rights at the individual level.[27] These struggles in themselves are born from a misunderstanding of the collective nature of ILO Convention No. 169. The Convention itself neither defines "indigenousness" (providing only elements to help to identify indigenous

23 Finnish Constitutional Committee, PeVL 38/2004 vp.
24 Act of the Sámi Parliament, 17 July 1995, 974/1995 (amendments up to 1026/2003 included) at Section 9.
25 Ibid.
26 Ibid.
27 See e.g. T. Joona, 'Ihmisoikeusnäkökulma ILO-sopimukseen No. 169' ['A Human Rights Perspective on ILO Convention No. 169'], *Agon* 2013, 37–38; S. Valkonen, 'Kuvaus saamelaisten itsehallinnon kehittymisestä sekä saamelaisuuden määrittelyn ja saamelais- ja alkuperäiskansakeskustelun taustoista ja tapahtumista Suomessa' ['The development of the Sámi self-governance and Sámi definition in Finland'], in L. Heinämäki, C. Allard, S. Kirchner, A. Xanthaki, S. Valkonen, U. Mörkenstam, N. Bankes, J. Ruru, J. Gilbert, P. Selle, A. Simpson and L. Olsén (eds), *Saamelaisten oikeuksien toteutuminen: kansainvälinen oikeusvertaileva tutkimus* [*Actualizing Sámi Rights: International Comparative Research*], Helsinki, Prime Minister's Office, Publications of the Government's analysis, assessment and research activities 4/2017, 2017, 176–223.

groups) nor promotes individual ownership of the lands. Whereas general human rights, applicable to all humans, seek to protect individuals, with the exception of a people's right to self-determination, Indigenous specific instruments, including ILO Convention No. 169, aim at safeguarding the cultural existence of Indigenous peoples as collectives, whose individuals naturally need to be protected as a part of the group.[28]

The management of the environment in the Sámi homeland of Finland is governed for the most part by the Wilderness Act and the Conservation Act, which are essential elements of the Finnish system. Despite the Wilderness Act mentioning as one of its purposes (Article 1) the safeguarding of the Sámi culture, sites in the Sámi cultural environment, in particular usufruct areas, have not been given any particular consideration.[29] Yet, given that Sámi usufruct of the landscape and the environment differs from the Finnish, it easily remains invisible. It lives in the cultural knowledge of small communities and, inasmuch as it has not been articulated and asserted verbally, it is ignored in decision-making.[30] Finnish legislation contains no definition of the concept "cultural environment", let alone "cultural landscape". The landscape in the Sámi region is classified essentially in its entirety as a natural landscape, although large tracts of it are areas in which the traditional Sámi livelihoods are practiced.[31]

The state-controlled land and water areas in the Sámi homeland are managed by Metsähallitus (National Forest Service), which controls 90 percent of the land and water areas in the region. Approximately 80 percent of this area is set aside for conservation under either the Conservation Act or the Wilderness Act. The Metsähallitus Act prescribes that the management, use and protection of the natural resources under the control of Metsähallitus in the Sámi homeland must be conducted in a way that guarantees the Sámi the conditions necessary for enjoying their culture. Metsähallitus does not, however, conduct systematic cumulative cultural impact assessments related to forestry or conservation plans. Sámi cultural values are thus not necessarily recognized or paid attention to in its operations, and Sámi have demanded a cumulative impact assessment to be carried out.

Metsähallitus has, however, increased the participation of Sámi to a degree in the management plans of the wilderness and nature protection areas as a part of the implementation of the Convention on Biological Diversity (CBD). Using voluntary guidelines of the CBD, the so called Akwé:Kon Guidelines on cultural, environmental and social impact assessment, Sámi values and

28 L. Heinämäki et al 2017, ibid, at 23.
29 S. Valkonen, J. Valkonen and V.P. Lehtola, note 5 at 166.
30 Ibid. See P. Magga, note 10 at 10–13.
31 A. Nuorgam, 'Saamelaisia koskeva lainsäädäntö ja sopimukset' ['The Legislation and Convention Pertaining to the Sámi'], in P. Magga and E. Ojanlatva (eds), *Ealli Biras, Saamelainen kulttuuriympäristöohjelma*, Inari, Sámi Museum – Saamelaismuseosäätiö, 2013, 220–225 at 220.

traditional knowledge and customary practices can be mapped and described by local Sámi groups in the management plans of wilderness and nature protection areas. Although the Akwé:Kon process has been viewed rather positively both by Sámi and Metsähallitus,[32] the current challenge is the lack of financial and timely resources for Sámi to conduct any proper impact assessment. Additionally, it might be generally difficult for Sámi to explicitly articulate their cultural values of certain areas. As Magga notes, it is difficult to explain fully what landscape and environment mean from the Sámi perspective. "To a Sámi the landscape is more than an object nor is the environment merely an object of one's actions; it is a person's partner – another subject with whom one has to act properly and wisely, because one's own survival depends on it."[33] As the Sámi conception of the landscape or environment incorporates a cognitive dimension, religiousness, myths, tales and communality in addition to the values and meanings, it entails that it is difficult to inventory and convert into discrete pieces of information in a database.[34]

Sacred natural sites are still of significant importance for the Sámi people, their ways of life, culture and identity.[35] Although several domestic legal instruments in Finland deal with the maintenance and safeguarding of Sámi sacred sites, effective protection is lacking, due to non-recognition of Sámi values related to these sites. As maintained by Eija Ojanlatva and Antje Neumann, fundamental differences exist between Western legal concepts of protection and Sámi traditional approaches towards their sacred sites.[36] All ancient monuments, including Sámi sacred sites, are automatically, without separate legal measures or any other legal procedures of designation, protected under the Antiquities Act.[37] Section 4, Paragraph 1 of the Act specifies that "ancient monuments" include the area of land necessary for the preservation of the remains in question and for providing sufficient space around

32 S. Juntunen and E. Stolt, *Application of Akwé: Kon Guidelines in the Management and Land Use Plan for the Hammastunturi Wilderness Area*, Vantaa, Metsähallitus, 2013.
33 P. Magga, note 10 at 10. See S. Valkonen, J. Valkonen and V.P. Lehtola, note 5 at 169–170.
34 S. Valkonen, J. Valkonen and V.P. Lehtola, note 5 at 170.
35 E. Ojanlatva and A. Neumann, 'Protecting the Sacred in the Finnish Sápmi: Settings and Challenges', in L.Heinämäki and T.M. Herrmann (eds), *Experiencing and Protecting Sacred Natural Sites of Sámi and other Indigenous Peoples, The Sacred Arctic*, Cham, Springer, 2017, 83–98 at 96; See also L. Heinämäki, E. Ojanlatva and A-M. Magga, 'Saamelaisten pyhät paikat kulttuuriperintöoikeuden ja tapaoikeuksien valossa' ['Sámi Sacred Sites in the Light of the Cultural Heritage and Customary Rights'], in T. Nykänen and L. Valkeapää (eds), *Kilpisjärven poliittinen luonto* [*Political Nature of Kilpisjärvi*], Helsinki, Suomalaisen kirjallisuuden seura, 2016, 199–242. See, also, generally, T. Äikäs, *Pyhät paikat saamelaisten rituaalisessa maisemassa*, Oulu, University of Oulu, 2011.
36 E. Ojanlatva and A. Neumann, note 35 at 96.
37 Antiquities Act, 17 June 1963, 295/1963.

them in view of their nature and significance, and the Act determines such an area subsequently as a "protective area".[38] Although neither defined nor specified by the Act of Antiquities, in practice, the protective area, determined by an archaeologist, usually comprises a radius of 2–4 m around the ancient monument or site, measured from the visible constructions or findings of the site.[39] However, most sacred sites do not have any boundaries, nor are they demarcated.[40] Ojanlatva and Neumann assert that in order to recognize and determine Sámi sacred sites, it is vital to have expertise in Sámi culture and languages. According to them, it would be very important to take into account Sámi participation and to respect the local Indigenous knowledge when dealing with sacred sites. This is key to understanding and interpreting the Sámi cultural landscape/environment. Since most Sámi sacred sites under the Antiquities Act are interpreted and determined by archaeologists, this imposes a major challenge to defining the protective area around the site or field.[41] Sámi may also not want to share information concerning their sacred sites; there is a fear that information on sacred places will end up being misused.[42] However, the Sámi cultural environmental unit has taken as its starting point that even though the "coordinates" of a sacred landscape must be withheld to some extent, the landscape, along with other archaeological cultural heritage, should be recorded so that it is taken into account in land use planning, forestry and other land uses.[43]

## 4 International legal instruments: challenges and prospects

Indigenous peoples' traditional landscapes and environments, including sacred natural sites, can become recognized and protected as World Heritage sites by the UNESCO World Heritage Convention.[44] The Convention embodies the idea that some places are so special and important that their protection is not only the responsibility of the States in which they are located, but also the duty of the international community as a whole. The Convention is concerned with only tangible, immovable heritage (i.e. 'sites'). These can be cultural sites (such as sacred sites, monuments or buildings), natural sites (such as biodiversity hotspots or outstanding geological formations), or mixed cultural/natural sites.[45] The

38 Ibid. at section 4, paragraph 2.
39 E. Ojanlatva and A. Neumann, note 35 at 93.
40 Ibid.
41 Ibid.
42 T. Äikäs, 'Avoin vai kätketty? Saamelaisten pyhien paikkojen sijaintitieto rekisterissä', in P. Magga and E. Ojanlatva (eds), *Ealli Biras, Saamelainen kulttuuriympäristöohjelma*, Inari, Sámi Museum – Saamelaismuseosäätiö, 2013, 232–233.
43 S. Valkonen, J. Valkonen and V.P. Lehtola, note 5 at 167.
44 United Nations Convention Concerning the Protection of the World Cultural and Natural Heritage, 23 November 1972, 1037 UNTS 151.
45 The Convention website: http://whc.unesco.org/en/about/; see, International Working Group on Indigenous Affairs (IWGIA), http://www.iwgia.org/human-rights/un-mechanisms-and-processes/world-heritage-convention.

World Heritage Convention can be, and in some cases has been, an important tool for the promotion and protection of the rights of indigenous peoples with respect to their traditional lands as cultural heritage.[46]

However, the protection of World Heritage has in many cases aggravated or consolidated Indigenous peoples' loss of control over their lands, led to restrictions on traditional land-use practices, and undermined their livelihoods. In many World Heritage sites, Indigenous peoples are still considered as threats to conservation objectives.[47] Stefan Disko concludes that for the World Heritage Convention to play a consistently positive role for Indigenous peoples, serious shortcomings in its implementation need to be rectified.[48] One such shortcoming relates to the differentiation between natural and cultural heritage in World Heritage sites. As UN Expert Mechanism on the Rights of Indigenous Peoples (EMRIP) has pointed out, the Convention's categorization of heritage into "cultural" and "natural" is inappropriate in the case of Indigenous peoples, for whom "cultural and natural values are inseparably interwoven and should be managed and protected in a holistic manner."[49] Another shortcoming is the problematic application of the concept of "outstanding universal value", a prerequisite for the nomination as a World Heritage site, which does not necessarily at all reflect Indigenous peoples' views and values.[50] Yet one more essential shortcoming is the lack of regulations and appropriate mechanisms to ensure the meaningful participation of Indigenous peoples in Convention processes affecting them.[51]

No Sámi cultural landscapes are so far listed as UNESCO World Heritage Sites in Finland. In Sweden, however, Laponia World Heritage site[52] is an important cultural landscape for Sámi. The area has a co-management regime in place, where Sámi have a substantial influence over the management of the area. Laponia World Heritage site is one of the successful examples of the potential of the World Heritage Convention, implemented in a manner that at

46 S. Disko, 'Indigenous Cultural Heritage in the Implementation of UNESCO's World Heritage Convention: Opportunities, Obstacles and Challenges', in A. Xanthaki, S. Valkonen, L. Heinämäki and P.K. Nuorgam (eds), *Indigenous Peoples' Cultural Heritage, Rights, Debates, Challenges*, Leiden and Boston, Brill Nijhoff, 2017, 39–77 at 41.

47 Ibid. See also L. Viikari, 'World Heritage Convention, Climate Change and the Arctic', in T. Koivurova, E. C. H. Keskitalo and N. Bankes (eds), *Climate Governance in the Arctic*, Dordrecht, Springer, 2009, 171–205 at 184.

48 S. Disko, note 46 at 42.

49 Human Rights Council, *Promotion and protection of the rights of indigenous peoples with respect to their cultural heritage – Study by the UN Expert Mechanism on the Rights of Indigenous Peoples*, A/HRC/30/53, 2015 at Paragraph 8; Human Rights Council, *Annex: Expert Mechanism advice No. 8 (2015): Promotion and protection of the rights of indigenous peoples with respect to their cultural heritage*, A/HRC/30/53, 2015 at Paragraph 7.

50 Human Rights Council, *Study*, A/HRC/30/53, 2015, ibid at paragraph 55.

51 See T. Herrmann, L. Heinämäki and C. Morin, note 11 at 67–68.

52 See UNESCO World Heritage List: https://whc.unesco.org/en/list/774.

least to a relatively high degree recognizes and respects Indigenous peoples' value base and ontological premises.[53]

Finland has also ratified the UNESCO Convention for the Protection of the Intangible Cultural Heritage,[54] doing so in 2013. So far, however, a national approach has been taken so that Sámi intangible cultural heritage has not been listed. According to the Convention, it would be, however, possible to define the different elements of the intangible cultural heritage in the Sámi homeland and to do so in cooperation with communities, groups and the relevant organizations.[55] According to Sámi scholar, Anne Nuorgam, where Indigenous peoples are concerned, it is problematic that the UNESCO conventions do not recognize ownership or possession of the traditional knowledge of Indigenous peoples; rather, the process of documentation and inventorying change the status of cultural heritage such that it is seen as benefitting all of humankind.[56]

In the human rights framework, Article 27 of the International Covenant on Civil and Political Rights (ICCPR) can be considered to be one of the most important provisions protecting Indigenous minority culture and traditional lifestyles of the Sámi. It states that persons belonging to minorities shall not be denied the right, in community with the other members of their group, to enjoy their culture. UN Human Rights Committee (HRC), the monitoring body of the ICCPR, recognizes that Indigenous peoples' subsistence and other traditional economic and social activities are an integral part of their culture. Interference with such activities may be detrimental to their cultural integrity and survival.[57] The HRC has acknowledged that, in the context of Indigenous peoples, the right to culture under Article 27 may apply to a *way of life* that is closely connected to a territory and the use of its resources. Furthermore, it has stated that the enjoyment of such rights may require positive protective legal measures and methods for ensuring the effective participation of minority communities' members in decisions that affect them.[58] The HRC has also stated that the protection of the above mentioned

53 See L. Heinämäki, T. Herrmann and C. Green, 'Towards Sámi Self-determination over Their Cultural Heritage: The UNESCO World Heritage Site of Laponia in Northern Sweden', in A. Xanthaki, S. Valkonen, L. Heinämäki and P.K. Nuorgam (eds), *Indigenous Peoples' Cultural Heritage, Rights, Debates, Challenges*, Leiden and Boston, Brill Nijhoff, 2017, 78–103.

54 United Nations Convention for Safeguarding of the Intangible Cultural Heritage, 17 October 2003, 2368 UNTS 1.

55 S. Valkonen, J. Valkonen and V.P. Lehtola, note 5 at 169.

56 A. Nuorgam 'Saamelaisia koskeva lainsäädäntö ja sopimukset' ['The Legislation and Convention Pertaining to the Sámi'], in P. Magga and E. Ojanlatva (eds), *Ealli Biras. Saamelainen Kulttuuriympäristöohjelma*, Inari, Sámi Museum – Saamelaismuseosäätiö, 2013, 220–225 at 220.

57 See UN Human Rights Committee, *Ivan Kitok v. Sweden*, Communication No. 197/1985, UN Doc. CCPR/C/33/D/197/1985, 27 July 1988, available online at http://www1.umn.edu/humanrts/undocs/197-1985.html.

58 Ibid. at 7.

right is directed at ensuring the survival and continued development of the cultural, religious and social identity of the minorities concerned, which also enriches the fabric of society as a whole.[59]

When studying the HRC's general comments as well as case studies, it becomes evident that more than emphasising Indigenous peoples' worldviews or values, the Committee tends to protect the economic sustainability of their nature-based livelihoods. The HRC has stated that Article 27 requires states to utilize the necessary steps in protecting Indigenous peoples' titles and interests in their traditional lands and to secure the continuation and sustainability of Indigenous minorities' traditional economies.[60] There are, however, some instances where Indigenous worldview is touched upon, particularly related to Indigenous peoples' places of worship (sacred natural sites). In its Concluding Observations on Australia (2000), the HRC expressed "its concern that securing continuation and sustainability of traditional forms of economy of indigenous minorities (hunting, fishing and gathering), and protection of sites of religious or cultural significance for such minorities, which must be protected under article 27, are not always a major factor in determining land use."[61] The HRC further stated that the Australian law reform related to the Aboriginal and Torres Strait Islander Heritage Protection Act (1984), which recognizes also sacred sites culturally and traditionally significant for Australian Aboriginals, should give sufficient weight to the *values* important to Indigenous peoples.[62]

It seems that the HRC, in principle, is willing to recognize aspects of Indigenous peoples' worldview, including spiritual, social and environmental values.[63] It could be argued that if Indigenous authors who bring claims to the HRC would strongly argue the need to protect their values and not solely a livelihood in an economically sustainable sense, there might be readiness in the Committee to expand the protection towards value-based rather than economic-based ground.[64] For instance, in one Sámi case, *Länsman et al v. Finland*,[65] the HRC did acknowledge that the mountain Riutusvaara continues to have a spiritual significance relevant to the culture of the Sámi

59 Ibid.
60 UN Human Rights Committee, *Concluding Observations on Australia*, UN Doc. CCPR/CO/69/AUS, 2000 at paragraphs 10–11.
61 Ibid. at paragraph 510.
62 Ibid. at paragraph 511. Aboriginal Land Rights (Northern Territory) Act, 16 December 1976, No. 191 (amendments up to Act No. 175, 2015 included), Part VII at 69.
63 See L. Heinämäki, S. Valkonen, J. Valkonen, 'Sámi Relationship with the Land: What does the Law Fail to Recognize?', D. Bunikowski (ed), *Philosophy of Law in the Arctic*, Rovaniemi, The University of the Arctic, 2016, 71–84.
64 Ibid.
65 UN Human Rights Committee, *Länsman et al v. Finland*, Communication No. 511/1992, UN Doc. CCPR/C/52/D/511/1992, 26 October 1994.

community, although the claim of the case was based on reindeer herding, not on infringement of the sacred site.[66]

One of the major challenges of the ICCPR regarding the protection of Indigenous, including Sámi, peoples' customary relationship to their lands, relates to the monitoring system of the Convention. It is individuals not the communities who are allowed to bring claims, so-called individual communications, to the HRC. This has prevented the HRC from considering the claims brought by Indigenous persons based on Article 1 of the ICCPR granting the right of self-determination of peoples. The HRC has noted that since the right of self-determination is not an individual but a collective right, it cannot be claimed by individuals.[67] This puts Indigenous peoples in an awkward position: they can only invoke individual rights and not a right of a people. According to the HRC, Article 1 on self-determination can only affect the interpretation of Article 27 on the right to a culture.[68] Having said this, peculiarly enough, in relation to statements (so-called Concluding Observations) that the HRC makes on individual States regarding their state reports to the Committee, the HRC had already recognized, in 1999, that Indigenous peoples have a right to self-determination under Article 1 of the ICCPR. The HRC has asked States to recognize this right, particularly in relation to Indigenous peoples' traditional lands, means of subsistence and natural resources.[69] Thus, although Indigenous peoples cannot argue their right to self-determination as a people in their own legal claims to the HRC, States should nevertheless, according to the Committee, implement this right in their policies and laws. For instance, in 2013, the HRC, in its Concluding Observations on Finland's country-report, referring to Article 27 as well as Article 1 on self-determination, expressed its concern that the Sámi people lack participation and decision-making powers over matters of fundamental importance to their culture and way of life, including rights to land and resources.[70] The HRC also noted that there might be insufficient understanding or accommodation of the *Sámi lifestyle* by public authorities and that there is a lack of legal clarity on the use of land in areas traditionally inhabited by the Sámi people.[71]

66 Ibid. at paragraph 9.3.
67 See UN Human Rights Committee, *Chief Bernard Ominayak and the Lubicon Lake Band v. Canada*, Communication No. 167/1984, UN Doc. CCPR/C/38/D/167/1984, 26 March 1990.
68 See, e.g. UN Human Rights Committee, *Tiina Sanila-Aikio v. Finland*, CCPR/C/124/D/2668/2015, 1.2.2019.
69 See UN Human Rights Committee, *Concluding Observations on Canada*, UN Doc. CCPR/C/79/Add.105, 1999.
70 UN Human Rights Committee, *Concluding Observations on Finland*, UN Doc. CCPR/C/FIN/CO/6, 2013 at paragraph 16.
71 Ibid.

The right to self-determination as a collective human right is often regarded by Indigenous peoples as the most important right, on which all the other rights are grounded. In international forums, it is argued that the right to self-determination of Indigenous peoples is essential to development that is sustainable. Sustainability and conservation rest on Indigenous peoples' knowledge of, and stewardship over, the larger part of the world's most diverse ecosystems. Self-determination consists of a bundle of rights which Indigenous peoples regard (primarily) as their responsibilities (rather than rights) to be exercised in their territories.[72]

When engaging in the negotiations of UNDRIP over two decades, the right to self-determination, first opposed by many states for a long time, was viewed as a crux that Indigenous peoples were invoking as the fundamental basis of their demands. When UNDRIP was finally adopted in 2007, it was celebrated as a paradigm shift and the beginning of new era in the relationship between States and Indigenous peoples.[73] UNDRIP is in many ways a historical document from the Indigenous peoples' point of view. First, although not legally binding – it is a declaration, not a convention – human rights bodies as well as national courts are nowadays referring to it as a legal source.[74] The view is often taken that

72 P. Havemann and H. Whall, *The Miner's Canary: Indigenous Peoples and Sustainable Development in the Commonwealth*, A Commonwealth Policy Studies Unit Memorandum to Commonwealth Heads of Government attending the World Summit on Sustainable Development (WSSD) on 26 August – 4 September, Johannesburg, South Africa, 2002 at 16–17.

73 See, generally, S. J. Rombouts, *Having a Say – Indigenous Peoples, International Law and Free, Prior and Informed Consent*, Oisterwijk, Wolf, 2014.

74 See UN Development Group, *Guidelines on Indigenous Peoples' Issues*, 2008. Similarly, the 31 UN specialised agencies that make up the Inter-Agency Support Group to the UN Permanent Forum on Indigenous Issues have announced to advance the spirit and letter of the UNDRIP. See *Statement on the UN Declaration on the Rights of Indigenous Peoples*, adopted at the Annual Meeting of the Inter-Agency Support Group, 2007; Food and Agriculture Organisation, *Policy on Indigenous and Tribal Peoples*, 2010 at 2 and at Chapter IV; UN Global Compact, *The Business Reference Guide to the UN Declaration on the Rights of Indigenous Peoples*, New York, United Nations Global Compact Office, 2013; Permanent Council of the Organization of American States, *Draft proposals by the chair emanating from the special meeting of the working group to prepare the Draft American Declaration on the Rights of Indigenous Peoples*, 12 December 2008, GT/DADIN/doc321/08 at 3. See Inter-American Court of Human Rights, *Saramaka People v. Suriname*, IACHR Series C No. 172, 28 November 2007; Inter-American Court of Human Rights, *Kichwa Indigenous People of Sarayaku v. Ecuador*, IACHR Series C No. 245, 27 June 2012; Shortly after the adoption of the Declaration by the UN General Assembly, the Supreme Court of Belize made a decision relating to the rights of the Maya community to their lands and resources, applying the Declaration: Supreme Court of Belize, *Aurelio Cal v. Attorney-General of Belize*, Claim 121/2007, 18 October 2007. The Constitutional Court of Colombia applied UNDRIP in its decision T-129: Constitutional Court of Colombia, *Case T-129*, 3 March 2011. See also examples in Canadian Supreme Court referring to UNDRIP. See C. Allard, 'Canada', in L. Heinämäki,

UNDRIP, rather than creating new norms, reflects the current generally accepted norms and principles related to Indigenous peoples.[75] Some scholars argue that many provisions of the declaration codifies customary international law.[76] Another major success of UNDRIP relates to the way it was negotiated, with a strong participation of Indigenous peoples and their advocates, and on an equal footing with the states.[77] This is why the text itself reflects Indigenous peoples' values more than any other international legal instrument to date. Not only does UNDRIP recognize Indigenous peoples' rights to self-determination[78] and consultation seeking to obtain free, prior and informed consent from Indigenous peoples,[79] and rights to lands and natural resources[80], but it also recognizes both tangible and intangible aspects of Indigenous peoples' cultural heritage[81] (which from Indigenous peoples' perspective are inseparable) and Indigenous peoples' spiritual relationship to their lands.[82] Related to their spiritual relationship to the land is the recognition in UNDRIP of Indigenous peoples' traditional land tenure systems,[83] traditional knowledge,[84] customs[85] and customary rights.[86]

C. Allard, S. Kirchner, A. Xanthaki, S. Valkonen, U. Mörkenstam, N. Bankes, J. Ruru, J. Gilbert, P. Selle, A. Simpson and L. Olsén (eds), *Saamelaisten oikeuksien toteutuminen: kansainvälinen oikeusvertaileva tutkimus* [*Actualizing Sámi Rights: International Comparative Research*], Helsinki, Prime Minister's Office, Publications of the Government's analysis, assessment and research activities 4/2017, 2017, 390–424 at 391. Referring to information gathered from a power point presentation (October 2016) by N. Bankes and a synopsis of case law prepared by the law student A. Matychuk. Note that in Manitoba there is a new piece of legislation that refers to the principles of UNDRIP, see the Path to Reconciliation Act, 2016, 5th Session 40th Legislature.

75 M. Åhren, *The Saami traditional dress and beauty pageants: Indigenous peoples' rights of ownership and self-determination over their cultures*, Avhandling leverert for graden Philosophiae Doctor i rettsvitenskap [Thesis supplied for the degree of Philosophiae Doctor of Law] (unpublished), 2010 at 103.

76 J. Rehman, 'Between the Devil and the Deep Blue Sea: Indigenous Peoples as the Pawns in the US "War on Terror" and Jihad of Osama Bin Laden', in S. Allen and A. Xanthaki (eds), *Reflections on the UN Declaration on the Rights of Indigenous Peoples*, Portland, Hart Publishing, 2011, 561–584, at 561.

77 See M. Davis, 'Indigenous Struggle in Standard-Setting: The United Nations Declaration on the Rights of Indigenous Peoples', *Melbourne Journal of International Law* 9(2), 2008, 1–33 at 2; see also, generally, R. L. Barsh, 'Indigenous Peoples and the UN Commission on Human Rights: A Case of the Immovable Object and the Irresistible Force', *Human Rights Quarterly* 18, 1996, 782–813, at 782.

78 United Nations Declaration on the Rights of Indigenous Peoples, note 6 at Article 3.

79 Ibid. at Articles 18, 19 and 32.

80 Ibid. at Articles 26–32.

81 Ibid. at Articles 11–13 and 31.

82 Ibid. at Article 25.

83 Ibid. at Article 26.

84 Ibid. at Article 31.

85 Ibid. at Articles 33–34.

86 Ibid. at Article 34.

In Finnish legislation, Sámi customary laws and land tenure systems, such as *siida* – a traditional land tenure system to manage reindeer herding in small family units[87] – are not recognized. According to Helander-Renvall, the Sámi connection to the land is based on customary rights that are integrated in the form of an oral tradition into the daily practices of the local community."[88] The members of the Sámi community do not even conceive of these as rules; the practices are renegotiated if someone for one reason or another departs from the land-use practices established by custom. Helander-Renvall takes the view that the use and applicability of traditional legal notions is further eroded by the fact that there is a constant collision between them and national legislation and orders issued by government authorities. Moreover, the non-Sámi population in the Sámi region does not necessarily adhere to or even know the Sámi's traditional norms when it comes to use of the land, a situation which might even prompt some members of the Sámi community to depart from the norms.[89] What is more, as Tim Ingold and Terhi Kurttila have shown, the Sámi's traditional system of knowledge underlying their use of the land is very difficult, if not impossible, to express in concrete terms, for it is far too dynamic and practically oriented and adapts too readily to the situation at hand.[90] However, as reminded by Helander-Renvall, this does not mean that the rules deriving from customary law cannot be taken as the basis for legislation or as part of it. There are examples internationally on how customary law has been taken into account in legal proceedings and negotiations dealing with Indigenous peoples' land rights.[91] The Inter-American human rights monitoring system, contrary to general universal or other regional human rights monitoring mechanisms, for instance, recognizes and highlights Indigenous peoples' values, customs and customary rights, which have to be taken into account when consulting Indigenous peoples, as well as when implementing their human rights into practice.[92]

According to Helander-Renvall, acknowledging the customary rights indicating in a state's land-use policies the connection of an Indigenous people to

87 See e.g. E. Helander-Renvall, note 4 at 88–90 and 125; S. Tervaniemi and P. Magga, 'Belonging to Sápmi – Sámi conceptions of home and home region', in T. H. Eriksen, S. Valkonen and J. Valkonen (eds), *Knowing from the Indigenous North. Sámi Approaches to History, Politics and Belonging*, New York, Routledge, 2019, 75–90.

88 E. Helander-Renvall, *Saamelaisten perinnetieto, tapaoikeudet ja biologinen monimuotoisuus* [*The Sámi Traditional Knowledge, Customary Law and Biodeversity*], 2011 at 3.

89 E. Helander-Renvall, note 16 at 133–134.

90 T. Ingold and T. Kurttila, 'Perceiving the environment in Finnish Lapland', *Body and Society* 6, 2001, 183–196.

91 See E. Helander-Renvall, note 4, 132.

92 Inter-American Court of Human Rights, *The Mayagna (Sumo) Awas Tingni Community v. Nicarague*, IACHR Series C No. 79, 31 August 2001 at paragraph 149; *Saramaka People v. Suriname*, note 74.

the land requires active elaboration of that connection through different practices and discourses so that the rights will be recognized more broadly and become part of society's commitments.[93]

## 5 Concluding remarks

In the protection of Sámi customary relationship with the land, including tangible and intangible manifestations of cultural heritage, the main challenge and threat is the inability and reluctance of the Western system and the prevailing political ideologies to recognize that Indigenous peoples' culture and their very existence is based on a special ontology, one which is difficult to grasp, translate and document in terms of the Western system. Safeguarding the Sámi culture, including their customary relationship with the land, however, requires that people's own understanding of the world and of its place in that world are taken seriously. The idea must be accepted that Sáminess is based on an ontology of its own, which creates a Sámi reality.[94]

In order to overcome the current non-recognition of Sámi values in domestic policies and legislation and to embrace Sámi values means simply that state actors engage in a meaningful dialogue with the Sámi in the form of participation in all relevant decision-making, from planning to implementation of policies, and legal instruments that are relevant for Sámi. In this dialogue, it would be vital to acknowledge and take into account Sámi customary rights, traditional decision-making structures, and ways to understand norms and related processes.

International human rights norms, such as the ICCPR, as interpreted by the HRC, have the potential to expand their understanding of Indigenous peoples' own premises and aspirations, when clearly articulated by Indigenous people in their communications to the Committee. Regarding the ICCPR, there might be positive prospects in the instrument, particularly if Indigenous peoples choose themselves to actively emphasize cultural values as a whole, not just emphasizing economic and material aspects of safeguarding the economic basis of their "traditional livelihoods". However, the lack of direct recognition of Indigenous peoples' collective right to self-determination (Article 1) in the case practice of the HRC makes it more challenging to recognize the fundamentally collective basis on which Indigenous cultures are grounded.

It would be important for Indigenous peoples not to repeat the Western rhetoric to view their culture mainly from an economical sustainability point of view. They should, instead, more actively and loudly challenge the

93 E. Helander, 'The nature of Sami customary law', in T. Koivurova, T. Joona and R. Shnoro (eds), *Arctic governance*, Rovaniemi, University of Lapland, 2014, 88–96.

94 See S. Valkonen, J. Valkonen and V.P. Lehtola, note 5 at 173.

prevailing ontologies and make their own ways of viewing their cultural heritage known by the members of human rights monitoring bodies. UNDRIP, which already uses the language that dwells substantially more than any instrument before on Indigenous peoples' own ontologies and worldviews, has a great potential to shift the paradigm in which Indigenous peoples' policies are viewed and expressed. In fact, UNDRIP has already influenced other international and domestic legal regimes bringing them in alignment with the modern human rights era, where anthropocentric and categorically divided interpretations slowly give room for a more holistic approach emphasized by Indigenous peoples.

Indigenous human rights mechanisms, UN Special Rapporteur, Permanent Forum on Indigenous Issues (UNPFII) as well as EMRIP have been pushing for implementation of UNDRIP in multiple ways. They have, for instance, requested that World Heritage Convention be applied aligned with the provisions of UNDRIP, particularly in relation to self-determination and free, prior and informed consent, calling upon stewardship of indigenous peoples over their cultural and natural heritage.[95] In fact, this has led the World Heritage Committee, for the first time, to include specific references to Indigenous peoples in the Operational Guidelines, encouraging state parties to prepare nominations with the widest possible participation of stakeholders such as Indigenous peoples and to demonstrate, as appropriate, that the free, prior and informed consent of Indigenous peoples has been obtained.[96]

Finland, together with other states, confirmed its commitment to implement UNDRIP in the World Conference on Indigenous Peoples in 2014.[97] So far, necessary changes in policies and laws have not actualized. It will probably still need more active work within Sámi communities to define and articulate their interpretations and aspirations regarding how legal regimes could embrace their own ontological basis as a starting point in the protection of their rights. This kind of paradigm shift can most likely emerge only from within Sámi communities, not from state authorities, which instead could and should support Sámi initiatives to safeguard their own culture and existence as an Indigenous people.

95 J. Anaya, *Report of the Special Rapporteur on the rights of indigenous peoples*, UN Doc. A/67/301, 2012 at paragraphs 33–42; J. Anaya, *Letter of the Special Rapporteur, James Anaya, to the World Heritage Committee*, UN Doc. A/HRC/25/74, 2013 at 127; UNPFII, *Report on the tenth session*, UN Doc. E/2011 42, 2011 at paragraphs 40–42; UNPFII, *Report on the twelfth session*, UN Doc. E/2013 43, 2013 at paragraph 23; EMRIP, *Report on its fifth session*, UN Doc A/HRC/21/52, 2011 at 7 (Proposal 9); EMRIP, *Study on cultural heritage*, UN Doc A/HRC/30/53, 2015 at paragraph 27.

96 World Heritage Committee, *Operational Guidelines 2015*, WHC.15/01 39 COM 11, 2015 at paragraph 123.

97 UN General Assembly, *Outcome document of the high-level plenary meeting of the General Assembly known as the World Conference on Indigenous Peoples*, UN Doc. A/RES/69/2, 2014.

Chapter 7

# Assimilation policy *contra* cultural viability in the North

*Tom G. Svensson*[1]

## 1 Introduction

Historically, indigenous people in the Arctic have been subject to assimilation enforced by and in the interest of majority societies, a process of change that has caused severe most detrimental effects on indigenous people and their cultural viability. This process, which indicates domination, is referred to as Norwegianizing, Japanizing and Canadianizing, a process which turned out to be explicit attacks especially on hunting-gathering and pastoralist ways of life, where a settled way of life by the majority society was considered a predefined ideal. In the same fashion the school system, the language and traditional beliefs had to be adapted to mainstream practice and norms.

The issue of assimilation is of moral-philosophical order and is still discussed and actualized among indigenous people in the political domain, not the least in the North. What is at stake is the right to their own life style. It is a human right to enjoy and preserve cultural distinctiveness, to be culturally unique in the world of peoples. This opens for a discussion of law in a broad sense, i.e. in both philosophical and anthropological terms.

Assimilation as a common feature and its consequences will be discussed based on three different ethnographic cases, the Sámi, the Ainu and the Nisga´a. A variety of strategies have been used to come to terms with and counteract the negative effects of such assimilation policy, strategic moves as a rule initiated by the indigenous people themselves. Such strategies refer to the use of the legal arena of the dominant society focusing on their historical, inherent rights. The demand for substantial negotiation is another tactic being used. The overall objective is the issue of recognition, i.e. formal acknowledgement of the majority society that the indigenous peoples are entitled to territorial rights, essential for the sustenance of their way of life, their livelihood. Rights to self-determination, i.e. increased autonomy concerning their own affairs, and cultural rights emphasizing their language, their school system and their ritual practice and belief system are equally significant. Only by

1 Museum of Cultural History, University of Oslo, Norway, tomgs@extern.uio.no.

means of such recognition will it be possible to meet the future as a distinct people regardless of number and where cultural diversity is key.[2]

The cases that follow give substance to a more general discussion of the most topical issue at present, truth and reconciliation, which will be covered in some detail. In this way the current position between the majority and the indigenous minority in the North will be informed, built on a process away from assimilation and towards recognition of the ultimate value of cultural difference.

The chapter presents legal, philosophical as well as anthropological dimensions of assimilation policy *contra* cultural viability in the North: a state of conflict between majority and minority.

## 2 The use of the legal arena – a strategic choice

In most parts of the Circumpolar area noticeable changes can be recorded, in particular from the World War II era to the present day. One thing worth paying attention to is the increased contact and collaboration between various indigenous peoples, where sharing experiences turn out as a decisive additional asset.

A set of fundamental *rights* appear to be critical if these usually small groups of people are able to achieve the ultimate goal of cultural survival. And as long as cultural diversity is associated with definite meaning, a political agenda is required where *law* is a superordinate factor. In trying to counteract assimilation, the use of the legal arena of the majority society, including its court system, is mandatory if any change and improvements of the position of indigenous people are able to occur. To reach such a goal, legal pluralistic thinking is required. International law, specifically human rights, and customary law, including peoples' own legal perceptions, are key factors to convey and actualize the value of cross-cultural understanding of rights. Legal pluralism does not necessarily assume two parallel courts or systems of law, but it asserts a dialogue on legal matters based on an open understanding of cultural difference. Such understanding is the opposite of assimilation and is indispensable for cultural continuity.

Cultural survival relates to the perspective of ethnic boundary, a situational construction which in the main is a social concern.[3] Defending rights to land which are traditionally used by indigenous people and which are subject to marked encroachments from the majority society, gives particular meaning when such boundaries, culturally defined, are strengthened. Such a boundary

2 For a more extensive account of the three ethnographic cases, see T. Svensson, 'Reconciling divergent normative orders: The struggle for recognition regarding customary law among indigenous peoples'. *Arctic/Antarctic International Jrl. of Circumpolar Sociocultural Issues*, 2, 2008.

3 F. Barth (ed), *Introduction Ethnic Groups and Boundaries*, London, George Allen & Unwin, 1969, 9–38.

is a dynamic concept situationally constructed depending on needs, where recognition of cultural diversity, including indigeneity, appears as a key factor. The question remains, in confrontations how effectively can indigenous people articulate the question of ethnicity?

In the legal arena, the use of a proficient translation which transforms culture-specific thinking about rights into a legal language acceptable in court is required. To reach a legally binding verdict in a cross-cultural confrontation on rights calls for a mutual understanding to become law. And this is what the use of the legal arena is aiming at, where respect for legal pluralism is essential.

In general terms, the discussion so far can be exemplified with a set of court cases dealing primarily with rights in principle, because it is in such cases that the articulation of cultural difference is fronted. The process of negotiation leading to final agreements, even treaties, and parliamentary inquiries turn out to be supplementary strategies, either as follow-ups from court cases or as independent actions aiming at a similar objective, i.e. *change* based on extended recognition and clarification of rights.

### 2.1 The case of the Ainu

Hokkaido in northernmost Japan is the homeland of the Ainu. Their history goes back to the middle of the 14th century, and their traditional livelihood consisted of hunting, fishing and gathering, what they consider a forest way of life.

In 1869 a more explicit policy of Japanizing was initiated with negative consequences for the Ainu, for example their traditional salmon fishing and deer hunting were banned. The idea behind such aggressive assimilation policy was that the Ainu were to be common small-scale farmers like the rest of the Japanese agrarian population. This policy of prohibition also had an effect on Ainu ritual practice and belief systems, which were deeply connected to their ecological adaptation. With such state enactment the Ainu were referred to as "former aboriginal", indicating they no longer existed as a distinct people. Thereby the process of Japanizing was formalized. And in 1899 this firm assimilation policy was summed up in a law, the Hokkaido Former Aboriginals Protection Act – a legal instrument with the purpose of accelerating the assimilation of the Ainu to Wajin culture by means of education in Japanese language and customs, in other words close to complete denial of anything but what was considered mainstream Japanese.

The Ainu reacted to the assimilation policy comparatively late, and it was not until the 1980s that activities in this respect could be seen, not least on the international scene. Inspired by worldwide movements among various indigenous peoples, the Ainu started to politicize their national association *Utary Kyokai* by seeking contacts abroad. This association was founded in 1930 and was mainly involved in social welfare programs. A first draft of a new Ainu law, *Ainu Shinpo*, was worked out between 1984 and 1988. This law was to replace the old law of 1899 spelling out in clear terms the contrast between "former aboriginal" and an actually existing people having their own distinct history and culture. The concept of indigenous was emphasized, being a people in Japan of the same category as very many small peoples in the world incorporated and acknowledged in international fora, for example under the United Nations. Basic human rights and the elimination of discrimination were central elements to be built into this new Ainu law.

With *Ainu Shinpo* the Ainu challenged an instituted assimilation policy making claims referring to political rights and rights to self-determination, which in the Ainu case referred to special forest rights, to which their rich ceremonial practice is associated. In a point addressed to the Japanese authorities the Ainu made it clear that "we do not seek separation but a high level of autonomy, based on our fundamental values of 'co-existence with nature' and 'peace through negotiations'".[4] For the Ainu the time was overdue to spell out that they were a unique group both culturally and historically, a nation therefore entitled to distinct rights.

In 1990, the Ainu central village in Nibutani was facing the development of a large hydro-power dam project on Sary River, an exploitation they were unable to prevent. Part of the land affected was considered holy by the local Ainu, and before the construction began, excavations were carried out which were sponsored by the state. As compensation for loss suffered, several additional measures were offered, for example a new museum, the Nibutani Ainu Culture Museum 1992, which would serve as an information center. Finally, as a follow up to this exploitation, a few active Ainu in Nibutani wanted to go to court to test the legality of the project, including their status as indigenous, the latter of which – according to international law – should give the Ainu a stronger voice against similar encroachments by the industrial society in the future. It turned out to be a case on Ainu rights in principle. In 1997, a verdict by the Sapporo District Court concluded that the Ainu were an indigenous minority in Japan, a legal recognition of indigeneity; furthermore, it affirmed the dam project to be illegal according to international law standards. Moreover, it ruled that the Nibutani dam development caused expropriation of sacred Ainu land, including the site for their traditional annual boat-launching ceremony, which was considered a violation of their human rights. This legal recognition presented for the first time an official acceptance that the Ainu were different to other ethnic minorities living in Japan. It is important to note that the decision was not appealed.

To a certain degree influenced by the court decision, the next step in this process of ethnification of politics was when *Ainu Shinpo* was passed in the national *Diet*. This new law – The Law for the Proclamation of the Ainu culture and for the Dissemination and Advocacy for the Traditions of the Ainu and the Ainu Culture – represents an epoch-making progress. However,

4 Utary Kyokai document, 1988–1994.

Ainu collective rights, including territorial rights, were not guaranteed to them as an ethnic group. The law is constrained to a more limited perception of culture, and far more needs to be accomplished should the Ainu reach a position close to other indigenous people in the North. Article 2, serving as the definition, states, "The Ainu Culture in this law means the Ainu language and cultural practice such as music, dance, crafts, and other cultural properties which have been inherited by the Ainu people, and other cultural properties developed from these".[5] A supplementary amendment meeting further demands by the Ainu was passed in 1999. Two extremely important advances on behalf of the Ainu are here legislatively resolved:

1 To make efforts regarding advance of human rights of the Ainu and awareness raising of this people.
2 To make efforts to disseminate the knowledge about Ainu traditions, including the indigenous nature of the Ainu, which is a historical fact.[6]

It can be added that this official recognition does not acknowledge any specific indigenous rights. Consequently, it appears, at least at this stage, as severely restricted, although with definite symbolic meaning compared to the earlier position held by the Japanese Government. Turning to the national court system in combination with increased activities on various international arenas demonstrated the use of an adequate strategy to attain stated goals.

### *2.2 The case of the Nisga'a*

The Thimshian-speaking Nisga'a live in the far north of British Columbia (BC) with a coastal/river way of life. As a non-Treaty people, in the 19th century they faced an uncontrolled encroachment by settlers on which they considered their land. During the same period an assimilation policy was initiated, from which emerged the establishment of residential schools, separating children from their parents, with the purpose to facilitate Canadianizing. Moreover, the significant feast practice, *potlatch*, was prohibited. This ban was explained by the authorities as putting an end to exuberant spending, the traditional circulating of goods and values, which would eventually ruin the population. However, the *potlatch* is so much more than extravagant spending on food and goods, it is the primary setting for sustaining the name-giving ceremony, indicating status transformation, and the appropriate place where important oral cultural knowledge is conveyed and learned.[7]

5 Law No 52, May 14, 1997. For a summary of Ainu Shinpo (Ainu New Law), see T. Tsunemoto, *The Ainu Shinpo: A New Beginning in Ainu Spirit of a Northern People. Arctic Studies Center*, Washington, Smithsonian Institution, 1999.
6 Amendment: Law No 160, Dec. 22, 1999.
7 For a more extensive account of the case of the Nisga'a in this respect, see T. Svensson, 'Indigenous rights and Customary Law Discourse. Comparing the Nisga'a and the Sámi', *Jrl. of Legal Pluralism and Unofficial Law*, 47, 2002.

In terms of protest against assimilation, the Nisga'a are pioneers among indigenous people. As early as 1887 a group of Nisga'a attempted to address their worries to the Canadian authorities. They went in a canoe along the entire coast of BC to the provincial capital Victoria with the main objective of trying to save the land they considered theirs. With no success, they later turned to the central authorities in Ottawa, and eventually in 1913 even to London to plead their case to the King. All these efforts though led to no result, and the assimilation and the increasing settlements continued.

The Nisga'a are divided into four clans, *raven, wolf, eagle* and *killerwhale*, and they live in four different villages with New Aiyansh in the upper Nass valley as the central community. To strengthen a geographically dispersed people, numbering 6,000, in 1955 the Nisga'a decided to form an association for all – the Nisga'a Tribal Council. In 1969, a law suit was initiated with the purpose of activating the land claims issue by means of testing their aboriginal title in Canadian courts, a claim referring back to the Royal Proclamation of 1763, i.e. Nisga'a rights in principle.

Chief Frank Calder brought the case on behalf of the Nisga'a, collectively supported by the Tribal Council, and in 1973 the Canadian Supreme Court ruled to a great extent in favor of Nisga'a claims, which is considered a landmark decision. Among indigenous people the year 1973 turned out to be a key date, for example the James Bay Cree (the Malouf case) and the Sámi in Sweden (the Taxed Mountains case) also made formal progress by court decisions concerning rights in principle.

Although still a non-Treaty people, following on from the Supreme Court ruling, the Nisga'a decided to take the issue of aboriginal title a step further and demanded negotiation, which eventually ended up with a Treaty, thereby securing enough traditional land for the Nisga'a Nation. The political rhetoric of the Nisga'a was clear on this point, only a Treaty would serve as a sufficient instrument to guarantee a Nisga'a land base.

Between 1976 and 1998 the Nisga'a were involved in a negotiation process as a direct prolongation of the court decision in 1973. It was a three-party negotiation, besides the Nisga'a Nation, the Provincial Government, BC and the Federal Government, Canada were parties. The negotiation was to look into the land rights issue collectively held by the Nisga'a in contrast to private property rights. In other words, the negotiation was to clarify, confirm and recognize what were regarded as specific Nisga'a rights, expressed in concrete terms as land rights and rights to self-determination. In this manner the outcome was to put a definite end to anything close to what is considered assimilation.

After 22 years of comprehensive negotiations a Final Agreement was reached, which was later converted into a Treaty, a most significant improvement for any non-Treaty nations. Based on this Treaty, a Nisga'a Constitution was worked out, which was to serve as a political guideline reflecting the step towards functioning self-determination, Nisga´a political autonomy.[8]

Looking into the implementation emanating from this negotiation, there is first a new political structure consisting of: (1) a central body the Nisga´a Lisims Government; (2) four village governments; and (3) a Council of Elders. In this way, tradition is fused with modernity. This dualistic view is, furthermore, brought out in regard to legal matters. Throughout the negotiation the Nisga´a insisted that their original justice system, *Ayuukhl*, based on custom and their own legal perceptions should remain. Its spirit and content is stated in the preamble of the Treaty, thus affirming a formal acceptance of the Nisga´a philosophical approach to justice, i.e. legal pluralism in real. An official recognition of such community-based justice is considered more important than having their own Nisga´a court. In the future, conflict resolutions can turn out to be culturally adequate without complete separation from the state law system, a key to legal pluralism in operation.

A final point to bring up refers to education and research. The Nisga´a have established their own college, *Wilp Wibco´oskwl Nisga´a* (Nisga´a House of Wisdom), cooperating with the University of Northern BC offering special BA programs in Nisga´a studies. In addition, there is an Ayuukhl Nisga´a Department in the central government, the purpose of which is to carry out and transmit research on Nisga´a customs and traditional knowledge.

As demonstrated, the Nisga´a Treaty is not only about land rights, but it is also about cultural heritage, i.e. comprehensive indigenous rights proper. The result of the strategic moves the Nisga´a chose will serve as a model for other indigenous people involved in Treaty-making processes, also concerning the use of the justice system of the majority society.

### 2.3 The case of the Sámi

In contrast to the other indigenous people referred to earlier who relate to one state, the Sámi are found in four different nation-states, Norway, Sweden, Finland and Russia. Historically, they are known as practicing an extensive land-use pattern, either reindeer pastoralism combined with other means of livelihood from outlying land, or coastal fishing and farming.

As a reaction to assimilation and increasing encroachment on traditional Sámi land, *Sápmi*, the Sámi entered on a process of testing their inherent rights turning to the court system of the majority society as the appropriate arena. In the 1970s a new trend emerged, i.e. focusing on rights in principle, recognition and specification of fundamental rights, e.g. those stated in the 1966 UN International Covenant on Civil and Political Rights, art. 27. This tactic was different to early attempts where the focus was put solely on trying to prevent a case of development or, if that was not possible, to secure

8 Nisga´a Final Agreement, Federal Treaty Negotiation Office, 1998.

sufficient compensation for estimated losses. Between 1971 and 1981 the Alta Case in Norway and the Taxed Mountains Case in Sweden stand out as epoch-making events, exclusively based on Sámi initiatives, and which in their aftermaths brought about extensive political change. And the hard felt assimilation policy was thereby eliminated for good.

The Alta Case refers to a hydro-power dam project in the, until that time, unspoiled Alta river. It is not the largest exploitation of its kind, but it occurred at the time when the Sámi had reached the point of putting up with no more exploitation. In political terms it was considered important for the Sámi to show a new voice, a voice which corresponded closely with other indigenous people and their claims. Two strategies were chosen: first, a litigation case ending up in the Norwegian Supreme Court; and, second, to arrange demonstrations, for example 'Chain gangs' close to the Alta river trying to stop developments, and hunger strikers putting up a Sámi tent (*lávvo*) in front of the Norwegian Parliament in central Oslo. As expected, such actions generated great attention in various media and among the general public. In this way the Sámi and their rights were placed on the agenda as never before.

The dam project could not be avoided, but what was stated in the verdict concerning rights in principle opened the way for the Sámi to demand a Parliamentary Inquiry, a Sámi Rights Commission, to examine and clarify comprehensive Sámi rights, work to be carried out by an expert committee.[9] In 1984, the first report was presented, setting out important proposals for change: (1) a Sámi Act; (2) a Constitutional Amendment § 110a; and (3) the establishment of a political assembly for the Sámi – the Sámi Parliament, *Sámi Diggi*.[10] In 1990, these transformations were followed by a Sámi Language Act, which gave the Sámi language official status.

A second report dealing with the material basis of the Sámi culture was completed in 1997.[11] Here, the emphasis was on Sámi rights to land and water, historical rights to a great extent built on the Sámi Codicil of 1751 (*Lappekodicillen*), which in diverse confrontations has served, and continues to serve, as a decisive instrument in defending rights based on the status of indigenous peoples (cf. the Royal Proclamation of 1763 in Canada).

Lacking the dimension of *custom* and Sámi legal perceptions –although stated in the mandate for the Commission – the Sámi demanded as a supplement that research on this culturally significant issue should be carried out. The Sámi Rights Commission had explained that the omission was made

9 *Alta-Domen 'Alta Verdict' Norges Høyesterett*, Oslo, 1982 (The Norwegian Supreme Court).

10 NOU 1984:18 *Om Samenes rettsstilling*, Oslo (*On Sámi legal rights* (NOU 1984:18)). NOU stands for *Norges Offentlige Utredninger*, "Public Inquiries Norway".

11 NOU 1997a:4 *Naturgrunnlaget for samisk kultur*, Oslo (*The natural basis for the Sámi culture* (NOU 1997a:4)).

because the issue of customary rights appeared too complicated and would presume new research which the Commission was unable to carry out. The Department of Justice approved of the Sámi demand, and between 1996 and 2001 this legal aspect was examined by an interdisciplinary group managed by a steering committee, consisting of three members from the Department of Justice and three appointed by the Sámi Parliament.[12] The fact that the Sámi put so much emphasis on customary rights is in many ways comparable to the point stressed by the Nisga'a, i.e. to retain the traditional law, *Ayuukhl*, in future specification of rights.

Finally, in 2004 the District Court for Inner Finnmark, *Finnmárku diggegoddi* was founded, a court having competence in Sámi culture and language, and based in Tana. In 2005, the Finnmark Act, based on the 1997/2001 reports, was passed by the Norwegian Parliament. Worth noticing here is the changed wording from "Sámi Act" to "Finnmark Act", as a compromise to include all people historically living in the Finnmark County.[13] Following on from this Act, what is called the Finnmark Estate (*Finnmarkseiendomen*) was established.

All actions mentioned represent firm expressions against the former assimilation policy and demonstrate a new trend in Sámi history.

## 3 On truth and reconciliation

As demonstrated, indigenous people in the North no longer accept the assimilation policy. On the contrary, and exclusively on their own initiative, they have chosen various strategies to come to terms with the negative implications of such policy. Cultural difference is a key against the notion of uniformity. In political as well as legal matters certain progress has been made. To consolidate the idea of cultural pluralism within a nation-state framework, a number of indigenous peoples have suggested that a truth and reconciliation process should be carried out, looking thoroughly at both the past and the future. In this matter, it was believed, cultural continuity could be secured even for small groups of people. This process should lead to a formal acceptance of cultural diversity in a nation-state context.

By 2008, Canada had already decided to meet the demand for such an inquiry, and the final report was presented in 2015.[14] The Commission defined reconciliation as a process to "establish and maintain a mutually

12 NOU 2001:34 *Samiske sedvaner og rettsoppfatninger*, Oslo (*Sámi customs and legal perceptions* (NOU 2001:34)). See also T. Svensson (ed), *On Customary Law and the Sámi Rights Process in Norway*, Skriftserie, No 8, Senter for samiske studier, Tromsø, 1999.

13 11 Ot.prp. 53, 2003. It refers to the formal proposal to the Norwegian Parliament prior to the enactment of the Finnmark Act, 2005.

14 *Honouring the Truth Reconciling for the Future. Summary of the Final Report*, Truth and Reconciliation Commission, 2015.

respectful relationship", with truth being the key to acknowledging all the damages caused by the assimilation. Many crucial aspects referring to cultural uniqueness are covered at great length in the report. The issue of education had a clear bearing on the intended assimilation. As stated, residential schooling was more than education, it was an integral part of an enforced assimilation policy. With the same aim, the right to use their own language and to practice their sacred ceremonies were examined. The ultimate intent regarding the government's policy was to assimilate indigenous people into mainstream Canadian society. In spite of such political force, occurring for more than 150 years, indigenous people in Canada did not surrender; and, as readily seen, they are still there, and they still have a voice.

The final report is considered a landmark document presenting no less than 94 recommendations for action. In general terms, the emphasis is on *change*, concluding with a list of measures necessary to get close to reconciliation, and based on nationwide actions. Reconciliation is a challenge, it is about respect and must become a way of life.

In Canada, the negative consequences of the assimilation are now mapped out and stated as a truth. Reconciliation has to do with actions which will connect the damaging effects caused by assimilation with recognition.

Turning to the Sámi, in all three Nordic countries with Sámi populations, the idea of truth and reconciliation has become a number one issue aiming at change, Norway being the first to appoint such a Commission with a mandate similar to the one in Canada. After intensive debate back and forth, the Commission was agreed upon by the Norwegian Parliament in June 2018, and its final date for submitting a report is set as September 1, 2022.

The Commission consists of 12 members, five of which were selected by the Sámi Parliament. Three themes to be examined stand out: (1) historical mapping of assimilation; (2) to examine the effects of the Norwegianizing policy today; and (3) to suggest measures for reconciliation.

As to the composition of the Commission, certain weak points have been brought up by the Sámi, for example there is an impression of a too heavy academic representation; in addition, there are no members from the South and East Sámi, which is problematic considering the distinct position of their history and language.

A first constituting meeting was held in September 2018. An important aspect pointed out by the Sámi is the mobilization of grass-roots participation, where extensive knowledge of people's own memory and opinions regarding the implication of Norwegianizing can be recorded. Independent of the Commission, the Sámi Parliament has prepared for 23 public meetings, and a few meetings have already taken place. The consecutive dialogue between the Commission and the Sámi Parliament will, to a great extent, fall back on such local engagement.

Without doubt, the inquiry represents a historically unique opportunity for the Sámi when it comes to exerting enough control to avoid future tendencies of assimilation, thereby falling back on a formal recognition of cultural diversity. It is a question of Sámi dignity as people which is at stake, and the expected reconciliation presumes the full truth to be uncovered, i.e. bringing out into the open all relevant knowledge.

Two historical dates are pointed out to have been especially discriminatory towards the Sámi: the year 1889, referring to the School Law, focusing on residential schooling with the firm denial of the value of anything Sámi; and the year 1902, referring to the Law of Land (*jordlov*). The latter law meant that only people who were proficient in Norwegian could buy and own land, an official policy close to apartheid.

Since the Commission is still in its initial stages, further comments must wait. A minor remark can be added concerning the name, which caused some debate. The Norwegian Parliament suggested the Commission should be called "Commission of righteousness", whereas the Sámi Parliament insisted on the internationally adopted term "Truth and Reconciliation".

Being an important part of Sámi history, the time is now overdue to examine in minute detail the effects of the assimilation policy. Recent cases underscore that need. The case of the young *Jovset Ánte Sara* trying to establish himself in reindeer herding was severely constrained by a split Supreme Court Decision in 2017, although both the District Court and the Court of Appeal had unanimously supported Sara. The issue concerned an assumed collective overgrazing, as a consequence of which, the opponent (the State) maintained that Sara must reduce his herd from 350 to 75 reindeer, making it impossible for him to carry on a reindeer pastoralist way of life, the culture he wants to be part of. Sara has appealed the ruling to the UN Human Rights Committee. While still waiting for a response from the Committee, the State surprisingly insisted on the forced slaughtering of reindeer, with the deadline of January 1, 2019, and if the requirement was not met, Sara would have to pay daily fines.

The plea by the Sámi Parliament in 2019 to revise the Norwegian Constitution § 108 (former §110a: the "Sámi paragraph"), changing the phrase "the Sámi group of people" to "the Sámi people, who are the indigenous people of the nation",[15] was turned down by Parliament (January 2019), as it did not achieve the two-thirds majority needed for a Constitutional Amendment. The change in wording will have no consequences concerning Sámi rights, but for the Sámi it is of great symbolic value that the Constitution corresponds with international law and legal practice. As in the Sara case, the decision can be seen as a step away from reconciliation and accentuates even further the indisputable necessity for a Truth and Reconciliation process.

15 A text proposal worked out by the former head of the Sámi Rights Commission, the expert on international law, Professor Carsten Smith, 2015, quoted in *Ságat*, 2019, Nr 13 and 21.

## 4 Brief summary

As demonstrated, most indigenous people in the Arctic have suffered severely from an assimilation policy. In many instances, an ethnic identity has been experienced as a social stigma, an identity which for a long time had been denied and avoided, especially in public spheres.[16] This social fact is part of what will be disclosed in the Truth and Reconciliation process. The most effective means available to cope with the issue of assimilation has been the combination of a legal strategy with political actions. This has brought about functional recognition, also in respect to indigeneity. A further step refers to coexistence based on equal value regardless of numbers.

16 See H. Eidheim, 'When Ethnic Identity is a Social Stigma', in F. Barth (ed).

Chapter 8

# The predicates of Chinese legal philosophy in the Polar Regions

*Nengye Liu*[1] *and Qi Xu*[2]

## 1 Introduction

The Polar Regions (Arctic and Antarctica) are changing rapidly due to human-induced climate change. This in turn generates pressure for development of Polar governance regimes which are underpinned by the law of the sea. A rising, industrialised China is playing an increasingly influential role in this process. For example, China was admitted as an Observer to the Arctic Council – the most important regional cooperation forum, in 2013.[3] Further, as an important high sea fishing state, China was invited by five Arctic coastal States (Canada, Denmark, Norway, Russia and the United States) to negotiate and conclude the 2018 Agreement to Prevent Unregulated High Seas Fisheries in the Central Arctic Ocean (CAO Agreement 2018).[4] Since acceding to the Antarctic Treaty in 1983, China has greatly expanded its presence in Antarctica.

Since President Xi Jinping took office in 2013, there has been a marked shift in Chinese diplomacy from a "low profile" to an "active participation approach". The Chinese delegation has, for example, become more and more vocal in the Antarctic Treaty Consultative Meetings (ATCMs) and annual meetings of the Commission for the Conservation of Antarctic Marine Living Resources (CCAMLR).[5] Most recently, on 26 January 2018, the State Council of the People's Republic of China (PRC) published its first ever official Arctic Policy White Paper (hereinafter Arctic White Paper),[6] which clearly

1 Adelaide Law School, University of Adelaide, Australia, nengye.liu@adelaide.edu.au.
2 Law School/Intellectual Property School, Jinan University, China.
3 Kiruna Declaration, The Eight Ministerial Meeting of the Arctic Council, 15 May 2013, available at: https://oaarchive.arctic-council.org/handle/11374/93.
4 Agreement to Prevent Unregulated High Seas Fisheries in the Central Arctic Ocean (3 October 2018), available at: http://www.dfo-mpo.gc.ca/international/arctic-arctique-eng.htm.
5 For an overview, see Nengye Liu, 'The Rise of China and the Antarctic Treaty System?', *Australian Journal of Maritime and Ocean Affairs* (2019) 11 (2), 120–131.
6 The State Council Information Office of the People's Republic of China, 'China's Arctic Policy' White Paper (January 2018), available at: http://english.scio.gov.cn/node_8002680.html.

presents China's position on Arctic affairs. China intends to build a "Polar Silk Road" (PSR) to increase its involvement at the Poles as part of a larger "Belt and Road Initiative" (BRI) launched by the Chinese Government in 2013.[7]

An enduring question arises: to what extent will a rising China shape the future of Polar governance? This question, especially China's ambitions, has been covered extensively in English literature.[8] Nevertheless, China differs from the western liberal tradition in many ways, including in its values and philosophical foundations.[9] In order to draw a full picture of China's future role in Polar governance, it is important to have an in-depth analysis of Chinese perceptions and legal philosophy towards current governance regimes in the Arctic and Antarctica.

In her book *Is International Law International?*, Roberts examines the concept of "comparative international law".[10] Roberts illustrates the different national and regional approaches towards understanding, interpretation and application of international law. She quotes Judge Hanqin Xue of the International Court of Justice, who states "notwithstanding its universal character, international law in practice is nonetheless not identically interpreted and applied among States". Roberts points out that national approaches to

7 The BRI is a huge infrastructure investment plan to link Europe to China across Eurasia and the Indian Ocean, with potentially significant economic, strategic and geopolitical impacts on existing world order. See Xi Jinping's Speech at Nazarbayev University, 7 September 2013, China Ministry of Foreign Affairs (8 September 2013), available at: http://www.fmprc.gov.cn/mfa_chn//ziliao_611306/zt_611380/dnzt_611382/ydyl_667839/zyxw_667918/t1074151.shtml (in Chinese); see also, Action Plan on the Belt and Road Initiative, State Council of P. R. China, available at: http://english.gov.cn/archive/publications/2015/03/30/content_281475080249035.htm; Vision for Maritime Cooperation under the Belt and Road Initiative, National Development and Reform Commission and State Oceanic Administration (Xinhua, 20 June 2017), available at: http://news.xinhuanet.com/english/2017-06/20/c_136380414.htm; Geoff Wade, China's 'One Belt, One Road' Initiative, Parliament of Australia, available at: https://www.aph.gov.au/About_Parliament/Parliamentary_Departments/Parliamentary_Library/pubs/BriefingBook45p/ChinasRoad.

8 For a literature review before the adoption of China's official Arctic Policy White Paper in 2018, see Nengye Liu, 'China's Emerging Arctic Policy – What are the Implications for Arctic Governance?' *Jindal Global Law Review* (2017) 8 (1), 55–68; For relevant literature afterwards, see e.g., Timo Koivurova et al., 'China in the Arctic, the Opportunities and Challenges for Chinese-Finnish Arctic Cooperation', 2019, available at: https://tietokayttoon.fi/julkaisut/raportti?pubid=URN:ISBN:978-952-287-636-2; Kamrul Hossain, 'China's BRI Expansion and Great Power Ambition: The Silk Road on the Ice Connecting the Arctic', *Cambridge Journal of Eurasian Studies* (2019) 3, 1–24; China & The Arctic – Special Section, *Arctic Yearbook* 2018.

9 Jianfu Chen, *Chinese Law, Context and Transformation* (Brill, 2016), pp. 6–8.

10 Anthea Roberts, *Is International Law International?* (Oxford University Press, 2017), pp. 19–23.

international law play an important part in "a transnational field that aspires to develop common rules to facilitate inter-state coexistence and cooperation".[11] Moreover, academics occupy an influential role in a State's international law practice, through their scholarship and practice.[12]

A comprehensive understanding of the Chinese approach towards international Polar law is essential when discussing China's role in the future of Polar governance. Most Chinese government officials who participate in contemporary Polar negotiations were trained by academics in prominent mainland Chinese universities, e.g. Peking, Tsinghua, Renmin and Wuhan. Although they (government officials and academics) spent their formative years in an open-door China, their view of the world order has been shaped by values and philosophies that are not necessarily the same as their American, European or Australasian colleagues. This chapter therefore applies the idea of "comparative international law" to the Polar Regions by examining Chinese academics' work over the past decade.[13] By examining over 350 papers published by Chinese scholars,[14] the chapter facilitates the comparison and inclusion of a broader array of world views. After presenting a brief overview of Chinese legal philosophy towards international law, the chapter examines the evolution of Chinese research on Polar law and policy. It concludes with some predictions about the future of China's role in Polar governance.

## 2 Chinese legal philosophy towards international law

Before the First Opium War, also known as the Anglo-Chinese War (1840), China (the Middle Kingdom) managed international relations through the Tribute System. The Tribute System placed China in the centre of the Chinese world between empires and "outside barbarians".[15] The 1842 Treaty of Nanking, an unequal treaty signed between the Qing Empire and Great Britain, introduced euro-centric international law into China. In the meantime, Chinese elites gradually realised that international law may be a useful

11 Ibid.
12 Ibid, pp. 28–32.
13 China hosted the Beijing Olympics in 2008. The Beijing Olympics is widely seen as a starting point for China's emergence onto the centre stage of world affairs. Therefore, we chose to examine papers published between 2009 and 2019, which are of most relevance for discussing China's Polar law and policy.
14 We did a thorough search on the China National Knowledge Infrastructure (CNKI/中国知网), a key national Chinese journal database that collects more than 100,000 Chinese academic journals. In the category of Social Sciences, we found around 300 relevant papers with the search term "Arctic", and more than 50 papers using the search term "Antarctica", published between 2008 and 2018. Available at: https://www.cnki.net.
15 Ssu-yu, John, K. Fairbank, *China's Response to the West, a documentary survey 1839–1923* (Harvard University Press, 1979).

tool to ensure Chinese sovereignty against western colonial powers. Therefore, albeit reluctantly, China started occasionally utilising international law to defend its national interests.[16] This pragmatic approach to the use of international law as a tool became institutionalised when *Zongli Yamen*, China's first ministry of foreign affairs, was established in 1861. The establishment of *Zongli Yamen* signalled the end of the Tribute System and the start of China's embrace of international law. After the collapse of the Qing Dynasty in 1911, the Republic of China actively integrated into the international community with some highs (e.g. the movement to abolish unequal treaties[17]) and lows (e.g. the failure to regain authority of Qingdao city in Shandong Province from Germany in the 1919 Paris Peace Conference[18]). However, after 1949 when the Communist Party took power, Mao Zedong's China once again closed its doors, and isolated China from the West. "The Five Principles of Peaceful Co-Existence" (The Five Principles),[19] which was first jointly proposed by India and the PRC in the 1950s, can be seen as inward-looking principles which aimed to secure China's sovereignty against any foreign interference. This is recognized by the Chinese Government as one of the PRC's major contributions to international law and is still officially the guiding principle of Chinese diplomacy.[20] Following Mao, Deng Xiaoping's strategy was for China to keep a low profile in the international arena. The focus then was attracting foreign investments and technology for economic development. As a result of the implementation of this approach, China ascended the World Trade Organization as a so-called "regime taker".[21]

In recent years, China has emerged as the world's second largest economy. Under President Xi Jinping, China has been making significant shifts from being a regime taker to becoming a "regime maker". The 19th General

16 Phil C. W. Chan, 'China's Approaches to International Law since the Opium War', *Leiden Journal of International Law* (2014) 27 (4), 859–892.

17 Edmund S. K. Fund, 'The Chinese Nationalists and the Unequal Treaties 1924–1931', *Modern Asian Studies* (1987) 21 (4), 793–819.

18 Bruce A. Elleman, *Wilson and China: A Revised History of the Shandong Question* (M. E. Sharpe, 2002).

19 The Five Principles are mutual respect for sovereignty and territorial integrity, mutual non-aggression, non-interference in each other's internal affairs, equality and mutual benefit, and peaceful coexistence. See China Ministry of Foreign Affairs, China's Initiation of the Five Principles of Peaceful Co-Existence, available at: https://www.fmprc.gov.cn/mfa_eng/ziliao_665539/3602_665543/3604_665547/t18053.shtml.

20 See for example, China Ministry of Foreign Affairs, The Five Principles of Peaceful Coexistence – The time-tested guideline of China's policy with neighbours (30 July 2014), available at: https://www.fmprc.gov.cn/mfa_eng/wjb_663304/zwjg_665342/zwbd_665378/t1179045.shtml.

21 Jacques deLise, 'China's Approaches to International Law: a Historical Perspective', *Proceedings of the Annual Meeting (American Society of International Law)* (2000) 94, 859–892.

Assembly of the Chinese Communist Party stated that China aimed to build a new great power relationship and a "shared community of mankind".[22] That is, to actively shape international law so as to maximise Chinese interests. That said, sovereignty is still China's biggest concern, given its maritime disputes in the South China Sea and the East China Sea, as well as the current separation between mainland China and Taiwan.[23] In any case, if there is any philosophy behind China's attitude towards international law, it would be "pragmatism". International law is a tool for China, either to secure its sovereignty at home or to expand its interests globally. In remote areas such as the Polar Regions, where China has no territorial claim, it can be expected that China could be relatively flexible in order to shape the regime to certain extent.

## 3 The Arctic

The Arctic is a hot topic in Chinese academia. Among 350 Polar papers we found in the China National Knowledge Infrastructure (CNKI) published between 2008 and 2018, over 300 articles deal with the Arctic. In general, three big questions are discussed in depth in the following subsections: (1) the legal status of Arctic shipping route; (2) who owns the Arctic; and (3) the PSR.

### *3.1 Legal status of Arctic shipping routes*

In 2007, two crafts from Russia erected a titanium Russian flag on the floor of the Arctic Ocean, which drew the world's attention.[24] This event was perhaps the beginning for Chinese academics to seriously look into Arctic issues from geopolitical and legal perspectives. Since then, some remarks have been published in the Chinese literature to explain the existing political and legal frameworks in the Arctic. For example, Huang Zhixiong analyses the significance of Arctic resources, transport and military.[25] Given China is the world's third largest shipping power by deadweight tonnage,[26] it is not surprising that the legal status of Arctic shipping routes, especially the Northeast

22 Xu Hong (Head of Department of Treaty and Law, China Ministry of Foreign Affairs), 'Creating a New Era for China and International Law', *People's Daily* (14 July 2018), available at: http://www.cssn.cn/zx/201807/t20180715_4503645.shtml (in Chinese).

23 For a comprehensive analysis of China's sovereignty, see Maria Adele Carrai, *Sovereignty in China: A Genealogy of a Concept since 1840* (Cambridge University Press, 2019).

24 'Russia Plants Flag on North Pole Seabed' (2 August 2007), *The Guardian*, available at: https://www.theguardian.com/world/2007/aug/02/russia.arctic.

25 Huang Zhixiong, 'Analysis of the Struggle in the Arctic Region from the Perspective of International Law', *International Forum* (2009) 6, 8–13 (in Chinese).

26 United Nations Conference on Trade and Development, Review of Maritime Transport 2018, available at: https://unctad.org/en/PublicationsLibrary/rmt2018_en.pdf, p. 30.

Passage (Northern Sea Route)[27] and the Northwest Passage[28] acquired much focus. While Russia and Canada view the Northern Sea Route and the Northwest Passage as their internal waters respectively, the United States and the European Union (EU) has consistently promoted the two Arctic shipping routes as "straits used for international navigation".[29] From a Chinese perspective, Bai Jiayu argues that the Northeast Passage constitutes a strait used for international navigation, since it accords with geographic and functional standards in the Corfu Channel case.[30] Guo Peiqing and Guan Qinglei consider Russia's "management system over Northern Sea Route" enhances its exclusive jurisdiction.[31] Liu Huirong and Liu Xiu, however, believe that according to the United Nations Convention on the Law of the Sea (UNCLOS),[32] the Northwest Passage can neither be defined as a strait used for international navigation, nor as internal water subject to exclusive coastal state jurisdiction.[33] They recommend the conclusion of an international convention similar to the Svalbard Treaty for the Northwest Passage, so as to balance Canada's sovereignty claim on the one hand and other States' navigational rights on the other hand.[34] Nevertheless, Chen Jinggen finds the idea

27 The Northeast Passage is defined as the set of sea routes from northwest Europe around North Cape (Norway) and along the north coast of Eurasia and Siberia through the Bering Strait to the Pacific. Arctic Council Protection of Marine Environment Working Group, *Arctic Marine Shipping Assessment Report*, p. 34, available at: https://oaarchive.arctic-council.org/handle/11374/54. The Northern Sea Route is defined in Russian Federation law as a set of marine routes from Kara Gate (south of Novaya Zemlya) in the west to the Bering Strait in the east. Several of the routes are along the coast, making use of the main straits through the islands of the Russian Arctic; other potential routes run north of the island groups. See *Arctic Marine Shipping Assessment Report*, p. 23.

28 The Northwest Passage is the name given to the various marine routes between the Atlantic and Pacific oceans along the northern coast of North America that span the Canadian Arctic Archipelago. Arctic Council Protection of Marine Environment Working Group, *Arctic Marine Shipping Assessment Report*, p. 20, available at: https://oaarchive.arctic-council.org/handle/11374/54.

29 For detailed discussions, see e.g., Nengye Liu and Kamrul Hossain, 'China and the Development of International Law on Arctic Shipping, Challenges and Opportunities', in Timo Koivurova, Tianbao Qin, Tapio Nykänen, Sebastien Duyck (eds), *Arctic Law and Governance: the Role of China and Finland* (Hart Publishing, Oxford) 233–251.

30 Bai Jiayu, 'Research on the International Law Issues about the Use of the Arctic Routes', *Journal of Ocean University of China (Social Sciences)* (2012) 8 (in Chinese).

31 Guo Peiqing, Guan Qinglei, 'Analysis on the Political and Legal Issues of Northern Sea Route', *Journal of Ocean University of China (Social Sciences)* (2009) 3–4 (in Chinese).

32 United Nations Convention on the Law of the Sea 1982, (1982) 21 ILM 1261–1354.

33 Liu Huirong, Liu Xiu, 'Research on the Legal Status of Northwest Passage', *Journal of Ocean University of China (Social Sciences)* (2009) 3–4 (in Chinese).

34 Ibid.

of an international convention almost impossible, due to strong resistance from Canada and Russia to applying the model of the Svalbard Treaty to Arctic shipping routes.[35] It therefore seems that Chinese academics tend to agree with the United States and the EU that both the Northeast Passage and Northwest Passage are straits used for international navigation. In a strait used for international navigation, transit passage will be allowed for foreign vessels and coastal States in most cases cannot stop the navigation. This would ideally serve China's shipping interest in the Arctic.

When it comes to where China should stand regarding the legal status of Arctic shipping routes under international law, Dai Zonghan suggests China should cooperate with Russia and Canada in scientific research, resource exploitation and to secure a most favoured state treatment agreement on the navigation of Arctic passages.[36] Zhang Huizhi and Wang Liding propose strengthening cooperation among East Asian countries (Japan and South Korea) to influence the development of international law on Arctic shipping.[37] This might be wishful thinking because of tensions and competition in East Asia. In any case, China, Japan and South Korea share interests as shipping powers to ensure freedom of navigation in the Arctic. Mi Chenxi further writes that China should take full advantage of its Observer status in the Arctic Council to participate in the Arctic shipping rule-making negotiations, with the aim to seek a balance between environmental protection and shipping interests, as well as to consolidate scientific research and cooperation alongside Arctic shipping routes.[38] China's Arctic White Paper mentions many times that ice-melt in the Arctic presents an "opportunity". However, rather than taking a clear position, the White Paper provides that "the management of the Arctic shipping routes should be conducted in accordance with treaties including the UNCLOS and general international law and that the freedom of navigation enjoyed by all countries in accordance with the law and their rights to use the Arctic shipping routes should be ensured."[39] Politically, China has grown close to Russia in recent years. China is therefore reluctant to openly challenge Russian authority over the Northern Sea Route. It is noted that China has taken a pragmatic approach by actively connecting

35 Chen Jinggen, 'Research on the Construction and Governance of Special Treaties Regulating Channel Pattern', *Journal of Political Science and Law* (2017) 91–93 (in Chinese).
36 Dai Zonghan, 'Examining the Legal Dispute over Arctic Passages under the UNCLOS and Analysing China's Diplomatic Strategy', *Journal of Comparative Law* (2013) 104–107 (in Chinese).
37 Zhang Huizhi, Wang Liding, 'Exploration on the Northeast Asia Cooperation of the Arctic Route', *Northeast Asian Forum* (2015) 74 (in Chinese).
38 Mi Chenxi, 'China's Role in the Governance of the Northeast Passage under New Circumstances', *Pacific Journal* (2015) 77–79 (in Chinese).
39 See China's Arctic Policy White Paper, note 6.

the resources-rich Russian Arctic with northern China,[40] without articulating its position on the legal status of Arctic shipping routes. This approach is reflected first in academic views (e.g. Liu Huirong and Liu Xu, cited earlier), then in the Arctic White Paper.

### *3.2 Who owns the Arctic?*

Apart from shipping, China's interests in the Arctic have expanded rapidly. Correspondingly, so has the width and depth of Chinese research on Arctic law and policy. The Arctic is not, however, legally considered by Chinese scholars to be the common heritage of mankind and most parts of the region lie under national jurisdictions. In order to effectively use the resources-rich Arctic, China has no other choice but to cooperate with Arctic States. Therefore, the next big question that Chinese academics deal with is "Who owns the Arctic?" More specifically, "What Arctic laws and policies have been adopted by Arctic States?" and "How might China collaborate with Arctic States?"

We found that the majority of the Chinese literature concentrated on Russia, Canada, the United States and the EU. These States plus the EU are seen by Chinese academia as the most powerful actors in the Arctic. Qian Zongqi analyses Russia's internal and external motivations to develop the Arctic: economic development; maintaining sovereignty; and strategic competition with western countries.[41] Su Peng sees infrastructure construction along Arctic sea routes and energy development as potential options for Sino-Russia cooperation under the BRI.[42] Guo Peiqing and Cao Yuan outline three principles of Russian Arctic policy – environmental protection, national security and social economic development – in order to advise Chinese policy-makers on Russian strategic focus and to effectively promote bilateral Arctic cooperation.[43]

Zhao Yadan points out that Canada formulates its Arctic policy by exercising sovereignty, improving economic and societal development, protecting the environment and promoting Arctic Governance.[44] To facilitate China-Canada Arctic cooperation, investment, scientific research, environmental

40 "China calls for stronger international cooperation on infrastructure construction and operation of the Arctic routes." See 'China's Arctic Policy' White Paper, note 6.

41 Qian Zongqi, 'Analysis on Russia's National Policy of Arctic Development', *Forum of World Economics & Politics* (2011) 79–83 (in Chinese).

42 Su Peng, 'The Essence of Russia's Current Arctic Policy and China's Response', *Jianghuai Tribune* (2017) 86 (in Chinese).

43 Guo Peiqing, Cao Yuan, 'An Analysis of Fundamental Principles of the Russian Arctic Policy', *Journal of Ocean University of China (Social Sciences)* (2016) 8–17 (in Chinese).

44 Zhao Yadan, 'An Analysis on Canada's Arctic Policy', *International Review* (2012) 72–79 (in Chinese).

protection and indigenous people's cultural heritage could be prioritised.[45] Zhang Xiaoyi believes that the Harper Administration overemphasized sovereignty and security concerns.[46] In contrast, the Trudeau Administration is more in favour of multilateral cooperation in Arctic governance.[47] Notably, in light of Canadian practice in safeguarding its historic water claim concerning the Northwest Passage, Zheng Lei recommends China promulgate a similar Vessel Traffic Services Zone so as to enhance its own historic rights claim in the South China Sea.[48]

Bai Jiayu's analysis on the evolution of American Arctic policy depicts national security as an enduring priority for the United States. This is followed by resource exploitation, scientific research and environmental protection.[49] While the United States has attempted to establish the outer limit of its Arctic continental shelf beyond 200 nautical miles, it has had legal difficulty in doing so as it is not a contracting party to UNCLOS.[50] During the Obama Administration, the United States was supportive of multilateral governance regimes, such as the Arctic Council for the protection of the Arctic.[51] Following the change from Obama to Trump, it looks like resources exploitation now prevails over environmental protection as a priority for American Arctic policy.[52]

When it comes to the EU, He Qisong highlights that the focus of the EU's Arctic policy is climate change, human rights, sustainable utilization of resources, and multilateral governance.[53] Similarly, Xia Liping considers that the EU defines itself as a normative power which adopts its own normative

45 Ibid.

46 Zhang Xiaoyi, 'Analysis on the Arctic Security Policy of Canada's Harper Administration', *Contemporary International Relations* (2016) 27–28 (in Chinese).

47 Guo Peiqing, Li Xiaowei, 'A Study of the New Trend of the Arctic Security Strategy of the Trudeau Government Based on Canada's New Defense Policy for 2017', *Journal of Ocean University of China (Social Sciences)* (2018) 13 (in Chinese).

48 Zheng Lei, 'Necessity and Feasibility of Promulgating Vessel Traffic Services Zone System in the South China Sea - With References to Canada', *Law Review* (2017), 134–136 (in Chinese).

49 Bai Jiayu, Li Jing, 'Research on the U.S. Arctic Policy', *Journal of Ocean University of China (Social Sciences)* (2009) 23–24 (in Chinese).

50 Shen Peng, 'A Study of U.S. Policy toward the Development of Polar Resources', *The Journal of International Studies* (2012) 112–113 (in Chinese).

51 Cheng Baozhi, 'New Development of Arctic Governance and European and U.S. Policy Practice', *Chinese Journal of European Studies* (2013) 50 (in Chinese); Ding Huang, Zhao Ningning, 'Analysis on Arctic Policy during Obama Administration', *Socialism Studies* (2013) 161 (in Chinese).

52 Yang Songlin, 'Trump Administration's Arctic Policy: Internal and External Environment and Development Trend', *Asia-Pacific Security and Maritime Affairs* (2018) 99–100 (in Chinese).

53 He Qisong, 'Climate Change and the EU's Arctic Strategy', *Chinese Journal of European Studies* (2010) 64–66.

rules to address Arctic affairs.[54] Specifically, Cheng Baozhi finds that the EU views the Arctic Council as the principal regional cooperation forum, but also tries to exert its influence in other international and regional organizations.[55] In addition, in the context of a Sino-EU strategic partnership, he believes that Arctic cooperation is a promising field between the EU and China.[56] Furthermore, learning from the EU's experience, China may participate in Arctic affairs in directions such as providing public goods (e.g. infrastructure), expanding the role of Chinese scientists, and bringing Arctic cooperation with the EU into the BRI agenda.[57]

Apart from major players, other Arctic States are on Chinese academia's radar. Zhao Ningning and Ou Kaifei describe Iceland's Arctic policy,[58] while Sun Kai pays attention to Finland's Arctic policy.[59] Norway's position has, however, been overlooked by Chinese scholars. This is certainly not because Norway is irrelevant or unimportant in Arctic governance. Rather, Norway is overlooked due to China's political tension with the country following Oslo's award of the Nobel Peace Prize to Chinese activist Liu Xiaobo. This resulted in a freeze of Sino-Norwegian diplomatic relations between 2010 and 2016.[60]

Chinese research on policies and strategies of other non-Arctic States with strong interests in the region keeps growing as well. Chen Hongbin's research shows that Japan, in its policy-making process is supportive of Arctic cooperation with China and South Korea.[61] According to Wang Jingchao, Japan actively participates in the law-making process relating to Arctic shipping routes so that the Japanese voice can be heard, and attaches importance to multilateral participation in Arctic affairs.[62] As revealed by Gong Keyu,

54 Xia Liping, 'On the Arctic Policy of European Union from the Perspective of Theory of Normative Power', *Social Sciences* (2014) 20–21 (in Chinese).
55 Cheng Baozhi, 'New Development of Arctic Governance and European and U.S. Policy Practice', *Chinese Journal of European Studies* (2013) 48 (in Chinese).
56 Cheng Baozhi, 'The European Union's Policy on the Arctic and the Possibilities of Its Cooperation with China', *Peace and Development* (2013) 59–61 (in Chinese).
57 Cheng Baozhi, 'The Practice of EU's Arctic Policy and Its Enlightenment on China', *Journal of Hubei University of Police* (2017) 91–92 (in Chinese).
58 Zhao Ningning, Ou Kaifei, 'Iceland and Arctic Governance: Strategic Considerations and Policy Practice', *Chinese Journal of European Studies* (2015) 117–121 (in Chinese).
59 Sun Kai, Wu Hao, 'Strategic Planning and Future Trends of Finland's Arctic Diplomacy', *International Forum* (2017) 21–22.
60 Statement of the Government of the People's Republic of China and the Government of the Kingdom of Norway on Normalization of Bilateral Relations, available at: https://www.regjeringen.no/en/aktuelt/normalization_china/id2524797/.
61 Chen Hongbin, 'Japan's Strategy of Participation in the Arctic', *Japanese Research* (2014) 6–7 (in Chinese).
62 Wang Jingchao, 'Research on Japanese Strategy of Developing Arctic Passages: Strategic Motives, Decision-making Mechanism, and Promotion Modes', *Forum of World Economics & Politics* (2017) 87–91 (in Chinese).

South Korea's Arctic policy serves its political and economic interests, which are "implemented through bilateral cooperation with Russia and Norway, and supplemented by multilateral cooperation".[63] In light of India's Arctic policy, as shown by Shi Hongyuan, India considers the Arctic as the common heritage of mankind and non-coastal States' interests should be respected.[64] India has been expanding scientific research in the Arctic, seeking Observer status in the Arctic Council, launching energy cooperation with Arctic States, and promoting Arctic diplomacy.[65]

In summary, Chinese scholars have expended much effort to introduce the underlying motivations and contents of the Arctic policies of major players in the region. Particular attention is paid to the formulation of the policy-making processes of these countries. Chinese scholars have deduced that Canada, the United States and Russia prefer Arctic stewardship rather than the internationalization of Arctic affairs. In contrast, small States such as Norway and Finland find multilateral cooperation more palatable. Based on these findings, it can be said that Chinese academia has played an important part in drafting China's official Arctic policy. For example, a number of scholars, such as Qian Jing and Zhu Xinguang,[66] recommend China publish its own Arctic policy that defines its role, clarifies its interests and determines the scope and fields of its participation in the Arctic. Moreover, Zhao Ningning and Zhou Fei suggest that China has to be innovative in order to establish its unique identity in the Arctic.[67] As can be seen in the Arctic White Paper, China declares itself as a near Arctic State with significant interest in the region.[68] This is a very interesting self-claimed identity, aiming to justify China's involvement in Arctic affairs as a country without coastline or territory in the region. Furthermore, Zhou Fei looks into French Arctic policy regarding how France develops Arctic ties, such as developing scientific research and education with Arctic States, or using sustainability as an opportunity to take part in Arctic affairs.[69] This was also taken into account in the Arctic White Paper, which provides that China's interests are to "understand, protect and use the Arctic".[70]

63 Gong Keyu, 'South Korea's Arctic Policy and Arctic Affairs', *Journal of North-east Asia Studies* (2014), 17 (in Chinese).
64 Shi Hongyuan, 'An Analysis on India's Arctic Policy', *South Asian Studies Quarterly* (2017) 46–47 (in Chinese).
65 Ibid, 48–50
66 Qian Jing, Zhu Xinguang, 'A Study on Iceland's Arctic Policy', International Forum (2015) 63 (in Chinese).
67 Zhao Ningning, Zhou Fei, 'The Evolution, Characteristic of UK's Arctic Policy and Its Implication for China', *International Forum* (2016) 21–22 (in Chinese).
68 See 'China's Arctic Policy' White Paper, note 6.
69 Zhou Fei, 'French Protection for Arctic Interests and Its Recommendations', *Wuhan University of Technology (Social Science Edition)* (2016) 51–53 (in Chinese).
70 See 'China's Arctic Policy' White Paper, note 6.

### 3.3 The Polar Silk Road

Figuring out "who owns the Arctic" helps to answer the question: "How best could China benefit from the Arctic?" The Chinese Government officially launched its Arctic version of the BRI – the PSR – in the Arctic White Paper in 2018. The PSR is a political rather than a legal concept with a focus on the Arctic. It is a vision for China to implement its Arctic policy, in order to build a so-called "shared community for mankind", which becomes the guiding principle of Chinese diplomacy in the so-called "New Era" (or Xi's Era).[71]

Since there are some suspicions from Arctic States regarding the real intentions or ambitions of Chinese activities,[72] Yang Jian suggests that China's Arctic policy needs coordination between an international mechanism and its own policy goals, and sufficiently takes the concerns of Arctic States, indigenous people and other stakeholders into account.[73] Yang Jian has also outlined China's Arctic interests, including environment, scientific research, security and legitimate rights in governance.[74] Common recommendations for China to participate in Arctic affairs include: first, China should respect sovereignty, sovereign rights and jurisdiction of the Arctic States.[75] Second, China should formulate specific policies in different fields, such as environmental protection, resources utilization, shipping and scientific research.[76] Third, in order to facilitate its participation in Arctic affairs, China should rely on existing international law in order to win respect from Arctic States. Zhang Cheng and Huang Deming advise that China could push forward "international cooperation through economic activities" in light of different circumstances of Arctic and non-Arctic States.[77] Ye Yanhua, Li Hanbin and Bai Jiayu write on Arctic cooperation among

71 Department of Treaty and Law, China Ministry of Foreign Affairs, *Selected Cases on Chinese Practice of International Law* (World Knowledge, 2018), pp. 7–22 (in Chinese).

72 Jia Guide, Shi Wuhong, 'On China's Participation in the Arctic Governance under New Circumstance', *Global Review* (2014), 26 (in Chinese).

73 Yang Jian, 'Arctic Shipping and China's Arctic Policy', *International Review* (2014) 137 (in Chinese).

74 Yang Jian, 'Strategic Thinking on the Development of China's Polar Cause', *Frontiers* (2017) 10–11 (in Chinese).

75 Jia Guide, Shi Wuhong, 'On China's Participation in the Arctic Governance under New Circumstance', *Global Review* (2014), 26 (in Chinese).

76 Tang Guoqiang, 'Arctic Issues and China's Policy', *International Studies* (2013), 15–25. Zhu Baolin, 'Analysis on China's Arctic Policy', *Wuhan University of Technology (Social Science Edition)* (2016), 38–39. Wang Chuanxing, 'China's Participation in the Arctic Affairs and the Formulation of Arctic Strategy', *Frontiers / Xueshu Qianyan* (2017) 39–41.

77 Zhang Cheng, Huang Deming, 'The Maintenance Route and Strategy Choice of China' s Arctic rights and Interests', *Journal of East China University of Science and Technology (Social Science Edition)* (2015) 80–83 (in Chinese).

Northeast Asian countries.[78] Pan Min and Xu Liling analyse potential Arctic cooperation between the United States and China.[79] Zhao Ningning looks into pathways of Arctic cooperation between China and Nordic countries.[80] Moreover, some legal scholars seek to make use of international law to legitimize China's participation in the Arctic. Wu Jun and Wu Leizhao explicitly point out that the international law of the sea endows China's rights and interests including freedom of navigation, scientific research, utilization of international sea bed area, exploitation of marine biological resources, investigation of marine incidents, and maritime rescue at sea in the Arctic.[81] China should therefore promote the application of UNCLOS in the Arctic, effectively take part in establishing legal system on the management of maritime activities, and reinforce scientific research under the Svalbard Treaty.[82]

Since the launch of the BRI and the PSR, it is noted that Chinese academics are also paying attention to linking the BRI with China's Arctic policy. Ding Huang and Zhu Baolin write that "community with a shared future for mankind" is possible to inspire the development of Arctic governance regimes.[83] China is obliged to develop this concept and take actions to build up an Arctic community with a shared future.[84] Nevertheless, they failed to draw a clear picture about what exactly a shared future would look like. Bai Jiayu argues that the PSR constitutes a basis for China to participate in Arctic affairs.[85] China's strategy in the Arctic should create a win-win situation by building a community with a shared future.[86] Encouraged by the progress of the BRI between 2013 and 2018,[87] several Chinese scholars are

78 Bai Jiayu, 'Research on the Feasibility of Cooperation about Arctic Affairs among China, Japan, and Republic of Korea', *Northeast Asian Forum* (2016) 112–123 (in Chinese); Ye Yanhua, 'International Cooperation for East Asian Countries to Participate in the Arctic Affairs', *Northeast Asian Forum* (2016) 92–103 (in Chinese); Li Hanbin, 'Research on Arctic Cooperation in Northeast Asia', *Northeast Asian Forum* (2018) 118–125 (in Chinese).

79 Pan Min, Xu Liling, 'Sino–US Arctic Cooperation: Institution, Fields and Methods', *Pacific Journal* (2016) 87–93 (in Chinese).

80 Zhao Ningning, 'The Motivation, Characteristic and Deepen Path of the Arctic Cooperation between China and Nordic Countries', *Journal of Boundary and Ocean Studies* (2017) 107–115 (in Chinese).

81 Wu Lun, Wu Leizhao, 'China's Rights and Interests in the Arctic Ocean', *Wuhan University Journal (Philosophy & Social Sciences)* (2014), 51–53 (in Chinese).

82 Ibid., 54–55.

83 Ding Huang, Zhu Baolin, 'Innovation of Arctic Governance Mechanism Based on the concept of "A Community with a Shared Future"', *Exploration and Free Views* (2016), 95–97.

84 Ibid., 98.

85 Bai Jiayu, 'The International Law Strategy for China's Participation in the Arctic Affairs', *Tribune of Political Science and Law* (2017) 143 (in Chinese).

86 Ibid.

87 Joint Communique of the Leaders Roundtable of the Belt and Road Forum for International Cooperation, 16 May 2017, available at: https://www.fmprc.gov.cn/mfa_eng/wjdt_665385/2649_665393/t1462012.shtml.

optimistic about China's cooperation with Arctic States, particularly Russia. Zheng Lei points out that the BRI can meet Russia's need for foreign investment in infrastructure construction on port, communication and rescue in the Arctic.[88] Xu Guangmiao recommends that cooperation between individual enterprises and local governments between two countries could be the first step for the implementation of the PSR, followed and supported by intergovernmental agreements.[89] Wang Zhimin and Chen Yuanhang propose that Russian Far East development plans could be effectively integrated with China's project of revitalizing Northeast Industrial Base, such as Heilong Jiang – China's northern most province bordering Siberia.[90] In addition, China, Russia and Kazakhstan can work together to construct an inland waterway connecting China's Irtysh River and the Arctic ocean, a new connectivity between China and Russian Arctic.[91] It is obvious that no other philosophy but pragmatism for reaping potential benefits is driving Chinese academia's research on the PSR.

## 4 Antarctica

In contrast to the Arctic, Chinese academics have paid much less attention to Antarctica. This is evidenced by the fact that only around 50 Antarctic papers were found in the CNKI, compared to more than 300 papers regarding the Arctic. Since 1958, Antarctica has been governed by the Antarctic Treaty and its related agreements, e.g. the Protocol on Environmental Protection to the Antarctic Treaty (the Madrid Protocol), the 1982 Convention on the Conservation of Antarctic Marine Living Resources (CAMLR Convention) – the Antarctic Treaty System (ATS). China has no territorial claim in Antarctica. China ratified the Antarctic Treaty in 1983, and became a consultative party in 1985 following the establishment of the Great Wall Station. China is also supportive of the Madrid Protocol as well as the CAMLR Convention. Chinese academic discussions can be seen as evolving in three stages over the past decade: (1) What is the ATS? (2) What are incumbents' Antarctic laws and policies? (3) What role could China play? These will be discussed in the following subsections.

88 Zheng Lei, 'Northern Sea Route: The Relationship between Coastal State's Jurisdiction and Freedom of Navigation', *International Forum* (2016) 10–11 (in Chinese).

89 Xu Guangmiao, 'An Analysis on the Prospect of Integrating "Northern Sea Route" Development Project into the Construction of The Belt and Road', *Journal of Boundary and Ocean Studies* (2018), 90–94 (in Chinese).

90 Wang Zhimin, Chen Yuanhang, 'China and Russia's Collaboration in Constructing the Supraglacial Silk Road: Opportunities and Challenges', *Northeast Asia Forum* (2018), 29 (in Chinese).

91 Ibid, 30.

### 4.1 The Antarctic Treaty System

For a long time, Antarctic law and policy research attracted little interest from Chinese academics. In 2009, the same year China established its third Antarctic research station (Kun Lun Station) at Dome A – the highest point of the Antarctic ice sheet[92] – Guo Peiqing writes about Antarctic exploration history and raises the concern that there is a "cold war" among great powers in the Antarctic competing for resources.[93] Guo describes the Antarctic Treaty as an exclusive club for consultative parties – countries with substantial research activities in the continent, which is a "collective hegemony" against developing countries.[94] In the meantime, because China is a consultative party of the Antarctic Treaty, Guo believes the ATS serves China's interests well and should be maintained.[95] Again in 2009, Hu Dekun and Tang Jingyao note that most Chinese Antarctic research focused on the natural sciences, while a shift on social sciences had just began. Hu and Tang review colonial history and the adoption of the Antarctic Treaty in the climax of US-Soviet Cold War.[96] Hu and Tang highly regard the Antarctic Treaty as an innovative regime that successfully governs Antarctica.[97] They call on China to invest more in studies on the regime of Antarctic governance, and to pursue further involvement in Antarctic affairs.[98] Chen Yugang introduces the theory of critical geopolitics to draw a picture about the evolution of geopolitical situations in Antarctica, and concludes that Antarctic geopolitics is motivated by territorial claims, scientific research and resources and environmentalism.[99] By examining the power structure in the development of the Antarctic Treaty Regime, Wang Wanlu provides a comprehensive analysis of the evolution of the regime. Wang concludes that climate change, tourism and bioprospecting are key governance issues in the future.[100] Shi Weihua notes that members of the ATS enjoy equal rights, evidenced by the requirement of

92 Australian Antarctic Division, 'New Antarctic Stations', *Australian Antarctic Magazine* (2009) 16, available at: http://www.antarctica.gov.au/magazine/2006-2010/issue-16-2009/international-polar-year/new-antarctic-stations.
93 Guo Peiqing, 'Antarctic Cold War, Resources Competition among Great Powers', *Xinwen Tiandi / News Universe* (2009) 2, 29–31 (in Chinese).
94 Ibid.
95 Ibid.
96 Hu Dekun, Tang Jingyao, 'Territorial Disputes in Antarctica and the Adoption of the Antarctic Treaty', *Wuhan University Journal (Humanity Sciences)* (2010) 63 (1), 64–69 (in Chinese)
97 Ibid.
98 Ibid.
99 Chen Yugang, Zhou Chao and Qin Qian, 'Critical Geopolitics and the Development of Antarctic Geopolitics', *World Economics and Politics* (2012) 10, 116–131 (in Chinese).
100 Wang Wanlu, 'Connotations, Driving Forces and Future Prospect of the Antarctic Governance Regime', *Chinese Journal of Polar Research* (2019) 31 (2) 198–208 (in Chinese).

a consensus based decision-making process, but countries are not equally powerful in shaping the development of the ATS.[101] Shi further raises the fact that the ATS is facing significant challenges posed by illegal, unreported and unregulated (IUU) fishing, a difficult balance between use and protection, as well as the application of the UNCLOS continental shelf regime to the Southern Ocean.[102] The paper written by Yang Ying is, so far, the only one that specifically discusses the interaction between UNCLOS and the ATS.[103] Yang notices that France, Australia, New Zealand, the United Kingdom, Norway and Argentina have made submissions to the United Nations Commission on the Limits of the Continental Shelf (CLCS), while Chile has submitted preliminary information. She believes that CLCS submissions by claimant States pose a substantial challenge to the ATS.[104] "It is unrealistic to rely on the ATS to solve future conflicts in Antarctica", says Yang Ying.[105] On the other hand, Yang urges China to make full use of the ATS and UNCLOS to maximise its interests in the region.[106]

In addition, Chinese scholars (Wang Hui[107] and Que Zhanwen[108]) kept an eye on Annex VI: Liability Arising from Environmental Emergencies of the Madrid Protocol. China has not yet approved Annex VI, after its adoption by the 28th ATCM in Stockholm in 2005. Nevertheless, neither Wang nor Que have made any recommendation in regard to where China should stand on this issue. Furthermore, Peng discusses the implementation of the ATS in China's domestic legal system.[109] So far, China has adopted a number of ministerial rules to regulate Chinese citizens' activities in Antarctica, including the 2018 Rules for Data Management of Polar Expeditions,[110] the 2018 Rules for Environmental Protection and Antarctic

101 Shi Weihua, 'An Analysis of Current Antarctic Governance Regime', *Chinese Journal of Polar Research* (2013) 25 (1), 90–95 (in Chinese).
102 Ibid.
103 Yang Ying, 'The Impact of the United Nations Convention on the Law of the Sea on Antarctic Governance', *Lilun Yuekan / Theory Monthly* (2015) (6), 174–178 (in Chinese). Xue Guifang also touched the issue in her paper: Xue Guifang, 'China's Strategy to Expand its Maritime Rights in the Polar Regions', *Frontiers / Xueshu Qianyan* (2017) 6, 50–55 (in Chinese).
104 Ibid.
105 Ibid.
106 Ibid.
107 Wang Hui, 'Liability Arising from Environmental Emergencies in Antarctica', *Journal of Nanjing University of Finance and Economics* (2009) 3, 91–94 (in Chinese).
108 Que Zhanwen, 'Liability Arising from Environmental Emergencies in Antarctica', *Jiangxi Social Sciences* (2011) 3, 170–174 (in Chinese).
109 Peng Peng, 'Implementation of the Antarctic Treaty System in China', *Ocean Development and Management* (2016) 2, 76–80 (in Chinese).
110 State Oceanic Administration of P. R. China, 2018. Rules for Data Management of Polar Expeditions, available at: http://f.mnr.gov.cn/201807/t20180709_2073215.html (in Chinese).

Activities,[111] the 2018 Rules for Visiting Chinese Antarctic Stations[112] and the 2017 Rules for Environmental Impact Assessment of Scientific Activities in Antarctica.[113] However, there are regulatory gaps, especially regarding the rapid growth of Chinese Antarctic tourism, which will be discussed later in the chapter.

### *4.2 Incumbents' law and policy*

Among more than 50 papers, almost half are devoted to the analysis of Antarctic law and policy of incumbents – seven claimant states and other major players. Chinese academics paid high attention to the United States – the most powerful state involved in Antarctic related affairs. Shen Peng writes that although the Antarctic Treaty is a successful initiative by the United States, the ATS lacks detailed management regimes for future resources development.[114] Shen looks into US domestic policies on Antarctic resources for inspiration. Chen Li published a detailed paper regarding Antarctic law and policy of the United States in 2013.[115] "As the designer and leader of the ATS, The United States plays a pivotal role for the future development of Antarctica", writes Chen.[116] China could certainly learn from the United States, on how to exert influence as a key player.[117] This is echoed by Pan Min in her analysis of US interests in Antarctica in terms of its geopolitics, science, environment and economy.[118] Further, Liu Han and Zhang Xia take a close look at how Antarctic scientific research is funded in the United States.[119] All of these efforts aim to guide China's Antarctic policy and can be seen as reflected in Chinese diplomacy in recent years. For example, in 2013, China submitted a proposal to establish an Antarctic Specially Managed

111 State Oceanic Administration of P. R. China, 2018. Rules for Environmental Protection and Antarctic Activities, available at: http://f.mnr.gov.cn/201807/t20180709_2074145.html (in Chinese).
112 State Oceanic Administration of P. R. China, 2018. Rules for Visiting Chinese Antarctic Stations, available at: http://f.mnr.gov.cn/201807/t20180709_2073614.html (in Chinese).
113 State Oceanic Administration of P. R. China, 2017. Rules for Environmental Impact Assessment of Scientific Activities in Antarctica, available at: http://f.mnr.gov.cn/201807/t20180709_2074145.html (in Chinese).
114 Shen Peng, 'A Study of U.S. Policy toward the Development of Polar Resources', *Journal of International Studies* (2012) 1, 97–116 (in Chinese).
115 Chen Li, 'America's Antarctic Policy and Law', *American Studies* (2013) 1, 65–86 (in Chinese).
116 Ibid, 65.
117 Ibid.
118 Pan Min, 'On the Antarctic Strategy and Policy Orientation of the US', *Frontiers / Xueshu Qianyan* (2017) 10, 62–71 (in Chinese).
119 Liu Han, Zhang Xia, 'Statistical Analysis of the United States' Antarctic Scientific Research Investment', *Chinese Journal of Polar Research* (2017) (29) 2, 245–255 (in Chinese).

Area (ASMA) around the Chinese Kunlun Station at Dome A, based on Article 4, Annex V of the Madrid Protocol.[120] The proposed ASMA covers an area of approximately 19,764 square kilometres.[121] China has modelled its proposal on American practice, which set up ASMA 5 around the Amundsen-Scott South Pole Station in 2007.[122] However, so far, the proposal has made little progress in gaining support of other consultative parties of the Antarctic Treaty.

In addition to the policy measures taken by the United States, Chinese academics are also considering the practice of Australia, Argentina,[123] Chile,[124] France,[125] New Zealand,[126] Norway,[127] the United Kingdom,[128] South Korea,[129] Germany,[130] Japan[131] and Malaysia[132] in Antarctic

120 WP008, Proposal for a new Antarctic Specially Managed Area at Chinese Antarctic Kunlun Station, Dome A, submitted by China, ATCM XXXVI / CEP XVI. See also Nengye Liu, 'The Height of China's Ambition in Antarctica', *The Interpreter*, available at: https://www.lowyinstitute.org/the-interpreter/heights-china-s-ambition-antarctica.

121 Ibid.

122 Annex A: ASMA No 5 – Amundsen-Scott South Pole Station, South Pole, Measure 2 (2007): Antarctic Specially Managed Areas: Designations and Management Plans, Final Report of the Thirtieth Antarctic Treaty Consultative Meeting, New Delhi, India, 30 April – 11 May 2007, 59–66.

123 Liu Ming, 'Argentina's Antarctic Policy', *Journal of Latin American Studies* (2015) 37 (1) 41–47 (in Chinese); Liu Ming, 'The Relationship between Britain and Argentina in the Antarctic Issues (1942–1961)', *Journal of Foreign Studies / Waiguo Wenti Yanjiu* (2014) 1, 32–39 (in Chinese); Mei Chuncai, Guo Peiqing, 'Antarctica: New Area for China-Argentina Diplomatic Relations', *World Affairs* (2017) 8, 60–62 (in Chinese).

124 Liu Ming, 'Chile's Antarctic Policy (1940–1982)', *Journal of Southwest University of Science and Technology* (2013) 30 (2), 6–14 (in Chinese).

125 Zhou Fei, 'France's Participation in Antarctic Affairs and Lessons for China', *Etudes Francaises* (2015) 3, 15–21 (in Chinese).

126 He Liu, 'The History and Current Status of New Zealand's Antarctic Sovereignty', *Theory Monthly / Lilun Yuekan* (2015) 5, 173–179 (in Chinese).

127 Ningning Zhao, 'Norway's Antarctic Affairs Participation: Interest Concerns and Policy Selection', *Journal of Boundary and Ocean Studies* (2018) 3 (4), 98–109 (in Chinese).

128 Bao Wenhan, 'The United Kingdom's Participation in Antarctic Affairs: Progress, Objectives and Strategy', *Forum of World Economics and Politics* (2016) 2, 70–84 (in Chinese).

129 Wu Lun, 'South Korea National Antarctic Activities: Causes, Measures and Tactics', *Chinese Journal of Polar Research* (2016) 28 (3), 381–389 (in Chinese).

130 Sun Zhumei, Hua Weina, 'An Overview of Germany's Antarctic Research – based on Web of Science Data', *Journal of Modern Information* (2015) 35 (7), 98–104 (in Chinese).

131 Wang Haibin, 'Japan's Whaling Diplomacy', *Xiandai Guoji Guanxi / Contemporary International Relations* (2011) 10, 30–35 (in Chinese).

132 Guo Peiqing, Shi Weihua, 'The Evolution of Malaysia's Antarctic Policy (1982–2008)', *Journal of Ocean University of China (Social Sciences)* (2009) 3, 14–17 (in Chinese).

governance. In particular, Chinese scholars have closely examined Australian law and policy. Wu Yilin introduces Australia's Antarctic Science Strategic Plan 2011–12 to 2020–21,[133] and notes that Australia's investment in Antarctica is driven by its determination to maintain its leadership in the ATS.[134] Wu Ningbo and Chen Li provide an overview of Australia's Antarctic interests and policies.[135] They believe that it is in China's interest to have a clear and in-depth understanding of Australia's Antarctic policy-making process, since Australia is China's closest partner in Antarctic cooperation.[136] Moreover, China should maintain the status quo of the ATS – neither denying nor supporting territorial claims. The bifocalism of the Antarctic Treaty serves China well in Antarctica, as three Chinese stations are located in the Australian Antarctic Territory (AAT).[137] Wu Ningbo further wrote a paper with a focus on Australia's Antarctic legislation.[138] He notes that Australia has established a comprehensive legal framework to enhance its jurisdiction in Antarctica. However, with increasing foreign governmental and commercial activities in the AAT, it is "a dilemma for Australia to maintain a delicate balance between its commitment under the ATS and territorial claims in Antarctica."[139] In March 2019, China's National People's Congress (NPS) decided to draft China's domestic Antarctic Law as part of the 13th NPC Standing Committee Legislative Plan (2018–2023).[140] The PRC's Antarctic Law is currently (at the time of writing) in the drafting process of the NPC Environmental Protection and Resources Conservation Committee and is categorized as "laws for which the conditions are relatively mature and which are planned to be submitted for deliberation during the term".[141] Wu suggests that lessons could be learnt from Australia's Antarctic legislation.[142]

133 Australian Government, Department of Sustainability, Environment, Water, Population and Communities, Australian Antarctic Division, Australian Antarctic Science Strategic Plan 2011–12 to 2020–21, available at: http://www.antarctica.gov.au/__data/assets/pdf_file/0019/27307/AASSP_final-published-version_Apr-2011.pdf.
134 Wu Yilin (Consulate General of the PRC in Sydney), 'Analysis of Australian Antarctic Science Strategy and Research Theme', *Journal of Ocean University of China (Social Sciences)* (2012) 1, 1–4 (in Chinese).
135 Wu Ningbo, Chen Li, 'Australian Antarctic Interests: Actual Challenge and Policy Response', *Chinese Journal of Polar Research* (2016) 28 (1), 123–132 (in Chinese).
136 Ibid, 130.
137 Ibid.
138 Wu Ningbo, 'Australian Antarctic Legislations and Its Dilemma', *Journal of Boundary and Ocean Studies* (2017) 2 (2) 116–127 (in Chinese).
139 Ibid, 124.
140 National People's Congress hold Press Conference on Legislative Work, State Council of P.R.C (10 March 2019), available at: http://www.gov.cn/xinwen/2019-03/10/content_5372482.htm (in Chinese).
141 13th NPC Standing Committee Legislative Plan, Xinhua (8 September 2018), available at: http://www.xinhuanet.com/politics/2018-09/08/c_1123397570.htm (in Chinese).
142 Wu, note 135, 125–126.

With the efforts of various scholars, some directly funded by the China Arctic and Antarctic Administration (e.g. Polar Countries' Policy Studies Project, CHINARE2014–04–05–05), it is fair to say that the Chinese Government now has a good understanding of the laws and policies of most key members of the ATS.[143] These papers are largely descriptive, but informative, which helps China to form its own policy and strategy on Antarctic affairs.

### 4.3 China's role

China hasn't adopted any official Antarctic policy yet. There is no urgency either, given China is a supporter of the ATS. Nevertheless, because China has been rapidly expanding its presence in the Antarctic over the past decade, there are internal[144] and external[145] calls for China to clarify its Antarctic interests and strategies. In May 2017, when China for the first time hosted an ATCM (40th ATCM in Beijing), the Chinese Government published the White Paper "China's Antarctic Activities" (Antarctic White Paper).[146] This is not an official policy document, rather it is a report that summarizes Chinese activities in Antarctica so far. At the end of the Antarctic White Paper, the Chinese Government states that "China is willing to join the rest of the international community in understanding, protecting and using Antarctica, in facilitation of establishing a more equitable and rational international Antarctic order, and forging the Antarctic 'community of human destiny'".[147] This reflects a vague vision of China for the future governance of Antarctica.

What are China's Antarctic interests? Chen Yugang and Wang Wanlu believe that China has political, security, scientific and economic interests in the Antarctic, and the ATS in general serves China's interests well.[148] Politically, China should maintain the stability of the ATS and aim to become an influential member of the ATS.[149] Economically, China could benefit from

143 Though we haven't found papers on Antarctic law and policy of Japan and Russia yet.

144 Wang Wanlu points out that China is the only great power that does not have a clear Antarctic strategy and interests. Wang Wanlu, 'An Analysis of China's Antarctic Strategic Interests', *World Affairs* (2015) 18, 23. See also Chen, note 115 and Pan, note 118.

145 Nengye Liu, 'Demystifying China in Antarctica', *The Diplomat*, 9 June 2017; Nengye Liu, 'What does China's Fifth Research Station Mean for Antarctic Governance?' *The Diplomat*, 28 June 2018; Nengye Liu, 'What are China's Intentions in Antarctica?' *The Diplomat*, 14 June 2019.

146 State Oceanic Administration of P. R. China, 2017. White Paper 'China's Antarctic Activities'.

147 Ibid.

148 Chen Yugang, Wang Wanlu, 'An Analysis of China's Antarctic Interests and Rights', *Jilin University Journal (Social Sciences)* (2016) 56 (4) 95–105 (in Chinese).

149 Ibid.

Antarctica's abundant resources,[150] such as krill fisheries.[151] Furthermore, demilitarisation in Antarctica would enhance China's space security, especially regarding the operation of the Chinese satellite system – Beidou.[152]

What strategy could China take in Antarctic governance? Zheng Yingqing echoes Guo Peiqing's view in 2009 that the ATS is still an exclusive "club", that a few rich countries are holding decision-making powers, while most developing countries and emerging countries (e.g. China) face difficulty in exerting a bigger influence.[153] Zheng also looks into potential pathways to improve Chinese diplomacy in the ATS.[154] In Antarctica, "science and power are two sides of the same coin", says Zheng.[155] At the end of the day, power is the most important instrument in Antarctic diplomacy.[156] Specifically, Ruan Jianping provides four policy suggestions for China's participation in Antarctic affairs: (1) maintaining the stability of the ATS, while consolidating and expanding substantial presence; (2) investing in Antarctic research; (3) enacting domestic Antarctic law to regulate Chinese activities; and (4) coordinating China's global and Antarctic strategy.[157] In late 2017, China for the first time sent a commercial flight to the South Pole, carrying 22 tourists.[158] Based on his field trip, Wang Wen and Yao Le argue for coordination of China's Antarctic strategy with its global strategy, especially under President Xi's idea of establishing a "Shared Community of Mankind" in Antarctica.[159] Wang and Yao suggest that China must: (1) be vocal against any territorial

150 Because China ratified the Madrid Protocol, which bans mining, few papers are interested in this issue. However, it is noted that Wu Yilin (Chinese Embassy in New Zealand) views the mining ban as temporary, rather than indefinite. He interprets the protection of Antarctica is for reasonable and sustainable use of its resources; and urges China should be prepared for any possible future development. Wu Yilin, 'The Evolution of the Antarctic Treaty System and Mining Issues', *Journal of Ocean University of China (Social Sciences Edition)* (2009) 5, 11–13 (in Chinese).

151 Chen and Wang, note 148.

152 Ibid.

153 Zheng Yingqing, 'The Pristine Wilderness, The Value of the Antarctic and Challenges for Governance', *World Affairs* (2017) 13, 52–53 (in Chinese).

154 Zheng Yingqing, 'Some Thoughts about Having a Say on Antarctica', *Journal of International Relations* (2014) 62–72 (in Chinese).

155 Ibid, 66.

156 Ibid, 72.

157 Ruan Jianping, 'The Process of Antarctic Politics. Its Challenges and China's Strategy for Participation: From Geopolitical Competition to Global Governance', *Pacific Journal* (2016) 24 (12), 21–30 (in Chinese).

158 Andreas Illmer, 'China hails "first Antarctica flight" for its tourists', BBC News (18 December 2017), available at: https://www.bbc.com/news/world-asia-china-42388788#.

159 Wang Wen, Yao Le, 'China's Development and Participation of Antarctica Governance under the Guidance of New Idea of Global Governance – Based on the Field Study', *Journal of Renmin University of China* (2018) 3, 123–134 (in Chinese).

claim in Antarctica and could consider a call for an Antarctic condominium covering the continent, continental shelf and adjacent waters; (2) adopt legislation to regulate Chinese tourism; (3) invest in the Antarctic infrastructure to safeguard scientific and tourism activities; (4) provide "public goods" in Antarctic governance, such as the use of the Beidou Satellite system for search and rescue; and (5) establish a National Antarctic Commission to coordinate Chinese Antarctic affairs.[160]

As already noted, tourism is an issue that has drawn a lot of attention from Chinese academics.[161] According to the International Association of Antarctica Tour Operators (IAATO), in the 2018/19 Antarctic season, 56,168 visitors travelled to Antarctica with IAATO Operators, representing an increase of 8.6 percent compared to the 2017/18 season.[162] China is now the second largest source of Antarctic tourists in the world, after the United States (33 percent in 2017/18).[163] However, it is rare to see detailed proposals from academics regarding how exactly the Chinese Government could regulate Antarctic tourism. Chen Danhong urges the adoption of a domestic management system of Antarctic tourism, including requirements of certification, environmental impact assessment, pre-departure training, monitoring and reporting obligations. Further, Chen suggests that the Chinese Government should leave the market to develop Antarctic tourism and only play a guiding and supervisory role.[164]

Apart from tourism, the most salient issue among Chinese academics is perhaps the negotiations on the establishment of marine protected areas (MPAs) in the Southern Ocean.[165] China joined the CCAMLR in 2007. At the beginning, China quietly followed discussions regarding the Southern Ocean MPAs in CCAMLR meetings. China expressed no opposition against the UK-proposed South Orkney MPA.[166] However, China began expressing concerns on the United States/New Zealand joint MPA proposal in the Ross

160 Ibid, 132–133.

161 See also, Tang Rong et. al., 'Development of Polar Tourism', *Ocean Development and Management* (2018) 6, 26–29 (in Chinese).

162 IP139, Report of the International Association of Antarctica Tour Operators 2018–19, XLII Antarctic Treaty Consultative Meeting, Prague, Czech Republic, 2019.

163 IP71, IAATO Overview of Antarctic Tourism: 2017–18 Season and Preliminary Estimates for 2018–2019 Season, XLI Antarctic Treaty Consultative Meeting, Buenos Aires, Argentina, 2018.

164 Chen Danhong (Deputy Director of China Arctic and Antarctic Administration), 'Study on the Development of Antarctic Tourism and the Countermeasures China Should Take', *Chinese Journal of Polar Research* (2012) 24 (1)70–76 (in Chinese).

165 For an overview, see Nengye Liu, Cassandra Brooks, 'China's changing position towards Marine Protected Areas in the Southern Ocean: implications for future Antarctic governance', *Marine Policy* (2018) 94, 189–195.

166 CCAMLR, 'Conservation Measure 91–03. Protection of the South Orkney Islands southern shelf', 2009.

Sea Region in 2012. Although the Chinese delegation changed position and became supportive of the Ross Sea Region MPA in 2016, it remains highly sceptical over three other MPA proposals to CCAMLR, proposed by the EU/Australia (East Antarctica), the EU (Weddell Sea) and Chile/Argentina (Western Antarctic Peninsula).

The issues of Southern Ocean MPAs were first raised by Tang Jianye[167] in Chinese academia in 2010.[168] While the Chinese delegation was having intense debates with other members in CCAMLR annual meetings, domestic discussions were going on as well. Tang Jianye further introduced the Chinese practice in the 2011 CCAMLR annual meeting.[169] Tang marks 2011 as a milestone for China's engagement with CCAMLR. Before 2011, China focused on delisting four Chinese-flagged vessels that were on CCAMLR's non-contracting party IUU list.[170] China was supportive of the adoption of Conservation Measure 91–04 in the 2011 meeting,[171] which is an Australian proposal that provides a legal basis for the establishment of MPAs in the Southern Ocean. Nevertheless, this was the beginning of China expressing concerns on the further establishment of MPAs. Tang notes that China raised the issue that conservation of marine living resources must take into account "Rational Use".[172] Further, the whole CCAMLR Area is already equivalent to an International Union for Conservation of Nature Category IV MPA.[173] Gui Jing generally discusses the pros and cons of high seas MPAs from a national perspective.[174] Gui thinks that high seas MPAs are a positive development for the protection of the marine environment.[175] At the other end of the scale, high seas MPAs might limit developing countries'[176] activities in the

167 As a law academic, Tang has been a legal adviser for the Chinese delegation to the CCAMLR Annual Meeting since 2010.

168 Tang Jianye, Shi Guihua, 'Management of Antarctic Krill and Its Implications for China's Distant Water Fisheries', *Resources Science* (2010) 32 (1), 11–18 (in Chinese).

169 Tang Jianye, 'China in the 30th Annual Meeting of the Commission for the Conservation of Antarctic Marine Living Resources', *Fishery Information & Strategy* (2012) 27 (3) 194–202 (in Chinese).

170 See also, Tang Jianye, 'China's Engagement in the Establishment of Marine Protected Areas in the Southern Ocean: From Reactive to Active', *Marine Policy* (2017) 75, 68–74.

171 CCAMLR, 'Conservation Measure 91–04 General framework for the establishment of CCAMLR Marine Protected Areas' 2011.

172 As reflected in para. 7, Preamble, as well as paras 1 and 2, Conservation Measure 91–04. Tang, note 169, 200

173 As reflected in para. 10, Preamble, Conservation Measure 91–04. Tang, note 169, 200.

174 Gui Jing, 'A Study of the Status and Trends of Protected Areas in the High Seas in Different Dimensions', *Pacific Journal* (2015) 23 (5), 1–8 (in Chinese).

175 Ibid.

176 In the context of Chinese academia, it goes without saying that China is a developing country in the world.

high seas, such as distant water fishing, deep seabed mining and marine scientific research.[177] Chen Li reviews the international legal basis for the establishment of Southern Ocean MPAs and questions whether: (1) the international legal basis is sufficient; (2) it is necessary; and (3) it is feasible to achieve its objectives.[178] Chen suggests that China should focus on the negotiations regarding how to best manage such kinds of MPAs, rather than challenging its legality.[179] Chen even thinks that China could make its own MPA proposal and submit it to the CCAMLR.[180] This is echoed by He Zhipeng, who believes a Chinese MPA proposal would enhance China's key interests as a major power in the ATS.[181] Tang Jianye, on the other hand, is suspicious of the legal basis and scientific evidence of those MPA proposals submitted to the CCAMLR.[182]

## 5 Concluding remarks

What will the future of the Polar Regions look like with a rising China? This chapter sheds light on this question by providing a comprehensive review of Chinese academic publications on Polar governance, previously untouched in English language literature.

In remote Polar Regions where China has no territorial claim, China, as a late comer, finds that existing governance regimes generally suit China's interests well. This is why China was keen to join the Arctic Council as an Observer. Moreover, China was particularly satisfied to be invited as an equal party to negotiate the CAE Agreement 2018 with Arctic states. Furthermore, contrary to some alarmist views that China has a secret plan to militarise Antarctica and overturn the ATS in the long run, Chinese academics strongly support the stability of the ATS, which would give China good access to conduct scientific research in Antarctica.

Nevertheless, Chinese diplomacy (as, presumably, is the case with the diplomacy of other states) always aims to serve its own interests at home and abroad. Shifting from "Five Principles of Co-Existence" to a "Shared

177 Gui, note 174.

178 Chen Li, 'Study on the International Legal Basis of Antarctic Marine Protected Area', *Fudan Journal (Social Sciences)* (2016) 2, 152–164 (in Chinese).

179 Ibid, 164.

180 Ibid, 164.

181 He Zhipeng, Mi Chenxi, 'China's Position on the Establishment of Antarctic MPAs', *Hebei Legal Science* (2018) 36 (7) 25–43 (in Chinese).

182 Tang Jianye, 'The Practice of Establishing Marine Protected Areas in the Southern Ocean and Related Legal and Political Debates', *Chinese Journal of Polar Research* (2016) 28 (3), 370–380 (in Chinese). Tang is in line with government views, see Yang Lei, Han Zixuan, Chen Danhong, Long Wei, Fang Lijun and Li Chunlei, 'Analysis on the Problems with the "General Framework for the Establishment of CCAMLR Marine Protected Areas"', *Chinese Journal of Polar Research* (2014) 26 (4) 522–534 (in Chinese).

Community of Mankind", China under President Xi is hoping to achieve an equally influential role as western developed countries in international decision-making processes. There are issues on which China has been, or will be, vocal in the international and regional arenas regarding Polar governance. For example, even if political relations between China and Russia have been close in recent years, Chinese academics are not necessarily happy about the Russian position that the Northern Sea Route is internal waters completely under Russian jurisdiction. In the Antarctic and Southern Ocean, Chinese scholars are highly alert about Antarctic claimants' submissions to the CLCS regarding the outer limits of Antarctic continental shelf. Needless to say, in order to secure potential krill fisheries opportunities for Chinese distant water fishing, China has been suspicious of, and vocally against, proposals to establish Southern Ocean MPAs.

It is clear that pragmatism has been driving China's participation in Polar affairs, and will continue to play a guiding role in China's strategy to shape Polar governance regimes in the future. It is predictable that a confident China will try its best to reflect national interests in any future development of international Polar Law.

## Acknowledgements

The authors would like to thank Dr Michelle Lim and Dr Alan Hemmings for their constructive comments on earlier drafts. This chapter also received excellent assistance from Cecilia Wang, through Adelaide Law School's Research Assistance Program.

# Part IV

# The environment

Chapter 9

# Climate change and the role of indigenous peoples in preserving nature and biodiversity with special emphasis on the Arctic

*Agnieszka Szpak*[1]

## 1 Introduction

There are about 370 million indigenous peoples in the world, which constitute about 5 percent of the world's population. They live in more than 70 countries and cover more than 24 percent of the Earth's surface. Of the territories with a high biodiversity level, 80 percent are indigenous territories.[2] Simply, indigenous territories are places where biodiversity is best preserved.[3] Some indigenous communities live in very 'sensitive areas of the world, where, as in the Arctic and the Nordic region, for example, the flora and fauna are extremely susceptible to irretrievable damage'.[4] For thousands of years, indigenous peoples have successfully managed their water/marine and land species. Indigenous peoples have built rich cultural and social systems based on their spiritual and close relationship with nature. As a rule, for thousands of years they have developed mechanisms of using natural resources in ways that guaranteed their sustainable use without undermining the needs of future generations. Indigenous peoples have contributed to the preservation of nature with their traditional knowledge and indigenous practices which have

1 Faculty of Political Science and Security Studies, Nicolaus Copernicus University, Poland, aszpak@umk.pl.

2 D. J. Nakashima et al. (eds), *Weathering Uncertainty Traditional Knowledge for Climate Change Assessment and Adaptation*, UNESCO, 2012, 7; R. L. Adamson, 'Indigenous Stewardship Preserves Biodiversity at Less Cost', 2007, available online at http://www.firstpeoples.org; 'Delivering on Paris Promise. Combating Climate Change While Protecting Rights', 2017, 6, available online at https://www.deliveringonparis.com/.

3 See also: 'Statement of Ms. Victoria Tauli-Corpuz, Special Rapporteur on the Rights of Indigenous Peoples, at the 71st session of the General Assembly', 17 October 2016, available online at http://www.ohchr.org/EN/NewsEvents/Pages/DisplayNews.aspx?NewsID=20748&LangID=E; Report to the UN General Assembly, *Conservation and indigenous peoples' rights* (29 July 2016), para. 15, available online at http://unsr.vtaulicorpuz.org/site/index.php/documents/annual-reports/149-report-ga-2016.

4 L. Watters, 'Indigenous Peoples and the Environment: Convergence from a Nordic Perspective', *Journal of Environmental Law*, 20, 2001–2001, 239.

been cultivated and developed through the ages and transmitted from generation to generation.[5] Hence, indigenous peoples are often referred to as aboriginal stewards of the environment who take care of ancestral lands for future generations. This sometimes places on them unrealistic expectations but certainly their sustainable way of using the resources contributes to the preservation of the environment.[6] They differ from the rest of the society and enjoy only limited ability to participate in decision-making processes and are also marginalized in development processes. It is also worth emphasizing that indigenous peoples have had many years of experience in self-government and they are also fully aware of their potential and ages-long experience in the mitigation and adaptation efforts in the context of climate change.[7]

Examples of indigenous peoples who undertake activities aimed at protection of their lands and the environment include peoples of the far North – the Inuit – who are involved in the protection of the Arctic against the corporations exploiting gas and oil and in this way endangering the ecological balance of the region, or the Sámi from northern Scandinavia who are involved in the protection of taiga, the latter being the place of winter pastures for reindeer which are a key element of the Sámi economy and culture. They also fight against the construction of river dams in Sweden (the most famous, although a lost fight, is the Alta river dam in Norway[8]).[9] Such constructions destroy traditional reindeer routes as well as impede salmon's migration to their breeding grounds. Generally, hydroelectric projects flooded indigenous lands and destroyed biodiversity. This is paradoxical as it clearly shows that climate change mitigation efforts such as hydroelectric projects actually compound the plight of indigenous peoples.[10]

After some introductory remarks, section 2 of the chapter introduces the larger picture of the threats that climate change causes – globally and to indigenous peoples in particular. The special emphasis on the Arctic is

5 J. Woodman, 'Conservation and the rights of tribal people must go hand in hand', *The Guardian*, available online at https://www.theguardian.com/environment/2015/apr/23/conservation-and-the-rights-of-tribal-people-must-go-hand-in-hand.

6 F. Berkes, *Sacred Ecology*, London, Routledge, 2012, 19; *Guidelines for Considering Traditional Knowledges in Climate Change Initiatives*, 2014, 247, available online at https://climatetkw.wordpress.com/.

7 See also the Kari-Oca 2 Declaration: Indigenous Peoples Global Conference on Rio +20 and Mother Earth, 2002, available online at https://www.culturalsurvival.org/news/kari-oca-2-declaration-indigenous-peoples-global-conference-rio20-and-mother-earth. See also the International Indigenous Peoples Forum on Climate Change established in 2008: http://www.iipfcc.org/.

8 L. Watters, note 4 at 279–282.

9 'Delivering on Paris Promise. Combating Climate Change While Protecting Rights', note 2 at 2.

10 R. S. Abate, E. A. Kronk, 'Commonality Among Unique Indigenous Communities: An Introduction to Climate Change and Its Impacts on Indigenous Peoples', *Tulane Environmental Law Review*, 26 (1), 2013, 7.

motivated by the fact that climate change is particularly intensely experienced there as well as by its global consequences. In this section the role of indigenous peoples in the preservation of the environment and biodiversity in the context of climate change is examined. Some solutions, such as an agro-ecological model, are proposed. Section 3 analyses legal (hard as well as soft law) regulations on the protection of indigenous lands and the environment in the context of climate change and biodiversity preservation. Its aim is to indicate the normative basis of the role of indigenous peoples in preserving nature and biodiversity. Lastly, some concluding remarks and answers to the research questions are offered.

The chapter is meant to answer the following research questions: What is the role of indigenous peoples in the mitigation and adaptation to climate change as well as in the environmental preservation? Are the international legal, hard and soft law regulations, sufficient to protect the rights of indigenous peoples in the context of climate change? Is the law capable of facing the reality? Does it give the indigenous peoples the instruments necessary to realize their rights and potential in the preservation of the environment? What are the indigenous alternative ways of development?

## 2 Climate change, the threats it causes and possible conservation models

Climate change and loss of biodiversity are among one of the greatest dangers to our planet, to populations of different countries and to indigenous peoples as climate change poses a threat to the implementation of human rights, particularly of those vulnerable and marginalized groups such as the indigenous peoples. Despite being the least to blame for destroying nature and causing climate change, they are the first to feel the effects of those negative processes and experience their direct consequences in the most dramatic ways.[11] Additionally, as mentioned, very often activities or projects aimed at mitigating climate change further undermine the rights of indigenous peoples, for example, by creating protected areas such as game reserves or national parks or by renewable energy projects such as building dams for hydroelectric power purposes.[12]

11 P. Havemann, 'Lessons from indigenous knowledge and culture: learning to live in harmony with nature in an age of ecocide', in *State of the World's Minorities and Indigenous Peoples*, 2016, 49, available online at http://minorityrights.org/publications/state-of-the-worlds-minorities-and-indigenous-peoples-2016/. According to the Intergovernmental Panel on Climate Change, climate change is largely human induced – see 'Climate Change 2007: Synthesis Report', 36–37, available online at https://www.ipcc.ch/report/ar4/syr/; para. 8 of the 'Declaration of Indigenous Peoples on Climate Change. Second International Indigenous Forum on Climate Change, The Hague, 15 November 2000', *Australian Indigenous Law Reports*, 7 (1), 2002, 98.

12 J. Eisen, 'Vicky-Tauli-Corpuz: "The better protected areas are those where indigenous peoples live!"', available online at http://www.theecologist.org/Interviews/

With reference to the Arctic, climate change is closely linked to issues such as environmental protection, preservation of culture and cultural identity as well as granting and maintaining autonomy and self-governance of indigenous peoples, in this case the Sámi and the Inuit. Industrialization, climate change and actual and potential economic exploitation of the natural resources in the Arctic pose threats to Sámi livelihoods and traditional lifestyles. As a result, the livelihoods linked to hunting, fishing and reindeer herding are threatened. As Kamrul Hossain claims, the major driver for the 'rapid transformation of the region' is climate change.[13] Climate change, including global warming, has a huge impact on the ecosystem and way of life of indigenous peoples in the Arctic. According to the *2004 Arctic Climate Impact Assessment*:

> '[…] climate changes are being experienced particularly intensely in the Arctic. Arctic average temperature has risen at almost twice the rate as the rest of the world in the past few decades. Widespread melting of glaciers and sea ice and rising permafrost temperatures present additional evidence of strong Arctic warming. These changes in the Arctic provide an early indication of the environmental and societal significance of global warming.'[14]

Temperature rises and a reduction in sea ice will, for example, drastically reduce 'the marine habitat for polar bears, ice-inhabiting seals and some seabirds, pushing some species toward extinction'.[15] Apart from species' migration there is also a risk of local overfishing (as a result of this migration) and – as the number of tourists is growing – also the risk of this growth's negative impact on the environment and sensitive habitats.[16] Traditional

2988254/vicky_taulicorpuz_the_better_protected_areas_are_those_where_indigenous_peoples_live.html.

13 K. Hossain, 'Securing the Rights: A Human Security Perspective in the Context of Arctic Indigenous Peoples', *The Yearbook of Polar Law*, 5 (1), 2012, 496.

14 *Arctic Climate Impact Assessment, Impact of a Warming Arctic*, Cambridge, Cambridge University Press, 2004, 8. For more details, see: G. M. Goldberg, T. Badua, 'Do People Have Standing? Indigenous Peoples, Global Warming, And Human Rights', *Barry Law Review*, 11, 2008, 59–76; T. Koivurova, 'Increasing Relevance of Treaties: The Case of the Arctic', AJIL Unbound, available online at http://www.asil.org/blogs/increasing-relevance-treaties-case-arctic-agora-end-treaties; E. A. Kronk Warner, R. S. Abate, 'International and Domestic Law Dimensions of Climate Justice for Arctic Indigenous Peoples', *Revue générale de droit*, 43, 2013, 116–17. On the consequences of permafrost thawing, see J. Fox-Skelly, 'Long-dormant bacteria and viruses, trapped in ice and permafrost for centuries, are reviving as Earth's climate warms', available online at http://www.bbc.com/earth/story/20170504-there-are-diseases-hidden-in-ice-and-they-are-waking-up.

15 K. Hossain, note 13 at 510.

16 J. Jokela (ed), *Arctic security matters*, ISS Report no. 24, 2015, 72.

hunting is becoming more and more difficult as certain species are no longer present in their traditional areas at specific seasons so the hunters must travel and search for them in different areas. Some of those threats to the Arctic are also threats to the Antarctic ecosystem, for example the growing number of tourists, rising temperatures leading to the melting of the ice which in turn contributes to the rising sea level. However, the warming trend stopped in the late 1990s and since then temperatures have been decreasing, but the glacier retreat is still ongoing. The main difference, however, is a lack of indigenous peoples or any permanent population at all in the Antarctic. For this reason the issue of climate change in the Antarctic is merely signalized.[17]

The Inuit's culture of hunting and food sharing may be destroyed as the sea ice is reduced, which leads to animals on which the Inuit depend to become less accessible, decline in number and possibly even become extinct. Because of the speed of the current changes, the Inuit's ability to adapt may not suffice.[18] For indigenous peoples of the Arctic, hunting polar bears, walrus, seals and caribou, fishing and reindeer herding are not only the basis of their food and local economy, but also of their cultural and social identity.[19] Hence, changes in the abundance and distribution of species, access to them, and the rise in the unpredictability of weather patterns, which are connected to travel safety in changing ice conditions, constitute challenges to the livelihoods of indigenous peoples, their food and health security and their cultural survival.[20]

These considerations allow for one conclusion: indigenous peoples and their role in the mitigation of climate change and the preservation of nature and biodiversity is inseparably linked to rights of indigenous peoples such as lands rights, a right to natural resources and food security. Protection of indigenous lands and their natural resources is strictly connected to the protection of nature and biodiversity.[21] Indigenous peoples are place-based

17 K. Hossain, note 13 at 514. For more details, see e.g.: 'Antarctic Climate Change and the Environment', 2009, available online at https://www.scar.org/science/acce/acce/ and 'Antarctic Climate Change and the Environment – 2017 Update', available online at https://www.scar.org/library/policy/antarctic-treaty/atcm-xl-and-cep-xx-2017-beijing-china/2966-atcm40-ip080/file/; T. Stephens, 'The Antarctic Treaty System and the Anthropocene', Legal Studies Research Paper Series, no. 18/22, 2018, available online at http://ssrn.com/abstract=3165816; M. Nevitt, R. V. Percival, 'Polar opposites: Assessing the State of Environmental Law in the World's Polar Regions', *Boston College Law Review*, 59 (5), 2018, 2–47.

18 E. A. Kronk Warner, R. S. Abate, note 14 at 133.

19 *Arctic Climate Impact Assessment, Impact of a Warming Arctic*, note 13 at 11. For more details on polar bears, ice-dependent seals and caribou/reindeer see *Arctic Climate Impact Assessment. Highlights* (2004), available online at http://www.amap.no/arctic-climate-impact-assessment-acia.

20 *Arctic Climate Impact Assessment, Impact of a Warming Arctic*, note 14 at 11.

21 'Delivering on Paris Promise. Combating Climate Change While Protecting Rights', note 2 at 6.

people with a kind of spiritual connection to their lands. They live in harmony with and within the ecological boundaries of the environment. They use natural resources but within those boundaries. Their way of life of fitting into the 'sustainable bio-cultural paradigm' stands in sharp contrast to the Western (or Euro-Atlantic) concept of continued economic growth.[22] The panacea to that illness as well as a solution to climate change and crises in food security lies in agro-ecology. The problems already mentioned make it necessary to transit from industrial agriculture to small agro-ecology farms. This need has been voiced inter alia by the UN Special Rapporteur for the right to food, Olivier de Schutter, FAO, UNEP and UNCTAD.[23] Agro-ecology is the basis or instrument of sustainable development. With reference to food security, it is worth mentioning that climate change has already reduced global agricultural production, therefore undermining food security.[24] Traditional livelihoods produce 10 percent of the global amount of meat and most of the fish that people eat. 'Small-scale farming based on agro-ecological methods informed by traditional knowledge provides 70 per cent of the world's food needs'.[25]

One of the climate change mitigation instruments is protected areas aimed at preserving biodiversity for the benefit of the whole of humankind, and have the potential to do this. Unfortunately, however, as already mentioned, their establishment very often leads to the violations of the individual and collective rights of indigenous communities who are removed from their traditional territories and to their culture being destroyed. For over a century, the aim of conservation projects was to establish protected areas of pristine nature devoid of any human presence.[26] One may easily undermine the argument of the 'pristineness' of the ecosystem because of the fact of previous and ages-long inhabitancy of those areas by indigenous peoples who kept the biodiversity at a high level. From the perspective of indigenous peoples, the protected areas' model is regarded as a colonialist or neo-colonialist model. As a result, during the last two decades, a significant shift took place and a new paradigm for nature conservation emerged. Within this new paradigm, the role of indigenous peoples in the preservation of biodiversity and mitigation of climate change was finally recognized, which was a result of growing awareness among conservationists of the importance of the indigenous knowledge in this process. The new paradigm joins the preservation of nature with respect for the rights of indigenous peoples. Consequently, their collective land rights are increasingly recognized in some States.[27] However, despite

22 P. Havemann, note 11 at 51.
23 Ibid.
24 'Delivering on Paris Promise. Combating Climate Change While Protecting Rights', note 2 at 9.
25 P. Havemann, note 11 at 49.
26 V. Tauli-Corpuz, note 3 para. 13.
27 Ibid., para. 37.

all the signs of progressive development there is a problem with the lack of effective implementation of new regulations. This is a general problem with the rights of indigenous peoples, even 13 years since the adoption of the UN Declaration on the Rights of Indigenous Peoples of 2007.[28]

## 3 International legal and political documents on the role of indigenous peoples in preserving the environment and biodiversity

While this section is mostly descriptive, its aim is to indicate the normative basis of the role and activities of indigenous peoples in preserving nature and biodiversity. The instruments are analyzed without any hierarchy between legally binding and non-binding documents, although it is always indicated if the document is legally binding. Even the non-binding resolutions may merely recognize the already existing rights of indigenous peoples, which makes their legal character irrelevant.[29] Due to space limits, I focus only on the most important documents.

It is desirable to start with the words from the *Report of the World Commission on Environment and Development: Our Common Future* of 1987:

> '[Indigenous] communities are the repositories of vast accumulations of traditional knowledge and experience that links humanity with its ancient origins. Their disappearance is a loss for the larger society, which could learn a great deal from their traditional skills in sustainably managing very complex ecological systems. It is a terrible irony that as formal development reaches more deeply into rain forests, deserts, and other isolated environments, it tends to destroy the only cultures that have proved able to thrive in these environments.'[30]

There it was also added that '[t]ribal and indigenous peoples' [...] lifestyles can offer modern societies many reasons in the management of resources in complex forest, mountain and dryland ecosystems'.[31] Those excerpts confirm the existence of the mutual relations between indigenous peoples' culture and environmental protection. In accordance with this approach, 'culture is

28 Ibid., paras. 18, 36 (protected areas were even seen as an instrument of coercive assimilation of indigenous peoples), 43.

29 S. Wheatley, 'The Legal Status of the UN Declaration on the Rights of Indigenous Peoples', *Inter Alia – Student Law Review* 60 (2010), 60–64; J. Gilbert, V. Couillard, 'Land Rights under international law: historical and contemporary issues', in *Land Rights and the Forest Peoples of Africa. Historical, Legal and Anthropological Perspectives*, 2009, 30–31.

30 G. Brundtland, *Report of the World Commission on Environment and Development: Our Common Future*, 1987, para. 74 (Chapter 4), available online at www.un-documents.net/our-common-future.pdf.

31 Ibid., para. 46 (Chapter 1).

described in terms of ecologically harmonious relationship between indigenous peoples and the environment'.[32]

The Indigenous and Tribal Peoples Convention, 1989 (No. 169) (ILO Convention 169) is today the only legally binding instrument devoted to indigenous and tribal peoples.[33] In its preamble, it mentions the contribution of indigenous and tribal peoples to the ecological harmony of humankind.[34] References to the environment may be found in Arts. 4 (1),[35] 7, 13 and 15. The most pertinent here is Art. 7, which gives the indigenous peoples the right to decide on their own developmental priorities and to participate in the formulation and implementation of developmental programmes that may affect indigenous peoples directly.[36] Governments are also obliged to conduct an environmental impact assessment every time developmental activities are planned as well as to cooperate with indigenous peoples in order to preserve the environment of the indigenous territories. Article 13 emphasizes the special spiritual relationship of indigenous peoples with their lands, which includes the environment of such territories.[37] Lastly, Art. 15 accords the indigenous peoples the right to the natural resources pertaining to their lands, including the right to participate in the use, management and preservation of these resources.[38] One may conclude that ILO Convention 169 reaffirms that the preservation of indigenous lands is a necessary condition for 'supporting indigenous peoples' survival as distinct social groups'.[39]

Similar provisions may be found in the UN Declaration on the Rights of Indigenous Peoples adopted in 2007, which is the most important –however, non-binding – instrument on the rights of indigenous peoples. Still, the Declaration 'consolidates the rights of indigenous peoples already recognized in other human rights instruments and through the jurisprudence of the international human rights treaty bodies'.[40]

32 Ch. Metcalf, 'Indigenous Rights and the Environment: Evolving International Law', *Ottawa Law Review*, 35 (1), 2003–2004, 108.

33 There was also the Indigenous and Tribal Populations Convention, 1957 (No. 107), Geneva (Switzerland), 26 June 1957, in force 2 June 1959, available online at http://www.ilo.org/dyn/normlex/en/f?p=NORMLEXPUB:12100:0::NO::P12100_ILO_CODE:C107, but because of its assimilationist approach it was replaced by the new Indigenous and Tribal Peoples Convention, 1989 (No. 169), Geneva (Switzerland), 27 June 1989, in force 5 September 1991, available online at http://www.ilo.org/dyn/normlex/en/f?p=NORMLEXPUB:12100:0::NO::P12100_ILO_CODE:C169.

34 Ibid., ILO Convention 169.

35 Ibid.: 'Special measures shall be adopted as appropriate for safeguarding the persons, institutions, property, labour, cultures and environment of the peoples concerned'.

36 Ibid.

37 Ibid.

38 Ibid.

39 Ch. Metcalf, note 32 at 109.

40 V. Tauli-Corpuz, note 3 para. 22.

The UN Declaration takes into account the special relationship of indigenous peoples to their lands. Article 26 provides that '[i]ndigenous peoples have the right to the lands, territories and resources which they have traditionally owned, occupied or otherwise used or acquired'.[41] Article 29 addresses the rights of indigenous peoples to conserve and protect the environment and their lands.[42] Article 32 regulates the right of indigenous peoples to determine and develop their own priorities and strategies for the development or use of their lands. The latter provisions also envisage an obligation of States to:

> 'consult and cooperate in good faith with the indigenous peoples concerned through their own representative institutions in order to obtain their free and informed consent prior to the approval of any project affecting their lands [...], particularly in connection with the development, utilization or exploitation of mineral, water or other resources [...].'[43]

Common in those provisions is free, prior and informed consent, which means that such consent must be given through, for example, consultation and good-faith participation, freely without coercion, manipulation or intimidation, and that indigenous peoples should be afforded a reasonable amount of time to formulate their opinion.[44]

Also, the Convention on Biological Diversity of 1992 (Biodiversity Convention) (legally binding) recognizes the rights of indigenous peoples in connection with their lands and environment. Article 8 (j) commits States parties to respect and maintain:

> 'knowledge, innovations and practices of indigenous and local communities embodying traditional lifestyles relevant for the conservation and sustainable use of biological diversity and promote their wider application with the approval and involvement of [their] holders [...] and encourage the equitable sharing of the benefits arising from the utilization of such knowledge, innovations and practices.'[45]

41 UN Declaration on the Rights of Indigenous Peoples (UN GA res. 61/295), 13 September 2007, preamble, available online at http://research.un.org/en/docs/ga/quick/regular/61.
42 Ibid.
43 Ibid.
44 D. M. Goldberg, T. Badua, note 14 at 70. For more details on free, prior and informed consent, see also: K. Powys Whyte, 'Justice forward: Tribes, climate adaptation and responsibility', in J. Koppel Maldonado, B. Colombi, R. Pandya (eds), *Climate Change and Indigenous Peoples in the United States. Impacts, Experiences and Actions*, Springer, 2014, 29.
45 Convention on Biological Diversity, Rio de Janeiro (Brazil), 5 June 1992, in force 29 December 1993, available online at https://www.cbd.int/.

Accordingly, in line with the Biodiversity Convention, indigenous peoples have a very important role to play in the preservation of nature and biodiversity. Hence, they are treated rather instrumentally: their environmental rights are recognized in order to strengthen the protection of the environment. Those provisions are supplemented and strengthened by the Rio Declaration on Environment and Development, 1992 (Principle 22).[46] According to those instruments, indigenous peoples and their knowledge are instrumental in achieving sustainable development taking into account environmental protection. Indigenous knowledge is not protected per se, but only in as much as it supports or contributes to sustainable development.[47] Chapter 26 of AGENDA 21, which is devoted to 'Recognizing and strengthening the role of indigenous people[s] and their communities', expands and complements the provisions of the Principle 22. It recognizes indigenous peoples' historical relationship with their lands as well as their traditional knowledge of their lands, natural resources and environment.[48]

Lastly, the binding Paris Agreement adopted at the UN Climate Change Conference, COP 21, in 2015 recognizes and emphasizes the role of indigenous peoples in the mitigation of climate change. According to Art. 7 (5) of the Paris Agreement, 'Parties acknowledge that adaptation action [...] should be based on and guided by the best available science and, as appropriate, traditional knowledge, knowledge of indigenous peoples'.[49] During COP 21, States-parties to the Paris Agreement established an indigenous peoples' knowledge-sharing platform for the exchange of indigenous views, experiences and practices on mitigation and adaptation to climate change.[50]

There is also a group of non-binding documents adopted by the indigenous peoples themselves where they strive for stronger protection of the environment than that which is currently granted: the Charter of the indigenous and tribal peoples of the tropical forests,[51] the Earth Charter of

46 Rio Declaration on Environment and Development, 1992, available online at http://www.unesco.org/education/pdf/RIO_E.PDF.

47 Ch. Metcalf, note 32 at 108.

48 United Nations Conference on Environment & Development, Rio de Janerio, Brazil, 3–14 June 1992. AGENDA 21, para. 26.1, available online at https://sustainabledevelopment.un.org/content/documents/Agenda21.pdf.

49 Paris Agreement to the United Nations Framework Convention on Climate Change, Paris (France), 12 December 2015, in force 4 November 2016, available online at http://unfccc.int/paris_agreement/items/9485.php.

50 'Delivering on Paris Promise. Combating Climate Change While Protecting Rights', note 2 at 6.

51 Charter of the indigenous and tribal peoples of the tropical forests, available online at http://www.fao.org/3/w7746e/w7746e0a.htm.

the Kari Oca conference (1992),[52] and the Declaration of Indigenous Peoples on Climate Change of 2000.[53]

With reference to the Arctic, one should mention the Arctic Council established in 1996 that may also be regarded as an instrument for indigenous peoples to participate in, and voice their concern about, climate change and the destruction of the Arctic environment.[54] The signatories of the Declaration on the Establishment of the Arctic Council confirmed their 'commitment to the protection of the Arctic environment, including the health of Arctic ecosystems, maintenance of biodiversity in the Arctic region and conservation and sustainable use of natural resources'.[55] This body was convened as a forum for international cooperation in environmental affairs affecting the Arctic. Indigenous peoples participate in the Arctic Council as permanent participants contributing to the legitimacy of the results of this cooperative body. Due to indigenous peoples' participation, their perspective on the environment is taken into account.[56]

To summarize, pointing to Cherrie Metcalf, on the basis of the normative instruments already mentioned, one may construe two approaches to the environmental protection in connection with indigenous peoples. The first may be termed the 'cultural integrity model' and the other the 'self-determination model'.[57] In accordance with the former, environmental rights are extended to indigenous peoples not only for the sake of preserving the environment, but also at the same time to protect and preserve their indigenous culture. In other words, the protection of indigenous culture serves environmental protection. The 'self-determination' model, on the other hand, recognizes indigenous rights with respect to the environment on the basis of indigenous peoples' right to self-determination. As a subject of self-determination, indigenous peoples are entitled to make decisions regarding their lands and resources.[58] The first model regards indigenous peoples and their

52 Kari-Oca Declaration and Indigenous Peoples' Earth Charter, World Conference of Indigenous Peoples on Territory, Environment and Development, Kari-Oca, 25–30 May 1992, available online at http://www.lacult.unesco.org/lacult_en/docc/Kari-Oca_1992.doc.

53 'Declaration of Indigenous Peoples on Climate Change. Second International Indigenous Forum on Climate Change, The Hague, 15 November 2000', *Australian Indigenous Law Reports*, 7 (1), 2002, 97.

54 Ch. Metcalf, note 32 at 104.

55 The Declaration on the Establishment of the Arctic Council (1996), Ottawa (Canada), 19 September 1996, preamble, available online at https://www.international.gc.ca/world-monde/international_relations-relations_internationales/arctic-arctique/declaration_ac-declaration_ca.aspx?lang=eng.

56 Ch. Metcalf, note 32 at 116. See also M. Poto, 'The Arctic Council as an Actor in the Global Governance', in T. Koivurova, W. Hasanat (eds), *Current Developments in the Arctic*, vol. 4, Rovaniemi, UArctic, 2016, 23–24.

57 Ibid., at 104, 105.

58 Ibid., at 105, 106.

rights as instruments of environmental protection (e.g. in the Biodiversity Convention), while the second one accords them the role of a subject that is capable of setting and developing their own environmental protection policy (UN Declaration on the Rights of Indigenous Peoples). Within the 'self-determination model', indigenous peoples not only have procedural rights but they also have substantial ones such as control over their lands, a right to formulate their own environmental policy and, lastly, the rights to autonomy and self-governance that pull those rights together.[59]

## 4 Concluding remarks

Here I would like to very briefly answer the questions posed in the introduction and summarize the main conclusions reached in this chapter:

- Indigenous peoples have a great potential to play a huge role in the preservation of the environment and biodiversity and mitigation, as well as adaptation to climate change. They already play such a role in their indigenous territories, which are the most biologically diverse ones. But their potential must be implemented, first of all by recognizing their indigenous ecological knowledge and indigenous practices and their right to participate in decision-making processes.
- International legal regulations are generally sufficient to ensure the protection of the rights of indigenous peoples. Still, what is lacking is the political will of States to implement those international standards. Unfortunately very often the 'law in books' does not transform into the 'law in action'.
- Indigenous ecological knowledge certainly offers alternative ways of development. The present, and still dominant, Western model of environmental protection is based on science and rationality, and aims at the preservation of environmentally valuable areas intact, without any trace of human activities such as agriculture or hunting. The indigenous model of environmental management regards humans as an integral part of the environment. An alternative to the Western conservation model is to include indigenous peoples in the control and management of protected areas in which they already live.
- There exists a correlation between respect for the rights of indigenous peoples, especially their land rights and a right to natural resources on the one hand, and the protection of the environment on the other hand.[60] The first contributes to the second. It is also connected to the vision of development construed by indigenous peoples – development is understood holistically as embracing environmental stability with socio-

59 Ibid., at 128.
60 J. Eisen, note 12.

economic development in the overall framework of human rights.[61] For those reasons, the role of indigenous peoples as stewards or guardians of the environment should be recognized.

To sum up, the role and contribution of indigenous peoples to preservation and conservation of the environment and biodiversity have not yet been fully acknowledged. There are some positive signs on the horizon, but they fall short of full recognition. Protected areas expand but still the participation of indigenous peoples in this process is not sufficient. There is a need to listen to and support indigenous peoples and to recognize their indigenous ecological knowledge. Conservation and the rights of indigenous and tribal peoples must go hand in hand. With reference to the Arctic, as the Arctic indigenous peoples bear the impacts and costs of adaptation and mitigation actions, such actions should be led by them, in other words 'local adaptation mechanisms ought to be developed by those that need to adapt to climate change. Holistic and multidimensional research initiatives [...] offer a promising model'.[62] And they, indeed, have used their natural resources in the difficult climatic and weather conditions and developed strategies of adaptation based on their unique observations and indigenous knowledge. Such knowledge and experience may be priceless in the current efforts to protect the environment and biodiversity in the Arctic and in the wider context of climate change.[63]

61 'Leaving no one behind. Practical Guide for Indigenous Peoples', Asia Indigenous Peoples Pact (AIPP) Foundation, 2017, https://aippnet.org/leaving-no-one-behind-practical-guide-for-indigenous-peoples/.
62 I. L. Stoyanova, 'The Saami facing the impacts of global climate change', in R. Abate, E. A. Kronk (eds) *Climate Change and Indigenous Peoples: The Search for Legal Remedies*, Cheltenham, Edward Elgar Publishing, 2013, 310.
63 Ibid., at 311.

Chapter 10

# Environmental perceptions and values of the Russian northern indigenous peoples

*Elena Gladun*[1] *and Olga V. Zakharova*[2]

## 1 Introduction

The Arctic is one of the most resource-rich regions on the planet, as well as being one of the most fragile and globally important. The Arctic territories are pristine and untouched lands, which retain climatic and geographical phenomena: extreme cold, snow and ice, permafrost, sunless days and midnight Suns. The Arctic is the global reserve, not only of biodiversity but also of unique indigenous cultures and economies.[3] The lands and natural resources in the Arctic have been used for hunting, grazing, fishing and other traditional activities for thousands of years;[4] however, more recently they are being used for industrial activities, such as oil and gas extraction, road construction and urban development.

In the Russian Federation, 40 indigenous nations are legally recognized as "indigenous, small-numbered peoples of the North, Siberia and the Far East". This status is tied to the conditions that a people has no more than 50,000 members, maintains a traditional way of life, inhabits certain remote regions of Russia and identifies itself as a distinct ethnic community.[5] In Russia, the northern indigenous peoples include the Aleuts, Koryaks, Eskimos, Chukchi, Evenks, Yakuts, Yukagir, Dolgans, Selkup, Nanai, Khanty,

1 Public Administration Department, Tyumen State University, Russia, efgladun@yandex.ru.
2 Public Administration Department, Tyumen State University, Russia.
3 See for more details: I. Krupnik, *Arctic Adaptation. Native Whalers and Reindeer Herders of Northern Eurasia*, UPNE, 1993; E. Gladun and G. Chebotarev, 'Legal Measures for Efficient Environmental Regulations of Oil and Gas Industry in Western Siberia', *The Yearbook of Polar Law*, 7, 2015, 352–374; Y.F. Lukin, 'Arkticheskij turizm v Rossii' ['Arctic tourism in Russia, in Russian'], *Arktika i Sever*, 25, 2016, 2011–2016.
4 M. Nuttall, F. Berkes, B.C. Forbes, G. Kofinas, T. Vlassova and G. Wenzel, 'Hunting, herding, fishing and gathering: indigenous peoples and renewable resource use in the Arctic', in *Arctic Climate Impact Assessment (ACIA) Scientific Report*, Cambridge University Press UK, 2005, 649–690.
5 International Work Group for Indigenous Affairs (IWGIA). Indigenous peoples in Russia, 2016 https://www.iwgia.org/en/russia.html.

Mansi, Nenets, Sámi and others.[6] The northern indigenous peoples traditionally inhabit huge territories stretching from the Kola Peninsula in the west to the Bering Strait in the east, which make up about two-thirds of the Russian territory.

In the Yamal region of the Russian Arctic,[7] the main groups of indigenous peoples – Khanty, Mansi, Nenets – have created a civilization which is viable and adaptable to the harsh northern conditions. Their life-support system is closely linked to traditional lands and land use, to the challenging climate and geography, limited natural resources, and dispersed settlements.[8] Partly because of these conditions, the Russian northern indigenous groups preserve their national identity and traditional knowledge that help them to survive and live sustainably. Russian researchers argue that the peoples of the North are “a genetic reserve of the country”: for thousands of years in the North they have undergone hard natural selection, with only the most stable and powerful people surviving.[9]

In the 20th–21st centuries, indigenous peoples of all Arctic states have experienced the catastrophic impacts of actively developing industries; as a consequence, human-induced climate change and diminishing landscapes have resulted.[10] This development has been seen as the legacy of the Yamal native population. The first commercial gas discovery in the Yamal Peninsula was in 1953, later discoveries of new larger fields in 1965 made this region one of the richest gas provinces.[11]

The oil and gas industry has had adverse impacts on the region’s ecosystem. It has affected not only the nature but also the traditional culture of the area. Nikolai Vakhtin wrote about the consequences of industrial development in the 1960s: “pipelines and railway lines cut off reindeer routes decreasing reindeer numbers, farms lost tremendous pasturelands due to construction of transport lines and field development, and traditional fishing and hunting areas were lost”.[12]

6 News Agency ‘Arctic-Info’. Indigenous peoples, 2016 http://www.arctic-info.com/encyclopedia/indigenous-peoples.

7 See *Yamal: at the Edge of Millenniums, Illustrated Essay on the Region’s History from Prehistoric Times*, Salekhard: ARTVID, Saint Petersburg: Russkaya Collectsia, 2000.

8 E. Park, ‘Searching for a Voice: the Indigenous People in Polar Regions’, *Sustainable Development Law and Policy*, 8, 2008, 30.

9 L. Judina, ‘Vossozdanie ehtnogeneticheskih portretov’ [‘Recreating ethnogenetic portraits’, in Russian], *Nauka v Sibiri*, 6, 2010, 30–31.

10 E.M. Zimmerman, ‘Valuing Traditional Ecological Knowledge: Incorporating the Experiences of Indigenous People into Global Climate Change Policies’, *New York University Environmental Law Journal*, 13: 803, 2005.

11 *Yamal*, note 7.

12 N. Vakhtin, ‘Native Peoples of the Russian Far North’, *Information Analyses. Minority Rights Group*, London, 1992 at 24.

Today, industrial development is drastically altering the culture of northern indigenous peoples.[13] There are three significant changes to the Arctic that dramatically impact their way of life: exploration and production on oil and gas sites, climate changes caused by the human activities[14] and an increasing Arctic population, "newcomers" to the Arctic lands.[15]

While Arctic indigenous peoples are known for their ability to adapt, these changes are likely to be so rapid and severe that, without mitigation, they will not be able to continue living sustainably in their Arctic home.[16]

In Russia, as in all Arctic states, northern indigenous peoples are striving to survive and to preserve their way of life, while their best practices, experiences and traditional knowledge have historically been ignored by researchers, policymakers and state authorities. Traditional rules of environmental management are not incorporated into the emerging environmental legislation, while the indigenous attitude towards nature is perceived by the "non-indigenous" community as prejudiced and eccentric.

Meanwhile, the economic policy of Russia in the new century focuses on the exploration of mineral resources in the northern Arctic territories and the development of Arctic energy resources.[17] With industrial development being prioritized in the country's development strategy, indigenous traditional rules and values become even more important and necessary to adhere to for sustainable development of the region. For example, if environmental and Arctic-related legislation is based on certain ethical standards recommended by groups historically inhabiting the region, it will increase the environmental awareness of all Arctic actors, encouraging them to understand the significance of this unique region and to operate in an environmentally sustainable manner.

The objective of our study is to describe and interpret the environmental perceptions of northern indigenous peoples in order to conceptualize and define the basic traditional environmental values crucial for the development of the Russian Arctic. Environmental values can serve as guiding principles for environmental legislation in the Arctic region and provide a basis for the decision-making process, helping to shape society's attitudes towards the

13 M.N. Ignatieva, V.G. Loginov, A.A. Litvinova, L.M. Morozova and S.N. Ehktova, 'Ekonomicheskaya Ocenka Vreda, Prichinyaemogo Arkticheskim Ekosistemam Pri Osvoenii Neftegazovyh Resursov' ['Economic Estimation of Harm Caused by Arctic Ecosystems when Developing Oil and Gas Resources', in Russian], *Ehkonomika Regiona*, № 1, 2014, 102–112 at 102.

14 H.P. Huntington, M. Boyle, G.E. Flowers, J.W. Weatherly, L.C. Hamilton, L. Hinzman and J. Overpeck, 'The influence of human activity in the Arctic on climate and climate impacts', *Climatic Change*, 82, 1–2, 2007, 77–92.

15 E. Gladun, 'Legal frameworks for the interaction of northern indigenous peoples with other nationalities and cultures', *Legal Aspects of Inter-National Relations and Their Harmonization, Tyumen International Forum*, 2, 2016, 253–259.

16 Zimmerman, note 10.

17 *Foundations of Russian Federation Policy in the Arctic until 2020 and beyond*, Presidential Decree dated September 18, 2008, № Pr-1969.

environment and adhere to current trends of careful use of natural resources and the interests of local people. Today, indigenous traditions and culture imply huge potential to develop environmental policy and legislation in accordance with sustainable principles and to contribute towards global sustainable development.

## 2 Northern indigenous peoples in Russia and their natural environment

The key factors of Khanty, Mansi and Nenets identity are their adherence to a nomadic way of life, discovering new territories, and living in accordance with basic elements of the environment – geological structure, topography and climate. For example, in the Holocene epoch, when changes in the natural conditions and the formation of modern flora and fauna began, fishing and gathering became more important. Later, fishing capacity reduced significantly as the tundra swamps decreased and people had to resettle. Waterlogging processes in the lakes caused the relocation of people to the rivers. These changes led to the spatial allocation of the local population and development of new migration routes. Seasonal zones of reindeer migration formed alongside major clans of people who followed them in search of food.[18]

Thus, early settlements in the Russian Arctic were dependent on the peculiarities of the natural environment, with people adapting to natural changes without causing a significant impact on the surrounding world. At the same time, indigenous peoples sought an increasingly balanced lifestyle, and the history of reindeer herding illustrates this phenomenon.

The first record of reindeer herding dates back to the 16th century. Deer pastures, hunting and fishing territories belonged to groups of families living in the region. By the 18th century, population growth led to deer hunting becoming an insufficient source of food resulting in the need for domestic reindeer herds.[19] Gradually, reindeer herding became the main activity of the indigenous population in the Russian Arctic. This traditional occupation had developed over centuries and proved to be the only possible way of life in the Arctic. Today, reindeer herding is a basic economic activity for the Yamal indigenous peoples, although the area of land suitable for grazing has been reducing due to oil and gas development. The total area of reindeer pastures in the Yamalo-Nenets Autonomous Area is 48.5 million hectares; this capacity enables the grazing of 370,000 reindeer out of a total population of over 730,000.[20]

Reindeer herding in the Yamal tundra has the following features:

18 See 'Drevnie kul'tury i korennye narody' ['Ancient cultures and indigenous peoples'] in *Istoriya Yamala* [*History of Yamal*, in Russian] V.V. Alekseev (ed.), Ekaterinburg, 2010 at 145–182.

19 T. Moldanov and T. Moldanova, *Ocherki tradicionnoj kul'tury hantov* [*Essays on the traditional Khanty culture*, in Russian], Khanty-Mansijsk, 2010 at 10.

20 Ignatieva et al., note 13.

- large size of herds (from 500 to 3,000 reindeer);
- reindeer herding dogs exploited all year-round;
- meridional seasonal travel routes across several hundred kilometres;
- grouped herds in the summer period;
- special technologies for breeding herds, to improve and increase the reproduction of livestock;
- reindeer as a means of transport;
- processing and using reindeer products.[21]

Until now, the indigenous way of life has been likened to the nomadism of the reindeer herds. In the Yamal region, 60 percent of the population is nomadic. This rate is the highest in the country.[22]

The economic experience of northern indigenous peoples is paradoxical in the context of the modern economy: their economy is complex, extensive and appropriating.[23] The indigenous groups are largely self-sufficient and self-sustaining. They are able to exist almost autonomously from one another. A small group (family) is a primary economic group, capable of providing itself with all the necessary products and requirements for sustainable living. The major division of labour is gender-based and age-based, moreover the indigenous way of life does not imply intensification in resource use, as this can destroy fragile ecosystems: "these effects are particularly important because the culture of indigenous peoples is often directly dependent on natural resources and changes are likely to create long-lasting, even permanent environmental harm".[24] Therefore, the nomadic lifestyle is contingent for indigenous peoples in the Arctic tundra, while in the forest-tundra the indigenous peoples need extensive tribal lands for their economic activities. Indigenous peoples in Yamal chose such types of economic activities that are appropriating "gifts of nature" – hunting, fishing, gathering, reindeer herding – rather than altering the natural environment. They did not take up industrial production and agriculture, instead, they chose the most optimal methods of farming based on a balance with the territory's capabilities. The

21 T.N. Vasilkova, A.V. Evaj, E.P. Martynova and N.I. Novikova, *'Korennye Malochislennye Narody i Promyshlennoe Razvitie Arktiki' (Ehtnologicheskij Monitoring v Yamalo-Neneckom Avtonomnom Okruge) ['Indigenous People and Industrial Development of the Arctic' (Ethnological Monitoring in the Yamalo-Nenets Autonomous District*, in Russian)], Moskva – Shadrinsk: Izdatelstvo OGUP, Shadrinskij Dom Pechati, 2011 at 3.

22 *State Program for the development of the northern indigenous peoples in the Yamalo-Nenets Autonomous Area*, Resolution of the Governor of the Yamalo-Nenets Autonomous Area, 28 December 2017, № 132-pg.

23 Moldanov and Moldanova, note 19.

24 L. Watters, 'Indigenous Peoples and the Environment: Convergence from a Nordic Perspective', in Lawrence Watters (ed), *Indigenous Peoples, the Environment and Law*, Durham, North Carolina, Carolina Academic Press, 2002, 311–335.

complexity, extensiveness and appropriating nature of their economy is explained by the peculiarities of the Arctic nature. For many centuries in the harsh Arctic latitudes, the Yamal indigenous peoples have developed effective tools for sustainable development based on a careful attitude towards nature. This seems a pragmatic demand for life in the Arctic, where nature is especially vulnerable with limited ability to recover due to low temperatures.[25] This way of life developed and proved its viability over centuries.

Close ties with the environment are central to the indigenous way of life, and this correlates with religious beliefs, social traditions and language. For example, Arctic indigenous people see themselves as belonging to the land rather than owning the land.[26] The duty to take care of the environment for the benefit of future generations is fundamental to the Arctic indigenous worldview.[27]

## 3 Method and results

Traditional values have a historical background and define the unwritten rules of economic life as well as the aesthetic perception of the surrounding world. They are reflected in religious beliefs, arts, traditional occupations and folklore,[28] where being durable and reliable, they continue to impact on attitudes towards nature and society. Researchers believe that the goals of sustainable development can be more efficiently achieved if they are based on traditional values and supported by environmental legislation.[29]

This study attempts to tie indigenous behaviours related to the environment with the explicit traditional indigenous values embedded within their culture. However, the common failure of research related to indigenous

25 Vasilkova et al, note 21.

26 R. Tsosie, 'Tribal Environmental Policy in an Era of Self-Determination: The Role of Ethics, Economics, and Traditional Ecological Knowledge', *Vermont Law Review*, 21, 1996, 225.

27 Zimmerman, note 10.

28 See for more details: K.J. Oosthoek, 'Environmental History: Between Science and Philosophy', 1999, available online at https://www.eh-resources.org/environmental-history-between-science-and-philosophy/; L. Abryutina and V. Chashchin, 'Lifestyle, Social and Economic Status of Indigenous Peoples', in *Persistent Toxic Substances, Food Security and Indigenous Peoples of the Russian North*, Final Report, Oslo: AMAP Secretariat, 2004, 17–39.

29 See P. Burgera, C.-H. Daubb and Y. M. Scherrerb, 'Creating values for sustainable development', *International Journal of Sustainable Development & World Ecology*, 17 (1), 1, 2010, 1–3; A. Berna Görmez and F.Y. Yaman, 'Ethical Foundations of the Sustainability and the Sustainable Development', in *3rd International Symposium on Sustainable Development*, 31 May–1 June 2012, Sarajevo, 2012, 425–436; E. Gladun and O.V. Zakharova, 'Ethical Foundations of International Environmental Law', *Tomsk State University Journal*, 413, 2016, 177–181.

peoples and their traditions falls within the realm of conjecture due in large part to limited written records.[30] The complexity of this research lies in the fact that for a long time traditions of the northern indigenous peoples were transmitted only orally and written fixation appeared since the development of ethnography. Moreover, some Russian ethnographers described these peoples as "uncivilized" and lacking cultural traditions and valuable knowledge, therefore ignoring the traditional indigenous culture. This research provides more in-depth analysis compared to previous studies due to its proximity to northern indigenous cultures, which still exist in the Yamal region. Thus, it is possible to provide a thorough evaluation of both cultural phenomena and traditional economics.

Therefore, hermeneutic analysis is applied to those cultural phenomena that remained unchanged during the period of industrial development and retained the inherited values of the northern indigenous peoples. We use hermeneutic analysis to interpret folklore texts, arts, fairy tales, rituals and the patterns of indigenous peoples' economic activities.

Our analysis results in disposing basic traditional environmental values of indigenous peoples in the Russian Arctic, namely:

- the interaction with nature and natural phenomena makes humans aware of the consequences of their activities;
- the traditional way of transferring social experience from older to younger generations provides a coherency of values;
- religious beliefs restrict the unjustified and inefficient use of resources and in this way provides a sufficient amount of food for present and future generations;
- an admiration of nature, local places and inhabiting creatures helps to perceive life as a blessing and to be grateful for it;
- the rational use of natural resources proves to be the only possible way to survive through harsh Arctic conditions and limited nature capacity.

A comparative methodology was used to contrast environmental perceptions and values of the northern indigenous peoples and transform them into the basic principles and norms regulating the industrial economy in the Arctic. We compare the traditional and modern attitudes towards nature through a number of characteristics that allow us to specify the formation of the relationship between humans and nature, the different types of relationship, the methods of human activity and the possibilities of human activities and their goals. Table 10.1 shows the results of our comparisons.

30 M. Venkatesan, 'Sustainable development, the significance of culture: Foundations of present practices and Indigenous reflections', in J. Paulo Davim and Leal Filho, Walter (eds) *Challenges in Higher Education for Sustainability*, University of Aveiro, Aveiro, Portugal, 2016, 103–118 at 104.

*Table 10.1*

| *Criteria of human interaction with the natural environment* | *Traditional attitude to nature* | *Attitude to nature in the industrial economy* |
|---|---|---|
| Form of interaction | Dialogue | Conquering the nature |
| Type of interaction | Adaptive | Consumer |
| Type of activities | Natural economy | Industrial technologies |
| Possibilities of human activities | Limited by ecosystem capabilities | Intensive use up to exhaustion |
| Goals | Care for future generations | Present generation interests |

## 4 Discussion

### *4.1 Traditional environmental values of indigenous people*

Generally, traditional environmental values, described in this chapter, are in line with the results of previous studies. For example, Darlene McNaughton, Michael Morrison and Cassie Schill (2016) point out four interrelated themes of the indigenous peoples' behaviour in the natural environment: respect, care, interaction and closeness.[31] Another example is by Julia H. Lawler and Ryan C. L. Bullock depicting core principles of the North America indigenous community, which are based on traditional phenomena such as sacred sites, education, habitat and the protection of traditional cultural assets.[32]

Traditional environmental values can be defined as a set of ethical and aesthetic attitudes and knowledge of indigenous peoples who perceive the environment as an interconnected whole. The worldview of indigenous peoples can be compared to a "network thrown over the world". It regulates the entire universe, ensuring its coherence, and at the same time being selective, flexible and fundamentally unfinished.[33] It makes the society highly adaptive. Their value system consists of norms and restrictions of behaviour and economic life, transferred from generation to generation, supporting life and coordinating community care in harsh environments.

31 D. McNaughton, M. Morrison and C. Schill, '"My Country is Like my Mother…": Respect, Care, Interaction and Closeness as Principles for Undertaking Cultural Heritage Assessments', *International Journal of Heritage Studies*, 22(6) 2016, 1–19.

32 J.H. Lawler and R.C.L. Bullock, 'A Case for Indigenous Community Forestry', *Journal of Forestry*, 115(2), 2017, 117–125.

33 A.M. Sagalaev, *Uralo-altajskaja mifologija: Simvol i arhetip* [*Ural-Altai mythology: Symbol and archetype*, in Russian], Novosibirsk: Nauka, 1991 at 23; L. Bloch, 'Tales of Esnesv: Indigenous Oral Traditions about Trader-Diplomats in Ancient Southeastern North America', *American Anthropologist*, 120(4) 2018, 781–794.

The environmental perceptions and values of indigenous peoples can be amplified into certain criteria crucial for the decision-making process and legal frameworks for economic activities. These criteria will provide effective regulations for the conservation of biodiversity,[34] rare species,[35] protected areas,[36] ecological processes,[37] and to ensure sustainable resource use in general.[38]

The Russian northern nations – Khanty, Mansi and Nenets – believe that interaction between natural phenomena makes humans think about the consequences of their activities.[39] The world, according to the Nenets and Mansi, is a coherent system of three "worlds": if someone is born in the upper world, someone dies in the lower one.[40] The upper world is eternal, the middle world is for the birth and death, the lower world is for the dead.[41] The mythology of indigenous peoples asserts the appropriateness of all living beings. For example, mosquitoes are not useless, they drive deer into one place.[42] Therefore, human beings must not destroy the existing world order and ties.

Indigenous peoples are aware of interconnectedness in the universe: "only if there are pastures, there will be deer, and Khanty, Mansi, Nenets remain in the world".[43] As a result, the pasture area must be proportionate with the reindeer capacity and should not be reduced.

The daily routine of indigenous peoples is also a part of the interconnections within the universe. Khanty, Mansi and Nenets do not plan ahead and their days are scheduled according to the weather. If a hunter gets up in the

34 M. Gadgil, F. Berkes and C. Folke, 'Indigenous knowledge for biodiversity conservation', *Ambio*, 22, 1993, 151–156.
35 J. Colding, 'Analysis of hunting options by the use of general food taboos', *Ecological Modelling*, 110, 1998, 5–17.
36 R.E. Johannes, 'The case for data-less marine resource management: examples from tropical nearshore fisheries', *Trends in Ecology and Evolution*, 13(6), 1998, 243–246.
37 J. B. Alcorn, 'Indigenous peoples and conservation', *Conservation Biology*, 7, 1993, 424–426.
38 M. Schmink, K.H. Redford and C. Padoch, 'Traditional peoples and the biosphere: framing the issues and defining the terms', in K. H. Redford and C. Padoch (eds), *Conservation of neotropical forests: working from traditional resource use*, New York, USA: Columbia University Press, 1992, 3–13; F. Berkes, *Sacred ecology. Traditional ecological knowledge and resource management*, Taylor & Francis, Philadelphia and London, UK, 1999.
39 A. Wiget and O. Balalaeva, 'Khanty communal reindeer sacrifice: Belief, subsistence and cultural persistence in contemporary', *Siberia Arctic Anthropology*, 38(1), 2001, 82–99.
40 A. Kim-Maloney and A. Kim, 'Magic Hunt with the Forest Spirits According to Siberian Folklore Data', *Vestnik Tomskogo Gosudarstvennogo Universiteta. Istoriya*, 5, 2016, 148–151.
41 V.M. Kulemzin, *Chelovek i priroda v verovanijah hantov* [*Man and nature in the Khanty beliefs*, in Russian], Tomsk: Izdatelstvo Tomskogo universiteta, 1984 at 170.
42 Ibid, at 166.
43 Moldanov and Moldanova, note 19, at 15–16.

morning and does not feel like leaving the house, he follows his feelings and decides to do household chores reasoning that on such a day the game does not fly, the animal rests, the fish does not appear.[44] In an integrated economy, everyone is engaged in very simple and efficient activities without any specialization in order to provide themselves with everything necessary for life.

Khanty, Mansi and Nenets have been living on their land for centuries and know their territories well, taking into account all of their limits and demands. Reindeer lichen is the most important food, a factor of survival in the harsh winter.[45] Therefore, indigenous peoples use certain rules to preserve the reindeer lichen during periods of economic activity. They move the reindeer on a damp day, so that the reindeer lichen does not crumble and they choose places to feed the reindeer with less burden on the pasture. In hot or bad weather, the herds do not stay in one place for long, so as not to disturb the land surface. Nomadic routes are changed every seven to eight years, so that the land can be restored.[46] Another example is places in tundra with a thin reindeer lichen ground layer and sand below it. Historically, it has been forbidden to scrape this land by rakes or to clear the land plot of debris. To follow these rules, Khanty have created a mythological context: one cannot scrape it, because this is the face of Mother Earth. If the reindeer lichen is damaged, such plots are laid with moss so that the sandy areas do not expand.[47]

Restrictions in people's activities and careful use of scarce natural resources are typical for different indigenous cultures. Madhavi Venkatesan comments on the indigenous people of North America: "Evidence does promote the view that Native populations used environmental resources sparingly in spite of the surplus available."[48] The indigenous peoples living in extreme northern conditions for many centuries follow the rule of "few people on a large territory" – this enables them to maintain the necessary level of hunting and fishing reserves and of pastures. This rule is determined by the slow rate of biological resource reproduction in the North[49] and is of much importance nowadays in regards to intensive industrial development within the northern territories.

44 Ibid, at 33–34.
45 O. Lavrinenko and E. Kuljugina, 'Use of State Natural Reserve in the Nenents District as reindeer pastures: Inventory of lichens', in P. Soppela, W. Ruth, B. Åhman and J.-Å. Riseth (eds), Proceedings of the 1st CAES Course 'Reindeer as a Keystone Species in the North – Biological, Cultural and Socio-economic Aspects', *Arctic Centre Report Series Reports*, 38, 2020, 80–88, in press.
46 Moldanov and Moldanova, note 19, at 24–25.
47 During the Soviet period, reindeer herders were hired from other places, and they used the scraping technology which resulted in broad sandy areas growing every year and turning the tundra into a lifeless desert.
48 Venkatesan, note 30; see also: Lavrinenko and Kuljugina, note 45.
49 See 'Indigenous Peoples of the North: Traditional Culture and Knowledge for the Environment', in *UNESCO Institute for Information Technologies in Education. Climate Change Adaptation: Traditional Knowledge of Indigenous Peoples Inhabiting the Arctic and Far North*, 2014.

Providing enough food for present and future demand requires a balanced use of resources. There are numerous examples illustrating traditional regulations of economic activity – certain bird species are considered commercial, and other species are protected by religious and mythical rules, meaning they cannot be hunted during nesting and rearing periods.[50] There are strict restrictions on the number of animals, birds and fish extracted. Indigenous peoples only use the amount they need for food. Greed is a sin that can cause the wrath of the gods.[51] Compliance with such rules contributed to the maintenance of bird species and biodiversity in the northern territories.

The dependence of indigenous peoples on the environment is manifested in the admiration of life in any of its forms. For example, there is a custom to shoot only the beast which comes within shooting distance. It is believed that if the beast wants to live, it will never approach the hunter. A seated bird can be killed, while a flying bird cannot.[52] During the nesting period, dogs are tied up, hunting is banned and reindeer are not grazed near nests.[53] Those who violate the rules of behaviour in nature are punished by the gods.

Complex rituals and gifts brought to the gods after hunting make the indigenous people realize the significance of all of their actions.[54] A spiritual connection with all living objects is the common element across all native peoples. "Hunting was a ceremonial activity as much as an economic necessity, since only if the proper rituals were observed would the animals consent to let themselves be taken, or agree to return." Even the bones of consumed animals are carefully preserved and burned to ensure proper respect for the life taken.[55] Similarly, in northern Russian cultures, bones of fish and animals are buried in a special way, so that it could bring good luck.[56] Bones of animals can be placed in a certain way for the animals to live again; aboriginal people often address local spirits or special natural objects with a request for resources. The rituals associated with traditional activities are aimed at securing the production of resources at present and in future.[57]

The household is organized rationally – big families can share a small space without disturbing each other. All things are multifunctional, for example, in the reindeer camp there are only necessities that can be quickly picked up and packed. For instance, the manipulation of various kinds of

50 'T.A. Moldanova, 'Ornitomorfnaja simvolika v fol'klore i verovanijah hantov' ['Ornithomorphic symbols in the folklore and beliefs of the Khanty', in Russian], *Vestnik TGPU*, 4 (41). Gumanitarnye nauki (Istorija, Arheologija, Jetnologija), 2004, 95–98.
51 Ibid, at 97.
52 Kulemzin, note 41, at 93.
53 Moldanov and Moldanova, note 19, at 33.
54 Kulemzin, note 41, at 95.
55 C.C. Calloway, *New worlds for all*, Baltimore, MD: The Johns Hopkins University Press, 1997 at 73.
56 Kulemzin, note 41, at 83.
57 Ibid, at 82.

"ropes" (from the arcana to the garters) allows herders to control the herd, "wind up and unwind" the nomadic route. The "ropes" are associated with a network which covers and curbs the territory with its resources.[58]

### 4.2 Ways to transfer the environmental values of indigenous peoples from generation to generation

The traditional environmental values of indigenous peoples described earlier in this chapter have provided the basic rules for governing the behaviour of northern indigenous peoples in the natural environment for centuries and have determined the possibility for their adaptation. These values have been handed down from generation to generation by special means: religious beliefs, fairy tales, traditional customs, social customs and practices. The traditional transmission mechanism of social experience from senior to junior ensured the unity of values and behavioural guidelines.

The traditions, indigenous knowledge, behaviour rules in the environment as well as traditional skills are considered to be a part of the cosmological and religious beliefs of the northern indigenous peoples.[59] They have transformed traditional methods of land use, resource use and ecological planning and see it crucial to preserving these rules for future generations.[60]

The transfer of traditional knowledge is also carried out through ritual songs, geographical songs, religious songs, personal songs and fairy tales.[61]

A fairy tale as an environmental education instrument is an important element of understanding nature.[62] The Khanty and Mansi fairy tales are of high value.

For example, through a fairy tale, a child learns that fire is dangerous for the forest, but water is stronger than fire; that land wins over water, absorbing it, but a water monster can swallow the earth; that boys armed with bows and arrows can kill the water monster. Boys can fall through the ice; the sun can

58 A.V. Golovnev, N.P. Garin and D.A. Kukanov, *Reindeer Herders of Yamal (research materials for the Atlas of Nomadic Technologies)*, Ekaterinburg: UrFO RAN, 2016 at 8–9.

59 See T.J. Kristensen and D.H. Holly, 'Birds, Burials and Sacred Cosmology of the Indigenous Beothuk of Newfoundland, Canada', *Cambridge Archaeological Journal*, 23/1, 2013, 41–53; 'Indigenous Peoples of the North', note 49; M.H. Bassett, 'Animals and Aztec religion: Keepers and cultivators of nature', *Religion Compass*, 12, 2018, 5–6.

60 Y.S. Lea, 'The Praxis of Cultural Sustainability: A Q'eqchi' Maya Case of Cultural Autonomy and Resistance against the Monsanto Law in Guatemala', *Theory in Action*, 11/4, 2018, 44–73.

61 Moldanov and Moldanova, note 19, at 120.

62 F.-L. Alvaro and C. Mar, 'Rediscovering the Potential of Indigenous Storytelling for Conservation Practice Conservation Letters', *A Journal of the Society for Conservation Biology*, 00(00), 2017, 1–12.

melt the ice, etc. A child needs to be aware that all natural phenomena are interconnected and to anticipate danger in some situations.[63]

The efficiency of traditional indigenous activities – of nomads, hunters and fishermen – depended on their knowledge of animals, birds, fish, the ability to navigate in space, on their understanding of natural and weather phenomena. The knowledge accumulated by many generations has been imprinted in traditional arts, everyday objects, such as clothing.[64] For example, traditional ornaments show gull wings, pike teeth, bear trail, fox-foot, transferring the knowledge necessary for hunting and fishing.[65] The researchers describe celestial bodies in the ornaments[66] which are, alongside traditional arts and crafts, the cognitive and acceptable model of the world and the person in it.[67]

Traditional ecological perceptions, values and knowledge are vital in sustainable development because they constitute a "culturally transmitted knowledge-practice-belief complex, which is concerned primarily with the relations between living beings, including humans".[68] This knowledge provides understanding and awareness of: interrelations between humans and their environment, species of plants and animals;[69] practices of traditional activities;[70] community-based resource management;[71] and social institutions which shape social memory and reinforce dynamic community norms.[72]

63 See 'Geroi Skazok Naroda Mansi i Khanty' ['Heroes of Fairy Tales of the Khanty and Mansi People', in Russian], available online at http://www.hintfox.com/article/geroi-skazok-naroda-mansi-i-hanti.html.
64 A.M. Syazi, *Ornament i veschi v kulture khantov Nizhnego Priobja* [*Ornament and clothing in the culture of the Khanty of the Lower Ob River*], Tomsk: Izd-vo Tom. un-ta, 2000 at 19.
65 Ibid, at 59.
66 S.V. Ivanov, *Ornament narodov Sibiri* [*Ornament of the Peoples of Siberia*, in Russian], M, L.: Izdatelstvo Akademii nauk USSR, 1963 at 441.
67 Sagalaev, note 33, at 20.
68 F. Berkes, *Sacred Ecology*, New York: Routledge, 2nd edn, 2008.
69 N.J. Turner, F. Berkes, J. Stephenson and J. Dick, 'Blundering Intruders: Extraneous Impacts on Two Indigenous Food Systems', *Human Ecology*, 41, 2013, 563–574; Bassett, note 59.
70 Iin P. Handayani and Priyono Prawito, 'Indigenous Soil Knowledge for Sustainable Agriculture', *Sociology, Organic Farming, Climate Change and Soil Science*, 3, 2010, 303–317; E. De la Montana, R.D. Moreno-Sanchez, J.H. Maldonado and D.M. Griffith, 'Predicting Hunter Behavior of Indigenous Communities in the Ecuadorian Amazon: Insights from a Household Production Model', *Ecology and Society*, 20, 4, 2015.
71 D. Kwan, H. Marsh and S. Delean, 'Factors influencing the sustainability of customary dugong hunting by a remote indigenous community', *Environmental Conservation*, 33/2, 2006, 164–171; F. Becker-Ritterspach and T. Raaijman, 'Global Transfer and Indian Management', *A Historical Hybridity Perspective Management International Review*, 53, 1, 2013, 141–166.
72 M.A. Bergamaschi and J.S. Medeiros, 'History, Memory and Tradition in Indigenous School Education: a Kaingang School Case Study', *Revista Brasileira De Historia*, 30/60, 2010, 55–75.

In addition to ethical and aesthetic assessments, an important element of traditional environmental values is the rational use of resources, which is ensured through the transfer of knowledge about the rules of economic activity. Indigenous knowledge is transmitted not only through practices, but also through special events, for example, 'nomadic seminars', an equivalent to scientific seminars. Within nomadic seminars, the transmission of knowledge occurs through discourse, collective case studies and gatherings in the evening, when nomads share their experiences after a day spent hunting and herding.[73]

The traditional way of transferring social experience from older to younger generations provides a coherency of environmental values and reproduction of the most effective sustainable practices.

## 5 Conclusion

The study of traditional environmental values identified the criteria under which a balance is maintained between human needs and the capabilities of Arctic nature, such as extensive economic activity, adaptability, frugality, consideration of constraints and care for future generations. Obviously, modern Yamal's industrial development is not guided by these time-tested values. Therefore, the consequences of industrial development are often destructive. In the transition to sustainable development, this current situation needs to change.

Many researchers state that sustainability and ethical principles are intertwined as sustainability concepts cannot be applied without strong ethical principles. Commitment to sustainable development agendas should therefore be a rational choice based on ethical reasoning, with the understanding that ethical behaviour is closely connected to the welfare of society as a whole.[74] Sustainability refers to a moral way of acting,[75] in which the person or group intends to avoid harmful effects on the environmental, social and economic domains, consistent with a harmonious relationship between those domains.[76]

Specific ethical standards and values which have governed northern indigenous peoples through centuries and helped them to survive in harsh Arctic

73 A. Lavrillier and S. Gabyshev, *An Arctic Indigenous Knowledge System of Landscape, Climate, and Human Interactions: Evenki Reindeer Herders and Hunters*, Fürstenberg/Havel: Kulturstiftung Sibirien, 2017 at 16.

74 B. Chen, 'Moral and Ethical Foundations for Sustainability: A Multidisciplinary Approach', *Journal of Global Citizenship & Equity Education*, 2 (2), 2012.

75 R. Attfield, 'Ethics and Environmental Responsibility', *Philosophical Books*, 31 (3), 1990 at 172; A. Grear, 'The Vulnerable Living Order: Human Rights and the Environment in a Critical and Philosophical Perspective', *Journal of Human Rights and the Environment*, 2 (1), 2011 at 23.

76 A.J. Bañón-Gomis, M.G. Parra, W.M. Hoffman and R.E. McNulty, 'Rethinking the Concept of Sustainability', *Business and Society Review*, 116 (2), 2011 at 171.

conditions are not followed consistently in modern Russian society during the period of intensive industrial development of the Arctic territories. Neither these values nor indigenous economic methods are incorporated in environmental policy and legislation. If this were to happen, the moral rules and legal norms would serve as a mechanism to support and reinforce each other.

As the value of traditional attitudes for living in the Arctic becomes increasingly important, there is a growing need for the academic and legal spheres to consider their methods of protecting and using the environment. This includes developing measures to hold those who engage with traditional knowledge accountable to non-indigenous communities. Existing domestic and international law has the potential to protect and foster traditional values and knowledge, contributing to global efforts of sustainable development and environmental protection in the Arctic.

In order to craft responses to the environmental changes caused by intensive industrial development in Yamal, political decision-makers and law-makers must seek input from indigenous communities and implement their methods of handling the environment in order to create legitimate action plans targeting adverse impacts in an effective manner.

# Index

For Product Safety Concerns and Information please contact our EU
representative GPSR@taylorandfrancis.com
Taylor & Francis Verlag GmbH, Kaufingerstraße 24, 80331 München, Germany

www.ingramcontent.com/pod-product-compliance
Ingram Content Group UK Ltd.
Pitfield, Milton Keynes, MK11 3LW, UK
UKHW020004200926
475702UK00015B/2477
*9780367528195*